read any good

math lately?

HEINEMANN
Portsmouth, NH

read any good math lately?

children's books for mathematical learning, K–6

DAVID J. WHITIN
University of South Carolina

SANDRA WILDE
University of Oregon

Foreword by Kenneth S. Goodman

Heinemann
A division of Reed Publishing (USA), Inc.
361 Hanover Street, Portsmouth, NH 03801-3912
Offices and agents throughout the world

The publishers and the authors wish to thank the children and their
parents for permission to reproduce material in this book.

Library of Congress Cataloging-in-Publication Data

Whitin, David Jackman. 1947–
    Read any good math lately? : children's books for mathematical
learning, K–6 / David J. Whitin, Sandra Wilde.
      p.   cm.
    Includes bibliographical references.
    ISBN 0-435-08334-1
    1. Mathematics—Study and teaching (Elementary) 2. Children's
literature in mathematics education. I. Wilde, Sandra. II. Title.
QA135.5.W468 1992
372.7'044—dc20   92-2643
                                                CIP

Book design by Wladislaw Finne
Cover design by Julie Hahn
Photographs by David Whitin
Printed in the United States of America
10 9 8 7 6 5 4 3 2

dedication

The seeds of this book were planted twenty years ago when the authors were students in a graduate mathematics education class at the University of New Hampshire. Dr. Deborah Stone taught us many things that semester, but probably most significant was the importance of children's literature as a springboard for mathematical investigations. The strong and resonant voice of Dr. Stone reading the rhythmical pattern of Four Fur Feet, *by Margaret Wise Brown, still rings in our ears. We still remember her sharing* Counting Lightly *by Leonard Simon, describing it as an avenue for investigating other numeration systems. And how could we forget the symmetry puzzles of Marion Walter in* Make a Bigger Puddle, Make a Smaller Worm? *We were learning about mathematics through the gift of story. We were coming to view it not as a prescribed set of formulas to master but as an open-ended system of patterns and relationships to explore. We were discovering mathematics as a practical tool for asking questions and solving problems. Children's literature helped us reclaim a context for mathematical learning, a lesson we have never forgotten. It seems only fitting that we come together twenty years later and celebrate that important lesson by writing this book. We dedicate it to Dr. Deborah Stone, now Professor Emerita at the University of New Hampshire, who lit the fire that has kept on burning.*

contents

foreword

Whole language is the term that has been central to a refocusing of school experience for teachers and learners in the last decade. It refers to two related but different views of school experience: (1) keeping the experience undivided—the whole authentic transaction, speech act, or literacy event—and (2) integrating within school experience all aspects of human experience—language, thinking, problem solving, schema building, knowledge acquisition.

Teachers, particularly elementary teachers, have embraced the notions of whole language, using it as a banner under which they integrate reading, writing, speaking, and listening in functional, authentic use in learning concepts of science and social studies through theme cycles and thematic units. They have found it easy and rewarding to integrate the arts (music, art, dance, drama) in their whole language classrooms. Literature is not only the preferred medium of reading instruction, it supports the social studies and science problem solving. Fiction and nonfiction provide rich, authentic explorations of time and place and human experiences that make the concepts children are exploring vivid, relevant, and involving.

But mathematics has tended to remain outside the integrated whole. Except for a few inclusions of counting and measurement in theme studies, mathematics has tended to be confined to arithmetic, taught from the book during a separate period. Yet the math field has also moved toward a holistic problem-solving focus. Math folks express concern that we tend to teach the parts—arithmetic "facts" and "skills"—through meaningless drill so that learners lose the context and do not develop a sense of mathematical functions. They are concerned that youngsters are not learning to think mathematically or to see math in all of their life experiences. They are concerned that teachers who fear math are producing learners who fear math.

This book provides a bridge, through literature, by which to bring mathematics into the integrated whole and to make it possible for children to have the same authentic experiences with math that they are coming to have with language, social studies, science, and the arts. The authors suggest many trade books, both fiction and nonfiction, that support various mathematical topics. They then provide examples at various grade levels of teachers using these books in their integrated teaching. These examples help teachers new to this use of literature see its potential, though the authors repeatedly urge their readers to see the examples not as activities to be copied but as illustrations of uses they can devise to fit their own pupils in their own classrooms; the authors seek "to support the open-ended exploration of possibilities."

Good literature emulates life and can in turn lead back to emulations of literature as mathematical explorations in the classroom. The book provides many examples of how teachers build on their pupils' experiences with literature to provide experiences in their classrooms.

This is not, then, simply a book that suggests supplementing the math curriculum with literature. It is a book that will help both teachers and learners explore through literature the mathematical aspects of human experience and our physical world. It is a book that will help complete the integration of school experience to include functional, meaningful mathematics.

While whole language teachers will find this book invaluable in bringing math into their whole language teaching, other teachers will also find that using literature as the book suggests will help their pupils see how math in school relates to math in the real world. They will find the literature suggestions very helpful in moving toward the Standards of the National Council of Teachers of Mathematics.

Many teachers will be amazed at the number and range of books available. This is the golden age of children's and young adult literature. As teachers and learners discover literature, their demand for it encourages writers, publishers, and booksellers. And as the volume of literature increases, so does its variety and quality. *Read Any Good Math Lately?* is a resource teachers will find useful in accessing and using this treasure chest of literary resources.

Kenneth S. Goodman

We are grateful to many people who have helped to make this book possible. We want to thank Grace Burton, who said such a book needed to be written and encouraged us along the way; Kathy Short for her helpful suggestions on the format of the book, as well as her lists of additional books for the bibliographies; Carolyn Burke for clarifying the importance of concepts in mathematical thinking; Heidi Mills and Timothy O'Keefe for offering their organizational recommendations and for making sure this book provided an open-ended invitation to teachers to explore mathematical ideas; Phyllis Whitin for her many readings of the manuscript and her helpful suggestions about how to make our writing more clear and direct; and many other readers, among them Pammy Wills, Clint Wills, and Susan Forgang, for their thoughtful comments and ideas. We also want to thank Janet Gorman for sharing so many good books and resources, and Leslie Barban of the Richland County Public Library of Columbia, South Carolina, who was so helpful in locating good stories to read. We owe thanks to Toby Gordon and Alan Huisman of Heinemann Educational Books for their constant support and sound advice along the way and to the anonymous readers who read the manuscript on several occasions and made suggestions that helped us view our writing from a different perspective.

Sandra Wilde would like to give a special thank you to David Wilkinson and the community of St. Francis in the Foothills United Methodist Church in Tucson, Arizona, for all their support over the years. Part of the royalties from this book will be donated to the church's discretionary fund, which is used to help those with urgent financial needs.

Most important, we want to thank the many teachers and children with whom we have had the privilege to work. It is their stories that demonstrate so marvelously the mathematical explorations embodied in children's literature.

acknowledgments

1

"does it really take twenty-three days to count to a million?"

One day fourth-grade teacher Joe Mingo read *How Much Is a Million?* (Schwartz, 1985) aloud to his students. It tells the story of Marvelosissimo, a mathematical magician who takes readers on a delightful exploration into the size of one million, one billion, and one trillion. We see a million children climbing onto each other's shoulders and stretching up farther than airplanes can fly; we see a billion goldfish swimming in a bowl the size of a football stadium; and we discover that it would take 200,000 years to count to a trillion. As Joe finished the story, a student asked, "Is that story really true?"

"What do you mean?" asked Joe.

"I mean that part about the twenty-three days. Does it really take twenty-three days to count to a million?"

"What do you think?" said Joe. "How do you suppose you could find out?"

The children knew they couldn't stay at school for twenty-three consecutive days and count all day and all night. Instead, they devised an experiment. Several students would count as high as they could for sixty seconds. The children realized that larger numbers would take longer to say than smaller numbers, so they assigned a range of starting numbers to some of their classmates, then calculated how far each person could count in one hour and then in one day at the same rate. Finally, they calculated the number of days needed to reach a million and found their estimate to be twenty-two-and-a-half days (Table 1-1). Satisfied that the book's total of twenty-three days was fairly accurate, they decided that the small difference between the two figures was probably due to variations in rates of counting. At least that part of the book was true! In this classroom the teacher capitalized on his children's questions, encouraging them to conduct an experiment to find an answer.

Other teachers have shared this same book with their students to explore other mathematical concepts. For instance, the idea of place value arose when Tracy Dunn read the story aloud to six-year-old Travis, who, when he saw the numeral for one million, said, "It looks like a hundred but it has more zeroes. A million has a *lot* more zeroes." When Nina McLaughlin shared it with eight-year-old Adam, he remarked, as he looked at the numeral for one trillion, "It's getting more zeroes on it, so I know it's getting bigger. Let me count the zeroes . . . . Yes, this number's got more zeroes so it's more." When Olivia Huggins shared the part about one billion with Paige, this third-grader commented, "A million and

1

	per minute	per hour	per day	number of days
Robert	85 (1–85)	5,100	122,400	1 (up to 122,400)
LaTisha	31 (900,001–900,031)	1,860	44,640	18 (122,401–900,000)
Jesse	20 (900,951–900,970)	1,200	28,800	3½ (900,001–1,000,000)
				22½ days total

TABLE 1–1. *Counting to a million*

a million is a billion." Then she paused and reconsidered. "No, a million mil-lions makes a billion." Since a thousand thousands equals one million, she ex-plained, a million millions must equal one billion. (In Great Britain, a billion is indeed defined as a million millions.) As Paige continued reading, she also ex-plored the concept of proportionality. When she discovered that a million gold-fish would need a bowl large enough to hold a whale, she attempted to see the problem in more personal terms: "If those goldfish were the size of a tiny dot, I think they would all fit in my swimming pool."

The story gave other children an opportunity to share their experiences and demonstrate their global understanding of the term "million" as a very large number. Lori (two years old): "I have a million mosquito bites." Stacey (eight years old): "My daddy said we'd have a million rabbits before long." Megan (eight years old): "We can't go to Myrtle Waves [a water park] because my mom says there are a million people there and it's just too crowded."

This one book, *How Much Is a Million?*, was the starting point for good learning in several ways: questioning numerical information, devising an appro-priate mathematical experiment, exploring a variety of mathematical con-cepts, and sharing personal interpretations of "one million."

Other books, although not as obviously mathematical, and dealing with con-cepts on a much simpler scale, can also be important learning tools. Randy Gill's first-grade class read *The King's Flower* (Anno, 1979), the story of a king who insisted that everything he owned be larger than life yet was unable to control the size of a flower. The students responded in art and writing to the ideas of large and small portrayed in the book. Jared said, "I wish that all of my toys were giant" (Figure 1–1).[1] Hannah's illustration reproduced the huge chocolate bar from the book (Figure 1–2), while Teresa was quite happy to draw small kittens (Figure 1–3). Their responses reflect an early understanding of size concepts—a generalized sense of largeness and smallness that underlies all further experiences with measurement.

The experiences the children had with these two books demonstrate the po-tential of children's literature to involve readers in a variety of mathematical in-vestigations. Books can provide a rich context for understanding mathematical

[1] Jared's text, as well as many of the other pieces of children's writing in the figures, uses invented spelling. See Wilde, 1992, for a fuller discussion of invented spelling.

May 30

I wish that all of my toys ur jient. Jared

FIGURE 1-1

tannah

wish I was a princess and I got my stuff as big as I wanted it.

FIGURE 1-2

Teresa

Apr 29

I wish I had the smallest Kittens.

FIGURE 1-3

concepts. Without a meaningful context, learners may come to regard mathematics as an abstract and irrelevant system. Decontexualized learning can be a bewildering experience.

In the *Curriculum and Evaluation Standards for School Mathematics*, the National Council of Teachers of Mathematics (NCTM, 1989) advocates significant changes in mathematics instruction. It recommends that students have opportunities to be active constructors of mathematical knowledge, to be problem posers as well as problem solvers. It urges schools to provide children with opportunities to represent mathematical ideas in different ways, not only numerically but through writing, drawing, and discussion. It views mathematics not as a series of rules to be mastered but as a way of thinking to be developed, a communication system that learners will need to use for a variety of reasons in a variety of contexts. It recognizes the importance of the affective dimension of mathematical learning and supports the development of experiences that "endow all students with a realization that doing mathematics is a common human activity" (p. 6). It also advocates the use of children's books as a vehicle for communicating mathematical ideas (p. 5). In fact, children's literature is a powerful way to implement many of the changes the Council has proposed. Incorporating children's literature into the mathematics curriculum can be justified in several ways, and the remainder of this chapter will explore some of them. Much of our rationale is related to the *Standards,* which we consider the best available statement of current thinking about mathematics education.

Children's literature provides a meaningful context for mathematics

Through books, learners see mathematics as a "common human activity," which can be used in various contexts. Mathematics provides a tool for dividing a set of cookies (Hutchins, 1986), measuring a pig (Johnston, 1986), organizing a messy bedroom (Mayer, 1987), or comparing the relative size of things (Hoban, 1985). Children's literature helps to break down the artificial dichotomy that sometimes exists between *learning* mathematics and *living* mathematics. In quoting from Richard Hamming, Davis and Hersh (1986) assert, "Computation should be intimately bound up with the source of the problem and the use that is going to be made of the answer . . . . It is not a step to be taken in isolation from reality" (p. 154). Children's literature restores a meaningful context to the use of numbers, since mathematical concepts are naturally embedded in story situations.

Laurie Sperry used the book *50 Simple Things Kids Can Do to Save the Earth* (EarthWorks Group, 1990) to explore environmental issues with her second-grade students. The book contained statistical information on pollution that provided a meaningful context for the children to initiate their own mathematical investigations. Laurie read the class "Presto, On! . . . Presto, Off!," a chapter that focused on the conservation of water, and then posed the following challenge: "Estimate how much water you could conserve by turning off the tap while you brush your teeth." The children's estimates ranged from 3 gallons to 3,000 gallons daily.

"How could we figure out the answer to this problem more precisely?" Laurie asked.

"We could put a bucket under the faucet and have someone brush their teeth," suggested one student. Before rushing off to conduct this experiment, however, the students felt that they also needed to know how long people actually spend brushing their teeth. They called a local dentist and discovered that most people spend two minutes twice a day brushing their teeth. With this last bit of information in hand, the children marched off to the janitor's closet with a timer, a bucket, a toothbrush, and some toothpaste. Amanda turned on the water at an appropriate rate, set the timer for two minutes, and brushed. The students returned to the classroom and used a measuring cup to determine the amount of water wasted. As they filled a gallon container, they learned that sixteen cups were equivalent to one gallon and that Amanda had used three gallons of water. They then calculated a total use of six gallons for the day.

Laurie asked the children to focus again on the original question. "Now we know how much we use when we leave the water running. But our question was, 'How much will we conserve by *not* letting it run?' How are we going to figure that out?" One student suggested repeating the experiment but turning the water off during brushing. Another child concurred, "Yeah, and then we'll measure what's in the bucket that time." When they tried it, they discovered that they used one cup of water per brushing, or two cups a day.

Again Laurie asked the children to consider their initial question. "Well, now we know how much water we used by turning the water off, but that still doesn't answer our question about how much water we save. How do we figure that out?" Several students suggested comparing the numbers by subtracting. The children used a calculator to convert gallons back to cups and then summarized their findings like this:

96 cups (water left running)
−2 cups (water turned off)
94 cups saved

In Laurie's classroom children were using mathematics to pose real questions and solve real problems. They were discovering that children's literature can be a starting point for looking at mathematics in a new way—as a tool for solving the important problems that are a natural part of daily life and for considering issues that concern them as present and future citizens.

Children's literature celebrates mathematics as a language

NCTM (1989) cites "learning to communicate mathematically" as an essential goal for mathematics instruction. By doing so it quite rightly acknowledges that mathematics is a natural communication system that we can use to describe our world and communicate our experiences. One discussion about the language of mathematics occurred in a classroom of first-grade students. Veronica had discovered an interesting number pattern with her fingers. She held up the index fingers of both hands and remarked, "Look, one and one is two." She then raised the middle fingers of both hands as well and observed, "Look, two and two is four." She continued to raise successive fingers on each hand to demonstrate her numerical pattern: $1 + 1 = 2, 2 + 2 = 4, 3 + 3 = 6, 4 + 4 = 8, 5 + 5 = 10$. Her discovery nicely conveyed the symmetry of even numbers. To extend this investigation the teacher, Timothy O'Keefe, read the class *Mirror Mirror* (Irons and Irons, 1987), which uses a mirror to investigate the doubling property of even numbers. Because the teacher viewed mathematics as a language, he encouraged the children to represent their ideas about even numbers in different ways. During the class's discussion of the book, he asked, "What do you think the word 'double' means?" Michael responded, "It means you get the same again, 'cause when you press the double button in the video game, you get two balls instead of one." Sabrina described the evenness of these numbers in another way. "It's the same on one side as the other." And Quinton remarked, "I seen two things, one at a time." In their own ways, the children were using language to describe the two equal sets of even numbers. By providing a basis for learners to explore mathematical ideas, children's literature can combat the frequent perception that mathematics is essentially a written system composed of symbols rather than words, that it is "something to be performed on paper and not . . . a vehicle for oral communication" (Pimm, 1987, p. 1). Children's literature invites people and language into the forum of mathematical ideas.

Mirror Mirror inspired a discussion of even numbers, but it also allowed the children to express their ideas in different ways. Sheree created her own array (Figure 1–4) to show two sets of five chips, writing "I see 10 chips." (An array is an arrangement of objects in equal rows.) Alex did not use an array format but drew an arrow next to the four chips that were reflected in his mirror, writing "I see 8 chips" (Figure 1–5). Sabrina used the vertical line of the mirror to indicate the symmetry of two sets (Figure 1–6).

As these examples show, "communication about mathematics requires genuine negotiation and sharing of meaning" (Pimm, 1987, p. 73).

Children's literature demonstrates that mathematics develops out of human experience

NCTM has recommended that students engage in "varied experiences related to the cultural, historical and scientific evolution of mathematics" (1989, p. 5).

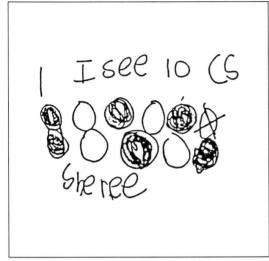

FIGURE 1-4

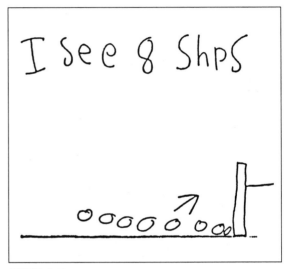

FIGURE 1-5

FIGURE 1-6

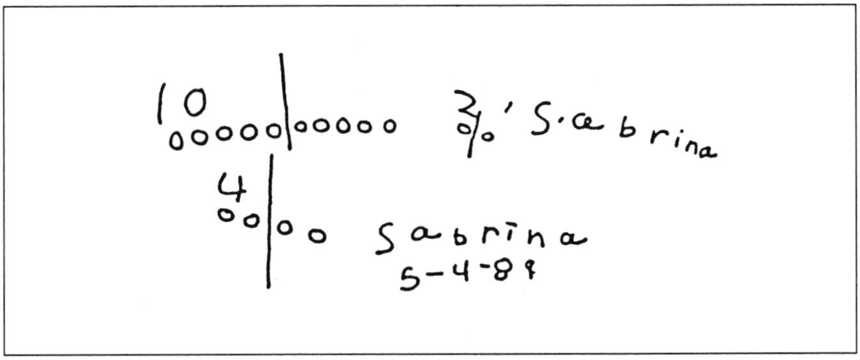

This focus on the interaction between mathematics and the historical contexts from which it developed emphasizes mathematics as a way of knowing rather than primarily a way of doing. From a historical and cultural perspective, "what are being shaped are ideas and meanings, not behaviors or techniques" (Bishop, 1988, p. 151).

Some of the six-year-olds in Timothy O'Keefe's first-grade class became involved in using nonstandard units of measurement when they were introduced to the book, *How Big Is a Foot?* (Myller, 1962). In this humorous story, a carpenter builds a bed for the queen, but it turns out the wrong size because he uses his own foot size to measure the lumber instead of the king's, which was the original measure used. After they heard the story, the children discussed the problem of the bed together. Some were still not sure why the bed didn't fit. Others explained the difference by matching their own shoe size to a classmate's and noting the discrepancy between them. The teacher invited the children to measure a chair with their foot and then look for other objects to measure. Aaron found several, including a pencil, pencil cup, shelf, ruler, person's back (BCR), and blocks (BCSS), as seen in Figure 1–7.

The children experienced firsthand the role nonstandard units have played in the history of our measurement system and began to understand concepts related to conservation of length.

FIGURE 1–7

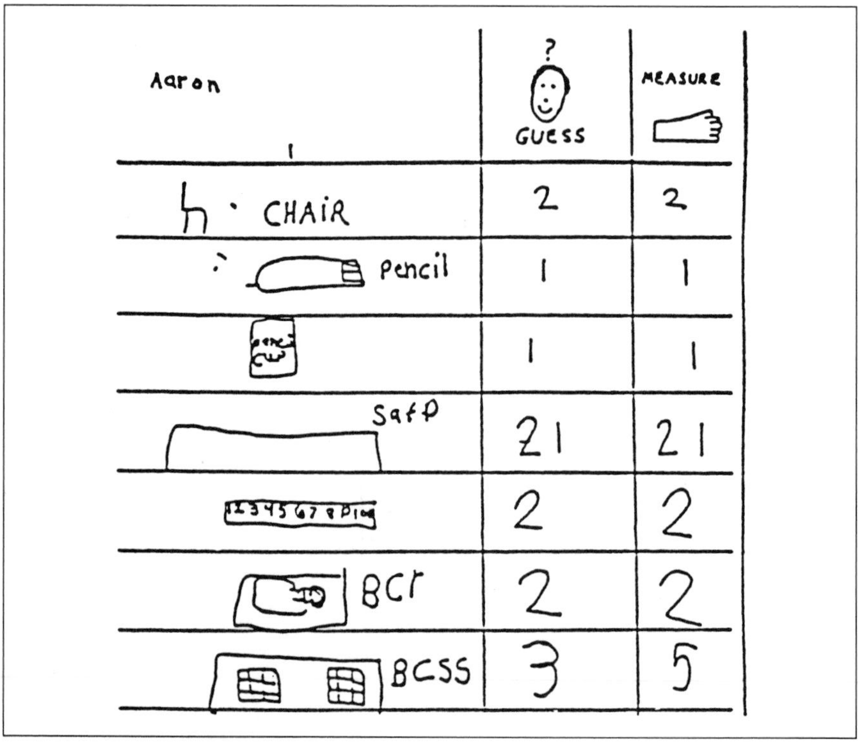

Aaron	GUESS	MEASURE
ꓶ · CHAIR	2	2
Pencil	1	1
	1	1
Safp	21	21
12345 67 8 Pico	2	2
BCr	2	2
BCSS	3	5

A class of third graders used *How Big Is a Foot?* to explore other nonstandard units. They marked off their body length using a strip of adding machine tape and then measured that length in terms of other nonstandard units—spans, feet, cubits, paces, digits, fathoms, and palms—and recorded the results on the strip. Once the children completed their measurements, Philip Chagnon, their teacher, asked them to line up according to height, from shortest to tallest, using their cubit measurement (the distance from their elbow to the tip of their middle finger) as the basis for comparison. As they formed a line the children soon realized that something didn't seem right.

"Hey, I should be in front," observed Peter, who was the tallest boy in the class according to the standard units of feet and inches, but found himself in the middle of the line when he was measured in cubits.

"Why do you suppose the line looks so uneven?" asked the teacher.

"We all have different size cubits," said Eric.

"Yes," confirmed Katy, "I have a big cubit so I didn't need so many cubits to measure, but if you have a small cubit you need a lot." The children were coming to understand the inverse relationship between the length of the measuring unit and the number of units contained in a given length. To extend the discussion the teacher asked the children, "If you were buying cloth from a tailor and you were charged by the cubit, would you want a tailor with a long or a short cubit?" Through this experience, these third graders began to realize the need for the standardization of measurement.

Children's literature addresses humanistic, affective elements of mathematics

Much has been written about "math anxiety" and its effects on the attitudes and literacy development of learners. Children's literature can help to alleviate some of that anxiety.

Gerry Oglan encouraged a positive attitude toward mathematics in his seven-year-old son Jerred when he read him *Two Ways to Count to Ten* (Dee, 1988). This African tale recounts a contest among all the animals in the jungle to determine who would succeed the tiger as king. Tiger claimed that whoever could hurl his mighty javelin into the air and count to ten before it hit the ground would be his successor. But none of the other animals could do it, not even the boisterous lion, until the clever hyena threw the javelin skyward and counted to ten by twos (2, 4, 6, 8, 10). At this point in the story, Jerred started to laugh. He understood the trick the hyena had played and recognized the shrewdness of the hyena's counting strategy. When the story was over, Gerry challenged his son to race him in counting to ten, and Jerred quickly responded, "I'll count by twos!" Poor dad counted by ones and lost. They raced several more times and Jerred won each time, laughing his way to ten. When Gerry asked, "Are there are other ways we could count to ten?" Jerred said, "I can count by fives." They raced again, Jerred counting by fives and his dad counting by twos, and Jerred won again! In this spirit of playful competition, Jerred learned about the relative speeds of different counting strategies.

Children's literature fosters the development of number sense

Number sense includes a variety of abilities: producing reasonable estimates, choosing the most appropriate calculating procedure, and just having a "feel" for numbers in their various uses and interpretations. NCTM (1989) recommends that estimation and number sense be considered important goals in school mathematics and lists various dimensions of number sense that need to be encouraged: developing number meanings, exploring number relationships with manipulatives, understanding the relative magnitude of numbers, developing referents for measures of common objects, and building a sense about the relative effect of operating on numbers. This last dimension of number sense can be explored through *Anno's Mysterious Multiplying Jar* (Anno, 1983). This book introduces a fascinating world of factorial numbers (the product of a series of digits) by inviting the reader into a mysterious jar. It contains two islands, with three mountains per island, four castles per mountain, and so on, up to a final ten jars in each of nine cupboards. Number operations enter in when, to determine the number of castles, for instance, one multiplies $1 \times 2 \times 3 \times 4$. To solve the final problem, one multiplies the numbers 1 through 10. The book's portrayal of the explosive power of multiplication is enhanced by arrays of dots in the latter part that directly illustrate the cumulative effect of continuous multiplying.

Some teachers have read Anno's book to their students and encouraged them to create their own factorial study. One student in fourth-grade teacher Joe Duprey's class used his geographic knowledge to pose the question, "How many states are in my world?" (Figure 1–8). Another student composed a story that took place inside the stomach of a dog, and asked, "How many trees were growing inside this dog?" (Figure 1–9). (Factorial numbers are written with an exclamation point. For instance, 4!, or 4 factorial, is equal to $4 \times 3 \times 2 \times 1$.)

Sixth-grade teacher Jeff Wallace also read the book to his class and invited his students to create their own variations. The problems the students devised inspired an interesting discussion of factorials and other kinds of multiplication. One student wrote: "If Ann had six boxes and each box had five plates, how many plates would there be?" Some of the students claimed that the answer to this problem would be determined not by the use of factorials but rather by multiplying 6×5. But it could be argued that this story is the beginning of a factorial sequence if further details are added, such as, "And each plate had four flowers; on each flower there were three bees; on each bee there were two spots; on each spot there was one speck of gold. How many specks of gold

Robert Gardner

There was 1 planet. It had 2 hemispheres. Each hemisphere had 3 continent. Each continent had 4 contries. and each contry had 5 states.

1! = 1×1 = 1
2! = 2×1 = 2
3! = 3×2×1 = 6
4! = 4×3×2×1 = 24
5! = 5×4×3×2×1 = 120

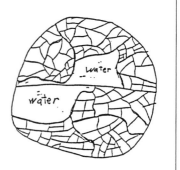

FIGURE 1–8

FIGURE 1–9

There was 1 dog
Inside the dog there were 2 cats
Inside each cat there were 3 mice
Inside each mouse there were 4 acorns
From each acorn 5 trees would grow.

1! = 1
2! = 2
3! = 6
4! = 24
5! = 120

were there?" In this case, the factorial story is written in reverse order. It is this kind of variation in problem construction that encourages learners to compare and contrast different story types and become more discerning problem solvers. Another sixth-grade student thought of this problem: "If John has four shirts and three pairs of slacks, how many combinations of clothes could be made?" Here again the children discussed the difference between this problem, which focuses on the number of possible pairings, and the original problem posed by Anno. The book encouraged the students to develop a stronger number sense by analyzing the distinctions between various problems and comparing different contexts for multiplication.

Children's literature integrates mathematics into other curriculum areas

Mathematics gives learners a unique perspective on various domains of knowledge. As Davis and Hersch (1986) assert, "in its origin, in its development, mathematics requires full association with all types of human activity, mental and physical . . . mathematics has drawn inspiration from business, from religion, from law, from war, from politics, from ethics, from gambling, from metaphysics, from mysticism, from ritual, from play (look what a mathematical thing the children's game of hopscotch is), and not just from a 'sanitized' physical science" (p. 304). Exploring the relationships between mathematics and the other disciplines it serves, such as the physical and life sciences, the social sciences, and the humanities, is one of NCTM's goals for students (1989, p. 5).

The well-known story *The Carrot Seed* (Krauss, 1945) gave a group of six-year-old children a way to incorporate mathematics into their current science topic: plants. Their teacher, Timothy O'Keefe, read the story to them after they had conducted a number of plant experiments. Although it has a happy ending (a seed begins to sprout despite the pessimism of many family members), the children knew that such an outcome was not always guaranteed. They discussed the reasons why a seed might not grow. "It might die without the sun." "Snow could fall." "It could not grow in a lot of sand." Their discussion reflected what they had learned from their own experiments trying to grow plants in a dark closet and in sandy soil.

The teacher then invited the children to create their own plant stories and encouraged them to incorporate some of their current knowledge about plants. Veronica wrote: "8 seeds in all. 4 was rotting in the dark. But the girl was happy because the plants were living" (Figure 1–10). Veronica remembered the class's attempt to grow seeds in a dark cupboard: The seeds germinated but grew very poorly. Her drawing illustrates their stunted growth. She includes mathematical vocabulary in her story—the words "in all"—but also a girl rejoicing in the number of plants that survived.

Amy drew two sets of seeds and explained why they didn't grow: "Some seeds grew: 3, 6. The man didn't water the plants. The man pulled the plants" (Figure 1–11). Amy knew from experience that if you do not water plants,

FIGURE 1–10

veronica
4-25-89

8 Seeds InAll.
4 was Riing In The Dork.
Bu t The gril was
HaPPy Becase
the Pntswere lereing.

FIGURE 1–11

either they do not grow at all or they grow very poorly. Amy recorded the number of seeds that grew and did not grow and then drew the gardener pulling up some of his harvest. Young learners are capable of incorporating rich details like these in their stories. Teachers can turn to children's literature to draw mathematics into the rest of the school day, whether in a science unit on plants, a social studies unit on economics, or a literary exploration of folktales.

Children's literature restores an aesthetic dimension to mathematical learning

Eisner (1985) argues that scientists and mathematicians are artists, like painters and sculptors, because they are involved in the process of form making. All things that are made have form, whether they are paintings and music, or taxonomies, theories, frameworks, and conceptual systems. When they are well made, they possess aesthetic properties. The aim of education, according to Eisner, is the creation of artists who are able to produce good form through various modes of expression, including mathematics. Elaborating on this aesthetic sensibility, he states, "To form is to confer order. To confer aesthetic order upon our world is to make that world hang together, to fit, to feel right, to put things in balance, to create harmony. Such harmonies are sought in all aspects of life" (p. 29). NCTM (1989) acknowledges the importance of the aesthetic dimension of mathematics when it emphasizes symmetry, balance, patterns, and numerical relationships. It supports the development of a curriculum that encourages children to recognize and create a wide variety of patterns and to represent mathematical relationships in different ways. Children need opportunities to see that regularity is an essential aspect of mathematics and that they can represent regularities of shapes, designs, events, and sets in multiple ways.

One children's book that graphically demonstrates the aesthetic dimension of mathematics is *Ten in a Bed* (Rees, 1988). The text is the familiar chant that begins with ten children nestled together in a single bed. The little one says "Roll over," and when they all roll over, one falls out of bed. The sequence begins again with nine in the bed, and continues in sequence until the bed is empty. When the six-year-olds in Timothy O'Keefe's first-grade class heard this story, they joined in by singing and even demanded a second reading. Their teacher invited them to create their own version of the story.

Sheree drew six children in a bed and wrote: "6 – 1, 5 – 1, 4 – 1, 3 – 1, 2 – 1, 1 – 1, 0. And wasn't no children in the bed" (Figure 1–12). When she was asked to read her text aloud, naturally she sang it: "There was six in the bed and one fell off; there was five in the bed and one fell off; there was four in the bed and one fell off . . . ." The rhythm of her voice as she sang nicely reflected the rhythm of the mathematical pattern she had created. Uncovering

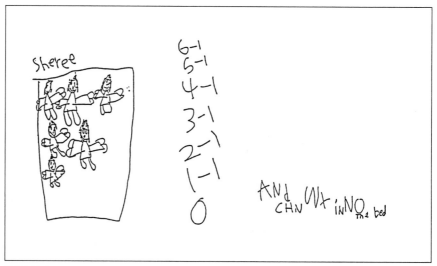

FIGURE 1–12

patterns and discovering relationships are part of the aesthetic order and structure of the mathematical system. Inspired by *Ten in a Bed,* Sheree generated her own numerical sequence and then represented that pattern through art and music.

Children's literature supports the art of problem posing

Mathematical stories have supporting details that learners can change in different ways to pursue other dimensions of a problem. The original story or problem thus becomes the basis for a multitude of related problems. The more opportunities children have to alter a particular story problem, the greater their understanding of the underlying mathematical concepts. This playfulness with problem variables produces an interesting irony: "We understand something best in the context of changing it" (Brown and Walter, 1983, p. 123).

An example of how children's literature can help children generate problems occurred in this same first-grade class. They were in the middle of an animal unit. They had read stories, conducted surveys, held class discussions, and shared their writing about animals. As part of their investigations their teacher read them *How Many Snails?* (Giganti, 1988), a predictable story that asks a set of three classification questions for each of its illustrations. When the teacher came to the end of the book, he showed the children a picture of various kinds of transportation vehicles. Although the author of the book had asked such questions as "How many fire trucks are there?" and "How many fire trucks with ladders are there?" the children looked at the illustration and began to generate their own questions. "We could say, 'How many planes?'" "Or 'How many dump trucks?'" "Or 'How many boats?'" "Or 'How many cars with people?'"

After each question, the children counted together to determine the answer. They had latched onto the story's predictable pattern and were fascinated by the details in this particular illustration. Quite spontaneously they posed their own questions to emphasize the particular attributes that were most interesting to them. Engaging in this kind of problem generation helps learners to break the right-answer syndrome and demonstrates the infinite array of possible modifications.

After this discussion, the children constructed their own stories, with accompanying questions. Since they had been studying animals for some time, their teacher asked them to use this theme for their stories. Many used the children's book as a basis for posing their own questions. Jessica, for example, drew a variety of animals (spider, snake, panda bear, cat, and rabbit) and wrote: "Who lives the longest? How many have legs? 4. How many have fur? 3" (Figure 1–13). Other children posed questions that focused on the speed and movement of animals: "Who goes the fastest?" or "How many crawl on the ground?" Still others emphasized an animal's diet: "How many eat bugs?" and "How many animals swallow their food whole?" Some children asked questions that focused on physical characteristics, habitat, reproduction, or unique behaviors.

FIGURE 1–13

How to use this book

Inspired by these classroom stories and many others, we want to encourage you to use children's literature, both fiction and nonfiction, to expand and enrich your students' mathematical knowledge. Children can learn to appreciate mathematics in ways that go far beyond computation: as a tool for solving real-life problems, a way of thinking and expressing knowledge, and a source of aesthetic pleasure and recreation. Teachers who are aware of the variety of children's books with mathematical themes have a tremendous range of resources available to them to help them accomplish these goals.

We have designed this book as a series of explorations of the major topics of elementary school mathematics. Thus, we devote chapters to specific mathematical strategies, such as classification and estimation, and we include chapters that involve the four basic operations of addition, subtraction, multiplication, and division. We have organized other chapters around more general topics, such as geometry and measurement. And we have included a chapter on games and puzzles to demonstrate the integral part mathematical thinking plays in this kind of intellectual recreation. The chapter on place value focuses on a specific mathematical concept, and we have likewise stressed other important concepts throughout: for example, equivalence in the addition chapter, partitioning in the fractions chapter, and symmetry in the geometry chapter.

In the first part of each chapter, we discuss some of the children's books we have discovered and how they might be used to present particular mathematical topics. We have made an effort to include both fiction and nonfiction, as well as to include books reflecting a variety of cultures, both within and beyond North America. Then, under the heading "Books in the Classroom," we share stories of how teachers have used these books, providing examples at three grade levels: K–2, 3–4, and 5–6. A section called "Further Explorations" gives additional brief suggestions for classroom applications. We hope these ideas will serve as sources of inspiration rather than as prescriptions. We encourage you to look for these titles and others in local libraries and bookstores and to develop your own ways of using them with your students.

Each chapter concludes with a list of the books we have mentioned in the chapter and, in most cases, a number of others on the same topic. (Naturally, a number of these books are included in more than one chapter.) Many of the books are recent, but some are older and often considered classics. Whenever posssible, we have used the book's original publication date, but be aware that many of the older books have been reissued, sometimes by different publishers. We have avoided identifying titles by suggested grade level because we feel that such labeling is too restrictive. Instead, we encourage you to use these books in ways that make sense to you and your students; we have known eighth-grade teachers who use picture books with their students as well as first-grade teachers who use "chapter books." Rather than prescribe any one particular way in which to use these books, we want to support the open-ended exploration of possibilities.

Some general suggestions for using children's literature

Although all the books in this resource guide have a mathematical dimension, it is important to remember that they are first and foremost good literature. We want to conclude with a few suggestions about how to use them appropriately with children.

1. Enjoy the story. Don't destroy the magic of a story by interrupting it with mathematical questions as you read it aloud. Each book is a unique literary experience and should be enjoyed for its own sake. The first step in any of the explorations we've suggested is an uninterrupted reading with time for spontaneous, unstructured personal response.

2. Read the book aloud. In fact, do so several times when the book is short, particularly if it's a storybook. It is impossible for listeners to attend to all the dimensions of a shared story at one time. They need repeated opportunities to make connections with different parts of the story.

3. Keep these book experiences open-ended to encourage multiple interpretations. Let children respond to the story personally by asking them such divergent questions as, "Tell me something you enjoyed about this story," or "How does this story relate to experiences you've had?"

4. Enourage your students to respond to these stories through poetry, drama, art, written narrative, or oral discourse. Each form of expression affords learners a way to view mathematics from a different perspective. Such multiple perspectives can deepen and broaden learners' understanding of mathematical concepts.

5. Integrate these books into current themes of study (both in your mathematics program and elsewhere in the curriculum) or relate them to impromptu questions raised in class. Learners can make more connections, ask deeper questions, and add richer details to their own writing when teachers use children's books in a context that is familiar or arises from students' own concerns.

6. Use your own students as a guide for deciding what to read, not a preordained grade-level index. Picture books are not only for the primary grades, and parts of more difficult books can often be used with younger children. You know your students better than anyone and can best predict what will appeal to them (although we are all surprised from time to time!).

7. Consider the age of your students and your intended use of a book to decide whether oral reading to a class or silent reading by individuals is more appropriate. Although many of the episodes we describe involve reading aloud, students' personal exploration of books, particularly the longer ones, should also play an important part in the learning process.

Children's books

Anno, Mitsumasa. 1979. *The king's flower.* New York: Collins.

———— . 1983. *Anno's mysterious multiplying jar.* New York: Philomel.

Dee, Ruby. 1988. *Two ways to count to ten.* New York: Holt.

EarthWorks Group. 1990. *50 simple things kids can do to save the earth.* Kansas City: Andrews and McMeel.

Giganti, Paul, Jr. 1988. *How many snails? A counting book.* New York: Greenwillow.

Hoban, Tana. 1985. *Is it larger? Is it smaller?* New York: Greenwillow.

Hutchins, Pat. 1986. *The doorbell rang.* New York: Greenwillow.

Irons, Rosemary, and Calvin Irons. 1987. *Mirror mirror.* Crystal Lake, IL: Rigby.

Johnston, Tony. 1986. *Farmer Mack measures his pig.* New York: Harper and Row.

Krauss, Ruth. 1945. *The carrot seed.* New York: Harper and Row.

Mayer, Mercer. 1987. *Just a mess.* Racine, WI: Western.

Myller, Rolf. 1962. *How big is a foot?* New York: Atheneum.

Rees, Mary. 1988. *Ten in a bed.* Boston: Little, Brown.

Schwartz, David. 1985. *Hom much is a million?* New York: Lothrop, Lee and Shepard.

Teacher resources

Bishop, Alan. 1988. *Mathematical enculturation.* Boston: Kluwer.

Brown, Stephen, and Marion Walter. 1983. *The art of problem posing.* Hillsdale, NJ: Lawrence Erlbaum.

Davis, Philip, and Reuben Hersh. 1986. *Descartes' dream: The world according to mathematics.* Boston: Houghton Mifflin

Eisner, Elliott. 1985. *Aesthetic modes of knowing.* In Elliott Eisner, ed., *Learning and teaching the ways of knowing: The 84th yearbook of the National Society for the Study of Education, part II* (pp. 23–36). Chicago: National Society for the Study of Education.

National Council of Teachers of Mathematics (NCTM). 1989. *Curriculum and evaluation standards for school mathematics.* Reston, VA: National Council of Teachers of Mathematics.

Paulos, John. 1988. *Innumeracy.* New York: Hill and Wang.

Pimm, David. 1987. *Speaking mathematically.* New York: Routledge and Kegan Paul.

Wilde, Sandra. 1992. *You kan red this! Spelling and punctuation for whole-language classrooms, K–6.* Portsmouth, NH: Heinemann.

Have you ever entered an unfamiliar grocery store and had difficulty finding a particular item? What aisle is unsweetened cocoa in? Some stores put it with flour and sugar because it is a baking product, while others shelve it beside coffee because it is used to make a beverage. And what about soy sauce? In some stores we may find it grouped with Chinese food, in others with condiments .

Why do we have trouble finding these items? Because we do not know the store's classification system. Foods can be classified in innumerable ways. When we search an aisle and cannot find an item under one category, we need to think of another category that might include it. We are forced to become more flexible thinkers.

Children too must have experiences that help them become flexible thinkers. Classifying objects in different ways encourages this kind of thinking. Classification is not only a basic operation in logic, it is also fundamental to learning about the physical world. We learn to distinguish between reptiles and mammals, oak leaves and maple leaves, blueberries and poisonous berries. Classification skills help us make some sense of the vast number of objects that surround us. Thank goodness that libraries, classified ads, and yes, even grocery stores are organized in a way that allows us to use them efficiently. Classification is also a crucial strategy for young children to understand before meaningful number work begins: before children can group objects, they must know what a group is. Sorting and classifying can help children build this understanding, and children's literature can provide a wide variety of such classification experiences.

Personal collections

All of us are habitual collectors of one thing or another. We find, pick up, trade, and keep all manner of objects. Children often stuff their pockets with treasures—rocks, marbles, insects, erasers, small toys, baseball cards—and bring them to school. Children's literature can involve children in discussing their collections and sharing their strategies for classification. Even with the smallest collection children constantly compare and contrast the items they have: "I have two players on the New York Mets." "These feathers have blue on the edges but

2

classification

these don't." "These rocks have little specks of mica that shine but these other rocks are just one color."

An excellent starting point for a discussion of collections is Shel Silverstein's poem "Hector the Collector" (1974). Hector, an obsessive collector, surrounds himself with all kinds of treasures, from ice cream sticks and twists of wire to old shoelaces and worn-out belts.

One common object that people often collect and that children enjoy sorting in the classroom is buttons. "The Lost Button" from Arnold Lobel's *Frog and Toad Are Friends* (1970) is an enchanting way to introduce classification. In this story, Toad and Frog go for a walk. When they return, Toad notices that one of the buttons on his jacket is missing. When Frog tries to help his friend find the lost button, he discovers buttons in all kinds of places, but none possess the particular attributes of Toad's. Toad finally finds his button lying on the floor in his own house. He sews it onto his jacket along with all the other buttons Frog has found and presents Frog with his "new" jacket, covered with all the different buttons.

Another appealing story about buttons is Margarette Reid's *The Button Box* (1990). A young boy explores his grandmother's box of buttons, classifying them according to a variety of attributes: sparkly, metal, leather, shiny, pearly, two-holed, four-holed, wooden, thick, and thin. He and Grandma also play a game called "Are these two buttons alike?" This classification game, and the accompanying illustrations of all kinds of buttons, invites readers to grab the nearest jar of buttons and do some of their own sorting.

Since buying new buttons for a classroom collection can be expensive, teachers can search them out in other ways. Yard sales and flea markets often sell jars of buttons inexpensively; buttons can be cut off of old clothes that are about to be discarded; and parents can be asked to contribute unneeded extra buttons. There is also a National Button Society, a nonprofit organization devoted to the promotion of button collecting, which has a wealth of information on the history of buttons; it disseminates guidelines for classifying many kinds of buttons and encourages the development of programs for junior collections. The address is 2733 Juno Place, Akron, OH, 44313.

The objects we collect are not always organized in ways that make sense. Mercer Mayer's *Just a Mess* (1987) makes a case for the functional usefulness of a classification scheme. In this book, a "little critter" must clean his disorganized room in order to find his baseball glove. He decides to group things that go together and then put them away in their proper places. Unfortunately, the critter does not do a very thorough job of organizing. He crams most of his belongings under his bed or into the closet without adequately sorting them into groups that make sense. This story is a useful starting place for discussing alternative ways of classifying a given set of materials based on children's descriptions of how they organize their own rooms.

Classifying animals

A good introduction to animal classification is Tana Hoban's *A Children's Zoo* (1985). The book presents a color photograph of a zoo animal on one page and a list of three words describing that animal on the opposite page. A seal is "sleek," "black," and "swims," while an elephant is "gray," "wrinkled," and "trumpets." The descriptive words relate to color, size, texture, strength, pattern, and movement. On the last page of the book a chart documents additional distinguishing characteristics, such as habitat and diet. Elementary school teachers at every grade level could use this book to begin a discussion of animal similarities and differences.

Several other books highlight the necessarily arbitrary nature of the scientific classification system. In *Benny's Animals and How He Put Them in Order* (Selsam, 1966), Benny and his friend John group birds, bats, and butterflies together because they all have wings. Later, they learn that the an animal's underlying structure (not an external feature like wings) is the critical attribute for scientific classification. In *Rabbit and His Friends* (Scarry, 1973), a confused platypus hatches from an egg and tries to find its mother. The other animals have difficulty in identifying it because it has such a mixture of attributes. Mr. Rabbit claims that it looks like a duck because it has a beak and webbed feet, while Mrs. Hen says it looks like a beaver with its tail and fur coat. The story ends happily but also serves to illustrate the imperfect nature of any scientific classification scheme. Children can use these stories to investigate some of the anomalies of the animal kingdom. For instance, how do we classify the duck-billed platypus? It lays eggs like a reptile yet nurses its young like a mammal. Children often seem surprised that a penguin is a bird. They might want to create a list of the distinguishing characteristics of birds that will include penguins. Another scientific anomaly is the euglena; it ingests food like an animal but contains chlorophyll like a plant. These examples underscore the fact that classification systems do not always incorporate the diversity of creatures and objects that surround us. We must often make arbitrary decisions about how to divide up a complex world.

Anno's Math Games (Anno, 1987) invites children to do their own classifying. The first section, entitled "What is Different?," presents a series of objects and asks the reader to select the one that looks the most different. At first the difference is easy to identify—a red circle in the midst of blue squares or a flower among a group of animals. Soon, however, the distinguishing characteristic becomes more difficult to recognize and the pictures invite multiple interpretations. In one illustration of animals, for example, readers must decide whether the elephant is different because of its weight, the tiger different because of its stripes, or the lion different because of its mane. Anno represents a wonderful variety of mammals, reptiles, fish, and insects and provides readers with an open-ended invitation to devise their own classification schemes.

No topic in science is more popular in the elementary grades than dinosaurs. There are many good reference books on dinosaur life, but one that does a particularly good job of explaining the dinosaur classification system is Aliki's *Dinosaurs Are Different* (1985), in which dinosaurs are distinguished by their diet, number of legs, hip structure, and other special features such as plates, horns, and duck-bills. Once students become familiar with these attributes, the class can play the game of "Twenty Questions." For instance, "I'm thinking of a dinosaur. Try to guess its name. You can ask me any question with a yes or no answer."

"Does it have four legs?" " Yes."

"Does it eat plants?" "No."

"Is it longer than Ankylosaurus?" "Yes."

"Does it have spikes on its tail?" "No."

"Was it known as the 'King' of dinosaurs?" "Yes."

"It's Tyrannosaurus Rex!"

How Many Snails? (Giganti, 1988) introduces the idea of subsets (groupings within larger sets). Readers are asked to look at a set of flowers, for example, and then answer a series of classification questions: "How many flowers are there? How many yellow flowers are there? How many yellow flowers with black centers are there?" Readers looking at pictures of clouds, fish, butterflies, and toys are invited to find specific sets and subsets within each. Once children sense the predictable nature of this text, they will often spontaneously pose additional questions for some of the pictures. *All About 1, 2, 3* (Thomson, 1987) also uses questions to focus on the characteristics of various animals. This counting book follows Sam into the jungle to find one armadillo, two jaguars, three alligators, and so on. On each page there are two questions about the particular activities of that set of animals. For instance, when children see six snakes, they are asked how many have their tongues out and how many are lying on the ground.

Spots, Feathers, and Curly Tails (Tafuri, 1988) uses the attributes mentioned in the title, as well as "mane," "bill," and "horns," to pose a simpler series of questions. Each page shows part of an animal and asks a classification question, such as "Who has spots?" On the following page there is a full illustration of the animal and the answer, "A cow has spots." Both of these stories can be used to launch the "Categories Game," which many teachers have made a part of their daily classroom routine. Third-grade teacher David Millstone asks children to line up for lunch with classifying statements like "You may line up if you are wearing something red." Sometimes he includes several attributes: "You may line up if you're wearing white socks and a brown belt," or "You may line up if you have two thumbs and a lot of freckles." Some of the smallest words in the English language—*and, if, but, or, not*—are among the most important words in the mathematics communication system. The game of categories provides a context for investigating the meaning of such words. Possible statements using *or* include: "Line up if you played kickball at recess or ate a banana for lunch," or "Line up if you solved the math puzzle or helped some of us clean up the playground." Qualifying conditions that incorporate the word *but* can be used as well: "Line up if you're wearing a piece of jewelry but it's not a ring." Teachers can also encourage their students to be the leaders of this game. The children will naturally draw upon their own personal experience and knowledge of classroom events to devise classification schemes.

Classifying other materials

Since children often talk about their shoes and sneakers, *Shoes* (Winthrop, 1986) can be an intriguing starting point for exploring classification. Using a rhyming format, the author describes all kinds of shoes —shoes for skating, shoes for skipping, and shoes for doing a double flip in. In a series of black and white photographs, Ron Roy's *Whose Shoes Are These?* (1988) introduces readers to twenty different kinds of shoes, including sneakers, slippers, boots, clogs, and toe shoes. Through a set of questions and responses readers also learn about the function of these different kinds of shoes and why some are made with wooden bottoms or thick soles or stretchy rubber. Inspired by these books, children may want to try classifying their own footwear.

Two good books about hats are Ron Roy's *Whose Hat Is That?* (1987) and Ann Morris's *Hats, Hats, Hats* (1989b). Roy's characteristic black-and-white photographs portray a variety of hats, among them a chef's hat, a bathing cap, a painter's hat, a cowboy hat, and a graduation mortarboard. Readers also learn about the reasons behind the design of each hat, for instance, why a fire fighter's hat has sloping edges. Morris captures the rich diversity of hats from around the world in a series of vivid color photographs. Her book presents the hats of twelve nations, from the festive hats worn by Nigerian dancers to the yarmulke, the traditional cap worn by Jewish males, and could generate a rich discussion on the traditions and customs of different cultures.

Foods provide another wonderful area for exploring classification. Ann Morris again supplies evidence of cultural diversity, this time in the different breads eaten throughout the world. In *Bread, Bread, Bread* (1989a), she uses stunning color photographs to illustrate the sizes, shapes, colors, and functions of breads from the United States, France, Ghana, Israel, Mexico, and elsewhere. "Beans, Beans, Beans," a humorous poem by Lucia and James Hymes (1960), celebrates the different kinds of beans, from string beans and lima beans to baked beans and even jelly beans!

Tana Hoban has created a set of books that emphasize several different attributes: color, size, texture, and spatial relations. *Is It Red? Is It Yellow? Is It Blue?* (1978) presents color photographs with colored dots below to encourage children to find those colors in the picture. On some pages there is only a single dot; on others there may be as many as five dots to classify, for example, cars in a parking lot. *Of Colors and Things* (Hoban, 1989) also focuses on color by representing a range of objects within a particular color category. Each page is divided into four quadrants. Inside three of the quadrants are objects of one particular color, such as an ear of corn, a basket, and a butterfly, all yellow. In the fourth quadrant is an object that contains some of that color as well as other colors, for instance, a set of red, green, yellow, and blue blocks. Each object is photographed against a white background, which helps to focus attention on the salient characteristic of color. Hoban's *Is It Rough? Is It Smooth? Is It Shiny?* (1984) explores the attribute of texture. Color photographs without text introduce readers to objects, such as bubbles, mud, pretzels, hay, and kittens, with many different textures. The photographs invite multiple interpretations— bread is crusty and smooth; hay is scratchy, prickly, or rough—a good place to begin a discussion of texture words. Finally, in *Exactly the Opposite* (Hoban, 1990), a variety of outdoor color photographs also lend themselves to multiple interpretations. For instance, does the photograph of two hands portray left and right or open and closed? Do the photographs of bears represent parent and child, big and little, or playful and calm?

Books in the classroom K–2

After Marilyn Barnes read "The Lost Button" (Lobel, 1970) to her first-grade classroom, some of the children began to tell stories about things they had lost at school. Maurice was still disappointed about a jacket he had recently lost, so the class marched down to the "Lost and Found" department in hopes of recovering it. As they lifted each jacket from the box, Maurice explained why it was not *his* jacket, just as Toad had done in the case of his lost button. Although in the end he still didn't find his jacket, Maurice enjoyed the attention and earned the nickname of "Toad" for several weeks. The story gave children a framework for thinking about classification in a personally meaningful context.

In another first-grade classroom, Timothy O'Keefe shared *How Many Snails?* (Giganti, 1988) with his students. The children were in the middle of a transportation unit, and the story gave them a chance to share what they had learned about vehicles. They made drawings of their own sets of vehicles and then asked classification questions highlighting the attributes they considered most interesting. Tray, a meticulous artist with a passion for detail, drew a series of boats and recorded three questions: "How many got engines? How many has fancy stuff? How many do not have motors?" (Figure 2–1).

FIGURE 2–1

After Julie Robinson shared *Just a Mess* (Mayer, 1987) with her second-grade class, the students wanted to discuss how they could have helped the little critter devise a better organizational plan. Joey had noticed that the critter jammed game boards in a trunk and remarked, "Game boards can't go in a box because they could get torn up."

"Are there other ways to group his toys and belongings?" asked Julie. The children created a variety of categories: indoor equipment, outdoor equipment, clothes, shoes, winter games, and summer games. Each child developed a classification plan, and one student, Jennifer, had some helpful suggestions, as well as some harsh words, for the little critter who "made the wrong decision" (Figure 2–2): "It would have helped if the little critter had kept all of his toys in families, like sports in one group and toy trucks in another group. He made the wrong decision about putting all of his toys under the bed and in the closet. The little critter made the wrong decision."

FIGURE 2–2

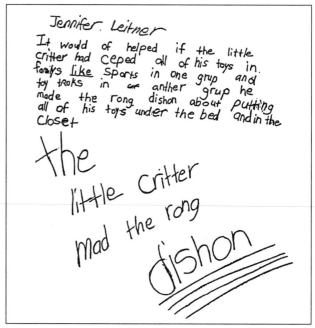

Books in the classroom 3–4

Fourth-grade teacher Nancy Wallace read *Shoes* (Winthrop, 1986b) aloud to the class. Then she asked her students to take off one of their shoes, place it in a common pile, and think of ways to classify this set. Some of their suggestions included shoes with and without laces, shoes with a common sole color or material, shoes with tassels or buckles or straps, shoes with writing on them, and shoes that are washable.

Other fourth-grade students used the book to canvass their peers about the kind of sneakers they wore. One student's findings—and the conclusions he drew from those findings—are shown in Figure 2–3.

Experiences like these promote flexible thinking. Learners come to see that a given set of objects can be sorted in a number of different ways, often overlapping. They begin to realize that classification schemes are arbitrary systems and that the sets they construct reflect their own background knowledge, interests, and intentions. They thus become aware, perhaps for the first time, that mathematics is a human construct for communicating ideas and sharing knowledge. As such, a variety of responses ought to be encouraged, debated, and discussed. When David Whitin invited third graders to compose their own classification poem based on "Beans, Beans, Beans" (Hymes and Hymes, 1960), Stacy wrote a version using cats (Figure 2–4). She used the structure of the original poem to describe a set of animals that were meaningful to her.

FIGURE 2-3

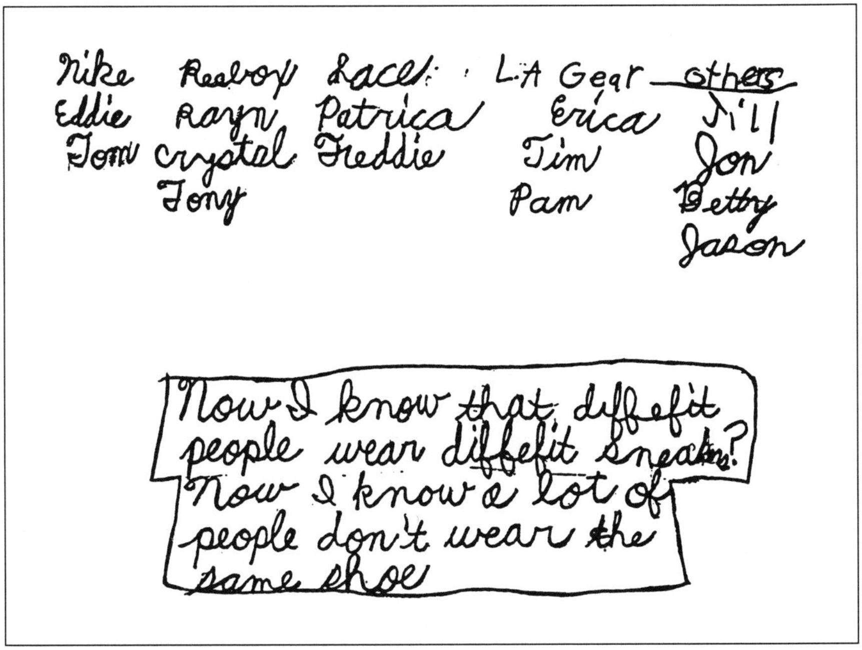

Nike   Reebok   Laces   L.A. Gear   others
Eddie   Rayn   Patrica Erica   Jill
Tom   Crystal   Freddie Tim   Jon
        Tony   Pam   Betty
                                        Jason

Now I know that diffefit people wear diffefit sneakers? Now I know a lot of people don't wear the same shoe

FIGURE 2-4

Cats
Cats
Cats

Big cats,
Little cats,
Diffrent kinds of tom cats,
Itsy, bitsy, kitty cats,
Those are just a few.
Fat cats,
Thin cats,
Big fat black cats,
Cuddly little yellow cats,
Crazy cats, too.
Brown cats,
Ichy cats,
Don't forget baby cats,
Last of all best of all,
I like wiches cats!!!

By Stacey
Anderson

Books in the classroom 5–6

Inspired by "The Lost Button" (Lobel, 1970), some of the fifth-grade students in Evelina Montgomery's classroom classified the buttons in the classroom button box. One student sorted her pile according to a variety of attributes, such as color, texture, and number of holes (Figure 2–5).

Another group of fifth graders created a fairy tale in which a set of twins wanted to marry the daughters of a king. The king posed "riddles" (Figure 2–6), a series of mathematics problems the twins had to solve in order to be considered proper suitors. The children organized the story to include contexts for division, subtraction, and the use of fractional parts and incorporated several classification attributes.

FIGURE 2–5

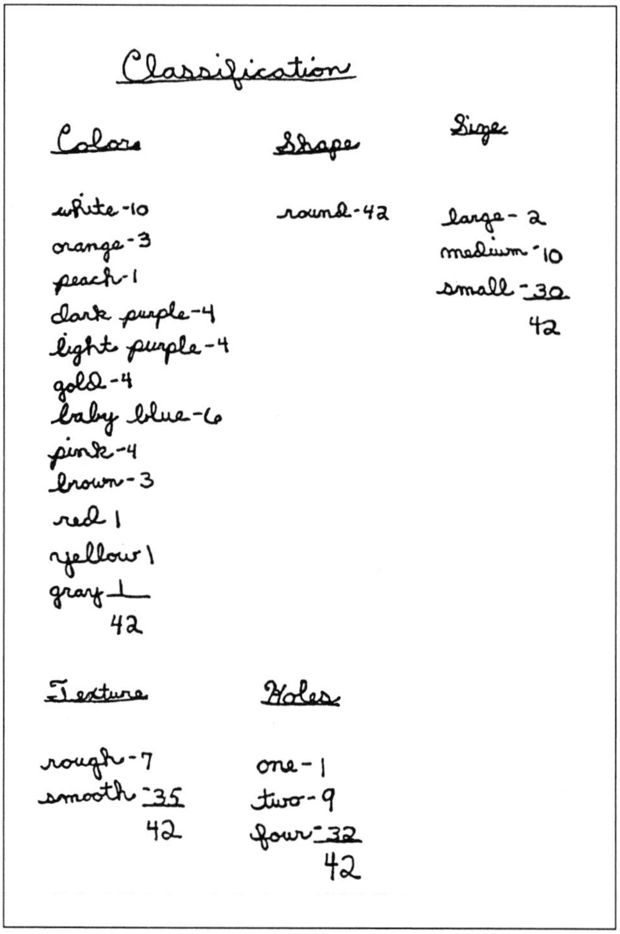

Classification

Colors	Shape	Size
white - 10	round - 42	large - 2
orange - 3		medium - 10
peach - 1		small - 30
dark purple - 4		42
light purple - 4		
gold - 4		
baby blue - 6		
pink - 4		
brown - 3		
red 1		
yellow 1		
gray 1		
42		

Texture	Holes
rough - 7	one - 1
smooth - 35	two - 9
42	four - 32
	42

FIGURE 2–6

<u>Riddles</u>

1. There are 56 buttons. There are 43 rough buttons. How many are smooth?

2. Out of 56 buttons 11 have one hole and 3 have two holes. How many have four holes?

3. There are 9 buttons. 3 are red. 3 are dark blue. How many are black?

4. There are 22 buttons. ½ are pink 2 are brown and 1 is orange. How many are light blue?

Further explorations

1. What classification decisions have you made as a teacher in organizing your classroom? How might you involve children in some of these decisions, such as sorting and arranging the books in the class library at the beginning of the year or categorizing games on the mathematics shelf or junk material in the art center?

2. What are your students' hobbies? Do they enjoy collecting dolls, matchbox cars, shells, pencils? How might you involve children in sharing their collections and describing the classification system they have used? How might you encourage those who don't have one to begin a collection of their own? *The Button Box* (Reid, 1990) could inspire students to write stories or books about their own collections.

3. Ann Morris's *Hats, Hats, Hats* (1989b) and *Bread, Bread, Bread* (1989a) can serve as appealing models for student-written books about other artifacts from around the world. For instance, children might want to research, write, and illustrate a book called *Houses, Houses, Houses* or *Toys, Toys, Toys*.

4. Peter Spier's *People* (Spier, 1980) illustrates and celebrates the great diversity of people in the world. A class exploration of human diversity could use this book to think about the interplay of similarities and differences among people and cultures.

5. Reference books provide raw data for classifying. For instance, students could use a book about mammals or plants to devise their own subcategory classification scheme.

Children's books

Aliki. 1985. *Dinosaurs are different*. New York: Crowell.

Anno, Mitsumasa. 1984. *Anno's flea market*. New York: Philomel.

———. 1987. *Anno's math games*. New York: Philomel.

———. 1989. *Anno's math games II*. New York: Philomel.

Carle, Eric. 1975. *The mixed-up chameleon*. New York: Crowell.

Ehlert, Lois. 1988. *Planting a rainbow*. New York: Harcourt Brace Jovanovich.

Froman, Robert. 1972. *Venn diagrams*. New York: Crowell.

Giganti, Paul, Jr. 1988. *How many snails? A counting book*. New York: Greenwillow.

Hoban, Tana. 1978. *Is it red? Is it yellow? Is it blue?* New York: Mulberry.

———. 1984. *Is it rough? Is it smooth? Is it shiny?* New York: Greenwillow.

———. 1985. *A children's zoo*. New York: Greenwillow.

———. 1987. *Dots, freckles, and stripes*. New York: Greenwillow.

———. 1989. *Of colors and things*. New York: Greenwillow.

———. 1990. *Exactly the opposite*. New York: Greenwillow.

Hymes, Lucia, and James Hymes. 1960. Beans, beans, beans. In *Hooray for chocolate*. Reading, MA: Addison-Wesley.

Imershein, Betsy. 1989. *Finding red, finding yellow*. New York: Harcourt Brace Jovanovich.

Konigsburg, E. L. 1990. *Samuel Todd's book of great colors*. New York: Atheneum.

Lionni, Leo. 1975. *A color of his own*. New York: Pantheon.

Lobel, Arnold. 1970. The lost button. In *Frog and toad are friends*. New York: Harper and Row.

Mayer, Mercer. 1987. *Just a mess*. Racine, WI: Western.

McMillan, Bruce. 1988a. *Dry or wet?* New York: Lothrop, Lee and Shepard.

———. 1988b. *Growing colors*. New York: Lothrop, Lee and Shepard.

Morris, Ann. 1989a. *Bread, bread, bread*. New York: Lothrop, Lee and Shepard.

———. 1989b. *Hats, hats, hats*. New York: Lothrop, Lee and Shepard.

Reid, Margarette S. 1990. *The button box*. New York: Dutton.

Roy, Ron. 1987. *Whose hat is that?* New York: Clarion.

———. 1988. *Whose shoes are these?* New York: Clarion.

Ruben, Patricia. 1978. *What is new? What is missing? What is different?* New York: Lippincott.

Scarry, Richard. 1973. *Rabbit and his friends*. Racine, WI: Western.

Selsam, Millicent. 1966. *Benny's animals, and how he put them in order*. New York: Harper and Row.

Silverstein, Shel. 1974. Hector the collector. In *Where the sidewalk ends*. New York: Harper and Row.

Sis, Peter. 1990. *Beach ball*. New York: Greenwillow.

Slobodkina, Esphyr. 1976. *Caps for sale*. New York: Scholastic.

Spier, Peter. 1980. *People*. Garden City, NY: Doubleday.

———. 1988. *Fast-slow, high-low*. Garden City, NY: Doubleday.

Tafuri, Nancy. 1988. *Spots, feathers, and curly tails*. New York: Greenwillow.

Thomson, Ruth. 1987. *All about 1, 2, 3*. Milwaukee, WI: Gareth Stevens.

Winthrop, Elizabeth. 1986. *Shoes*. New York: Harper and Row.

Teacher resources

Chase, William, and Helen Chase. 1990. *Chase's annual events*. Chicago: Contemporary Books.

Whitin, David J. 1989. Bring on the buttons. *Arithmetic Teacher, 35:* 4–6.

Quick, what number comes after one thousand ninety-nine? If you answered two thousand (rather than one thousand one hundred), your grasp of place value isn't as intuitive as it could be! Place value is one of the most important mathematical concepts children need to understand, and since it is rather abstract, they need to use a variety of materials to represent, manipulate, and explore it. Children's literature can help by providing, in pictures and through language, a range of models for place value.

Proportional representations

The heart of the concept of place value is the relationship between ones, tens, hundreds, and so on in our numerical system. Children need a concrete grasp of the fact that the first *3* in *33* represents ten times as many units as the second *3*. Important mathematics manipulatives for helping children to conceptualize place value are *proportional aids,* defined as concrete materials with a readily apparent size difference, so that the object representing ten is ten times as long, wide, heavy, thick, or numerous as the object representing one. The familiar base ten blocks are an excellent example of a proportional model. The long wooden stick representing 10 is ten times longer than the single unit representing 1, the large flat piece representing 100 units is ten times bigger still, and so on. Three counting books[1] that illustrate the proportional relationship between one and ten are *Anno's Counting Book* (Anno, 1977), *Count and See* (Hoban, 1972), and *Counting Wildflowers* (McMillan, 1986). *Anno's Math Games II* (Anno, 1989) also addresses the concept of place value proportionally.

Anno's Counting Book depicts the numbers 0 through 12 with pictures of a landscape that changes month by month throughout the year. This wordless picture book invites readers to look at the illustrations and find as many sets as they can for each number. For instance, in the picture for "three" there are sets of three buildings, children, flowers, trees, butterflies, boats, and so on. There is a large numeral 3 on the right-hand side of the two-page spread, while on the left-hand side there is an outline silhouette of ten blocks, three of

3

place value and

numeration

systems

---

[1] Counting books are dealt with at length in Chapter 4, which focuses on counting and addition.

which have been filled in with color. The numbers 11 and 12 are represented by one stack of ten blocks plus part of a second stack. The illustration for 11 nicely shows how the stack of ten is ten times longer than a single cube. Children could use their own counting blocks or snap-together cubes to represent this same proportional relationship.

Anno also uses a series of blocks in *Anno's Math Games II*. The two characters in the book, Kriss and Kross, are involved in a variety of mathematical explorations. At one point they are stacking up squares inside a shed. They are able to represent each number from 1 through 9 but cannot fit in a tenth block because of the sloping roof of the shed. So Kriss and Kross tie the row of ten squares together in one long stack and put them in the warehouse next to the shed. They then begin to build other numbers, such as 12 and 13, by using a set of ten in the warehouse and individual squares in the shed. These blocks also help to demonstrate the proportionality between ten and one. Later in the book they apply this same grouping principle to the concept of capacity in measuring a large bowl of water. Instead of measuring it cup by cup, they stack ten cups on top of each other to create a beaker, enabling them to measure sixty-eight cupfuls quite efficiently. This is an unusual demonstration of the place value concept, since it employs a continuous material, water, rather than discrete (countable) materials, such as blocks, which are more frequently used in this context.

In *Count and See*, Tana Hoban counts using a series of black-and-white photographs. Each photograph is accompanied by three representations of its number: a large numeral, the number word, and a series of dots. Once the line of dots reaches 10, a second line of dots begins with the number 11. The counting proceeds to 15 and then jumps to other multiples of ten: 20 watermelon seeds, 30 bottle caps, 40 peanuts, 50 nails, and 100 peas in a pod. The photographs for 40, 50, and 100 are particularly effective because they show the objects displayed in sets of ten, echoed by dots that are also grouped in tens.

Bruce McMillan's *Counting Wildflowers* uses a series of color photographs of wildflowers to represent the numbers 1 to 20. Each page has a large, crisp photograph of a particular flower. As in *Count and See*, below each photograph is a numeral, a number word, and a silhouette of dots. An attractive feature of this book is the color coordination of the wildflower and the counting dots. For example, the pale blue of three forget-me-nots is used to fill in three of the circles below that photograph. The remaining circles are colored green to correspond to the green vegetation that provides the background for each photograph. Also, as in Hoban's book, the dots for numbers 10 or greater show a grouping of ten.

Grouping in a more general sense is represented in *More Than One* (Hoban, 1981). A series of black-and-white photographs portray a variety of grouping words, such as a *herd* of elephants, a *flock* of geese, a *pile* of tires and a *crowd* of people. A term like *flock* does not refer to a specific number of geese; rather these terms usually refer to any large number of the being or object in question. This book explores indeterminate terms for grouping, which can then be contrasted to specific numerical groupings like *ten*.

Nonproportional models

A place value number system represents proportional differences in numbers in a nonproportional way; for instance, the first *3* in *33* is not written ten times as big as the second one. Children can also learn about the concept of place value by using a variety of nonproportional manipulative materials. These materials represent this concept in a more abstract way because they often signify quantity differences through an attribute such as color and/or position. The abacus is a good model of this system. If we were to represent the number 33 on a typical classroom abacus, the three beads that represent the tens look the same as the three beads that represent the ones; place value is expressed through the beads' position on adjacent wires. An interesting introduction to the Chinese abacus is *The Abacus* (Dilson, 1968), which provides a historical look at this particular abacus and gives directions on how to use it. Children might want to create their own abacus to use in the classroom. One of the benefits of nonproportional aids such as the abacus is that children can represent very large numbers quite easily, just as we can with our numeration system. (Imagine having to use proportional representation to write numbers of a billion and more; it would be impossible!)

Another example of a nonproportional aid is money. The coins we use have a predetermined value, but the relative differences in those values are not visibly apparent. The confusion that this monetary system causes children is represented in Shel Silverstein's poem "Smart," in *Where the Sidewalk Ends* (1974). A young boy receives a dollar bill from his father and proceeds to "trick" other people through a series of exchanges; he trades the dollar bill for two quarters because two is more than one; he then trades the two quarters for three dimes because three is more than two, and so forth. Of course, the trick is on him because he ends up with only five pennies in place of the dollar he started out with.

Understanding zero

A unique feature of our numeration system is that we have a symbol for zero. The Romans, Babylonians, and Egyptians devised numeration systems that had no zero, which made them less efficient. The Romans had to write 108 using five symbols (CVIII) and needed special symbols for ten (X), one hundred (C), and one thousand (M). In the case of 108, our zero acts as a placeholder for "no tens." We can write the number using only three symbols and do not need separate characters for each power of ten. Zero is therefore an important aspect of a place value system.

Several children's books focus on zero. *Anno's Counting Book*, mentioned earlier, is unusual for a counting book because it begins with zero. The "zero" illustration shows a stark, snowy landscape that rapidly fills up with houses, trees, people, and so on as the book proceeds. This picture would be a good place to start a discussion of zero and children's various interpretations of this concept. Another book that also explores various contexts for zero is *Zero: Is It Something? Is It Nothing?* (Zaslavsky, 1989). In some instances zero means nothing, such as no animals under the bed; in other situations zero is a place-holder, as on an odometer; in still other cases zeroes are used when rounding off large numbers. Further contexts for zero are the zero on a kitchen timer that indicates no time remaining, the zero on a ruler that indicates a starting place, the zero of a countdown sequence that signifies the time to begin an action, and the zero on a Celsius thermometer to show the point at which water freezes. These contexts for zero help to broaden a child's understanding of this rather abstract concept.

Other numeration systems

Mathematics is a human endeavor, a communication system devised by people to meet their culture's changing needs and interests. In ancient times, people invented trigonometry, which relates distances to directions, to assist navigators in crossing the seas. In later centuries, as commerce continued to grow and certain calculations had to be repeated frequently, people invented algebra as a more efficient means of computing. Mathematics was continually shaped and revised to address changing human needs. Unfortunately, children sometimes lose sight of the human dimension of mathematics when they are required to spend countless hours in computational practice. No topic can better restore the human touch to mathematical learning then the history of other numeration systems. Children can begin to see mathematics as an evolving historical record of people and their numerical ideas.

Leonard Simon's story "Counting Lightly" (1972) introduces readers to the concept of one-to-one correspondence in a cross-cultural context. A young boy wants to become a great hunter but first he must learn to report the total number of buffalo he sees. He tries to convey the number through general comparisons like "There are more buffalo than stars in the sky." When his father presses him for a more specific count, he decides to carry back one stone for every buffalo. But he has difficulty carrying such a heavy load and decides to use a set of sticks to represent the number of buffalo. All this lifting and carrying makes him almost too tired to hunt! His sister finally comes to the rescue by explaining that he can count with only one stick if he makes a series of notches in it to represent what he has seen. She tells him about number names, and he realizes that by using them he will truly be "counting lightly."

This story highlights the different strategies people have used to communicate the size of a set, such as general comparisons, one-to-one correspondence, and number names, and fosters an appreciation of the convenience and efficiency of a standardized numeration system.

How Did Numbers Begin? (Sitomer and Sitomer, 1976) also traces the early historical development of numbers and counting and emphasizes the language of general comparisons (*as many as, less than,* and *more than*). The authors suggest that matching could very well have been the first important step in the development of number ideas and encourage children to think of activities that reflect this concept, such as playing dominoes or musical chairs. An especially interesting part of the book considers the origin of particular number names. In China the word for two is the same as the word for eyes, and in Tibet the word for two is the same as the word for ears. In many other languages the words for five and hand are synonymous. Using fingers in counting also influenced the derivation of the word *eleven,* whose etymology reflects the concept of "one left over when counting by tens." This survey of the historical development of number words adds an important human dimension to mathematics.

The use of finger counting in African cultures is described by Claudia Zaslavsky in *Count on Your Fingers African Style* (1980), which presents different kinds of finger-counting strategies. For example, the Kamlia people show eight by using the right hand to hold three fingers of the left hand, (five plus three more). The Taita show eight by raising four fingers on each hand, while the Masai wave four fingers of the right hand to represent eight. Most authorities agree that our base ten system is derived from our ten fingers. This book underscores this point and describes the diverse range of counting strategies in African cultures. Zaslavsky has also written a book for adults, *Africa Counts* (1973), that provides a fascinating overview for teachers who would like a deeper understanding of Africa's mathematical systems.

How to Count Like a Martian (St. John, 1975) surveys a variety of numeration systems: Greek, Roman, Chinese, Babylonian, Mayan, and Egyptian. This is an excellent book for clarifying the similarities and differences between numeration systems. The Egyptians had many symbols and no fixed order for writing down their numerals. The Babylonians, on the other hand, had only one mark, a wedge-shaped symbol that was pressed into clay tablets. It allowed them, however, to represent very large numbers because they incorporated the important feature of place value into their numeration system. They reasoned that if they placed wedges in different places, the value of its position would give an old wedge a new meaning. The Babylonians were thus one of the first cultures to develop a true base system in which there is a process of repeated grouping—in this case, base sixty. The Mayan system was one of the first to include the use of zero as a placeholder. Children can contrast the Egyptian, Babylonian, and Mayan systems, which used tally marks (the same symbol repeated over and over again) to represent their numbers, with the Greek, Chinese, and Hindu systems, which used a varied set of symbols that constituted a code.

Another popular book relating to counting, *Knots on a Counting Rope* (Martin and Archambault, 1987), has been criticized as an inauthentic portrayal of Native American culture in both its pictures and its text. A better introduction to the counting rope, also known as the quipu, can be found in *Code of the Quipu* (Ascher and Ascher, 1981), an adult book that can serve as a resource for teachers. The quipus of the Incas reflected a base ten positional system. Each counting rope had various cluster positions separated by spaces to distinguish one set of knots from another. These positions represented the ones place, the tens place, the hundreds place, and so forth. Children could use quipus to represent larger numbers, and thus explore another nonproportional aid.

Books in the classroom K-2

When first-grade teacher Cassandra Gary shared Tana Hoban's *Count and See* (1972) with her students, she called their attention to the book's representation of eleven. "Does this picture remind you of anything?" One child remarked, "Yes, it's like what we do with the popsicle sticks and our calendar." The children had been keeping track of the date by placing a popsicle stick in a plastic cup labeled "ones." Once the tenth day of the month arrived, the children followed a rule of obligatory grouping into tens by bundling those ten sticks together and placing them in the cup to the left marked "tens."

After she had read the story to the class, Cassandra invited the children to pick their favorite number, illustrate it, and place their page in a class number book. She gave them a paper punch and some glue so that they could also represent their number using dots. Lauren drew thirteen rainbows and made an interesting decision in using the dots (Figure 3–1). The ten dots on the left were blue and the three dots on the right were pink. As she explained, "I used this different color for ones because they haven't got to tens yet. When it gets to ten it changes color." Lauren knew that "ten-ness" often involves grouping or changing, because of her experience of using popsicle sticks to group by tens. Here she used color, a somewhat more abstract method than the physical operation of bundling, to represent a change in category, thus paving the way for later nonproportional representations of place value.

Marissa chose to illustrate a watermelon with seeds (Figure 3–2). Her text reads, "There are 17 watermelon seeds. 17. Seventeen." One of the photographs in Hoban's book was of a watermelon, and Marissa's decision to draw one provided a striking contrast between the random display of a watermelon with seeds and the logical, systematic grouping scheme of the place value system.

FIGURE 3–1

FIGURE 3–2

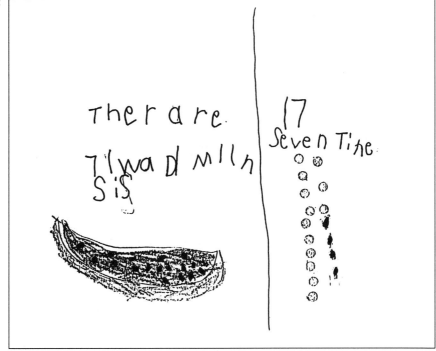

FIGURE 3–3

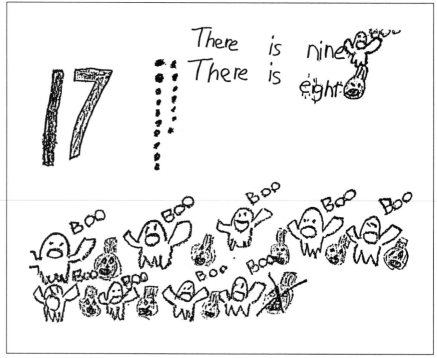

James's drawing (Figure 3–3) presents a number of interesting mathematical ideas. His text reads, "There is nine. There is eight." James demonstrates the concept of equivalence by describing through pictures two names for seventeen: 9 + 8 = 17 (ghosts and pumpkins) and 10 + 7 = 17 (dots). At the top of his paper he includes a symbolic key to show the total number of ghosts and pumpkins. The place value representation of 10 + 7 records the total number of objects joined together, although no visual distinction is made between the set of ten and the set of seven. James thus represents seventeen in three ways—picture illustrations, a symbolic key, and the more abstract grouping of tens and ones—making his own connections between concrete and abstract representations.

Books in the classroom 3–4

David Whitin read parts of *How to Count Like a Martian* (St. John, 1975) to his third-grade class. Each month the class studied a different numeration system described in the book. They compared and contrasted each one with our Hindu-Arabic system and kept track of the date using that month's system. When they studied the Egyptian system, David asked the class to write the numeral 31 in Egyptian numerals in as many different ways as they could. The children produced the possibilities seen in Figure 3–4: the heel-bone represents ten and the tally mark represents one.

David then challenged the children to try changing the position of the digits in our numeral 135. They discovered these possibilities, from smallest to largest: 135, 153, 315, 351, 513, 531. David asked if they all represented the number 135, and the children claimed that the numbers represented different amounts. "How is it possible," David asked, "that we can switch around the Egyptian symbols in different ways and still represent the same amount, but we can't perform such changes on our own numbers?" The children gave various explanations: "Our numbers are in a particular order, and they have to stay in that order or they mean a different number." "They didn't have a ones, tens, and hundreds place like we do. You could just put them any old way." Their comments helped to highlight a central aspect of the place value concept, the value of the place, particularly when compared with the Egyptian non-place-value system. Because the children were encouraged to discover and describe the concept in their own words rather than being given a rule, their knowledge was grounded in their own thinking.

David contrasted the two systems in another way by asking the children to write down the number 87 in Egyptian numerals as fast as they could. He noted that it took students about twenty-five seconds to complete the task. "Now I'm going to give you another number and I want you to write this one down as quickly as possible, too, but this time you can use our own system of numerals. Raise your hand again when you finish. The number is 127." Not surprisingly, the students needed only about four seconds.

"Why did you take such a long time using Egyptian numerals and such a short time using our own?" David asked. Again the children made some perceptive observations: "We didn't have to write as much with our own numbers." "Yeah, we don't have to write the same thing over and over; like for 80 we can just write one 'eight,' but they have to write 'ten' eight times." "Ours is quicker." "Yeah. It saves time. It's a lot faster."

FIGURE 3–4

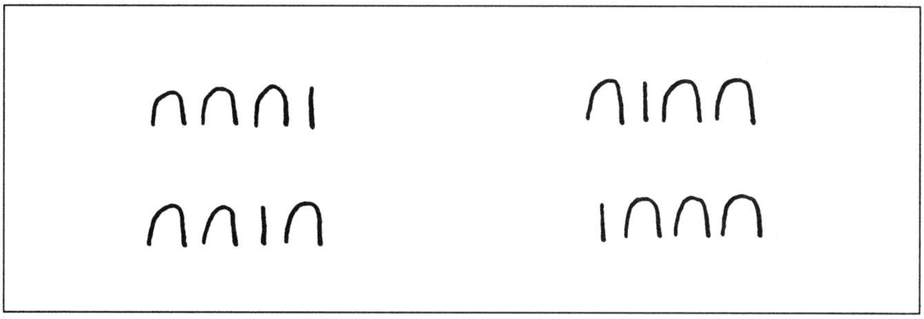

Here again the discussion centered on the value of the place as an important dimension of our numeration system. The children were gaining an appreciation for the convenience and efficiency of their own place value system by comparing it to a more cumbersome one.

Books in the classroom 5–6

Since zero can be a difficult concept for children to understand, David Whitin invited some fifth-grade students to create a book about zero for children in the primary grades. At first David asked these fifth graders why they thought zero was such a difficult idea to understand. They suggested several possible reasons:

1. "When you start counting you always begin with 1, like 1, 2, 3 . . . and you never mention zero."
2. "Because you can't hold it or see it."
3. "Because you can't show how many. You can't illustrate it."
4. "There is always something there, because even an empty jar has something in it."

These comments were insightful. The students recognized the abstract nature of zero and knew it was difficult to represent. They also knew it was often omitted from the regular counting sequence (except when a number line model is used). One student even realized that the very concept of zero can be ambiguous, since in one sense an empty container is not really empty.

David then asked, "Where have you seen zero being used both in and out of school?" The children volunteered some novel responses:

Context	Meaning
In outer space	"Zero is a state of nothingness."
Time	"In army time zero is midnight, zero hundred hours."
Stories	"You sometimes read stories and there's nothing in a treasure chest."
Stock market	"Zero means that the market stayed in the same place; it was steady and there were no changes."
Tracks in the mud or snow	"Zero means that the person who made the tracks isn't there right now."

Speedometer   "Zero means you are standing still and you
                                       aren't going anywhere."

David then read *Zero: Is It Something? Is It Nothing?* (Zaslavsky, 1989) to the
class, a book that highlighted still other contexts, such as the place of zero on a
thermometer, a kitchen timer, and a ruler.

David invited the children to create an illustration about the concept of
zero to include in a book for the primary grades. Their representations showed
a rich diversity of contexts. Luther was intrigued by the passage in the book
that described zero as a place holder: 205 Maple Street did not designate the
same house as 25 Maple Street. Since Luther had several allergies and was cur-
rently receiving weekly shots for these allergies, he created a story that reflected his own particular circumstances (Figure 3–5). Robin reported that she
had often worked with first graders on various projects and she knew the

FIGURE 3–5

Dr. Minks gave Billy 60 cc# of medicen for a snake bite. If Dr. Minks had taken off the zero he would have given Billy 6cc# of medicen, and. Billy might have died!

Fire!!!

FIGURE 3-6

Ashley goes to the toy store. She sees 4 toys on the top shelf and 1 toy on the next shelf. But she sees nothing on the bottom shelf.

How many toys are on the shelves?

There are 5 toys altogether.

FIGURE 3-7

If you found some tracks but there is no one there who made the tracks.

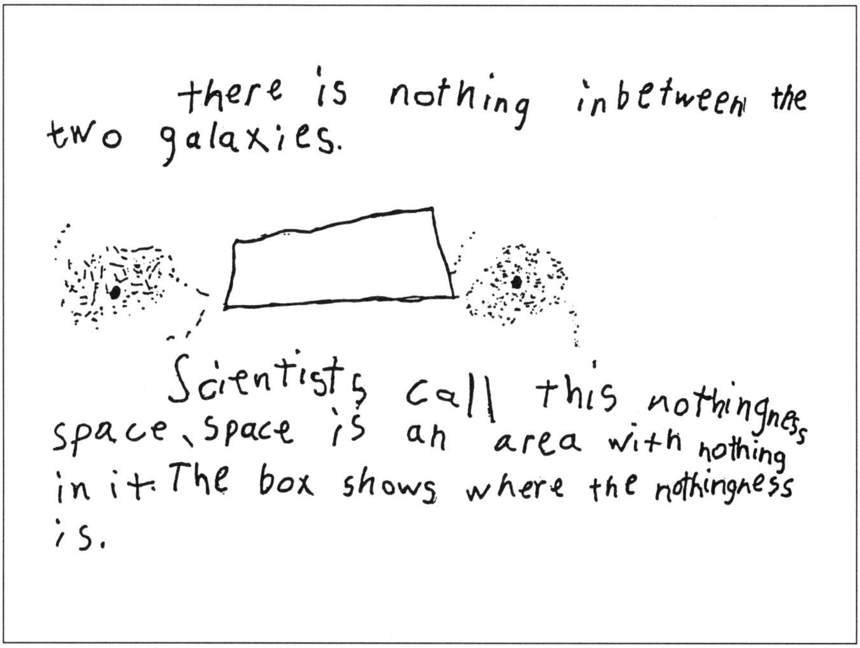

there is nothing inbetween the two galaxies.

Scientists call this nothingness space, space is an area with nothing in it. The box shows where the nothingness is.

FIGURE 3–8

"kind of toys and things those kids talk about." When she created her story, she included items on the toy shelf that her audience would know about, such as stuffed animals and Ninja turtles (Figure 3–6). Robin's story was typical of several of the children's stories: zero was often only one of the numbers used. As Robin explained, the younger children could better understand zero if they could compare it to other numbers.

The notion that zero can really represent something was illustrated by Beau in his footprint story (Figure 3–7). The footprints are a helpful, concrete reminder of the person who used to be there. Nathan also represented zero visually when he illustrated his concept of nothingness (Figure 3–8). In Nathan's story, zero acts as a "spatial" placeholder between two galaxies.

Further explorations

1. After reading *More Than One* (Hoban, 1981) as an introduction to the language of grouping, you might explore children's own grouping schemes. David Millstone and David Whitin noticed that children in one third/fourth-grade room employed their own personalized trading plan on the playground as they shot marbles, using the following exchange rates:

1 Jumbo = 2 Biggies	1 Biggie Puree = 2 Biggies
1 Biggie = 10 Littlies	1 Little Ball Bearing = 5 Littlies
1 Puree = 2 Littlies	1 Cat's Eye = 2 Littlies

In this informal trading context the children were able to explore the principle of grouping and exchanging.

2. How do your students use their fingers to perform calculations? The children might like to read *Count on Your Fingers African Style* (Zaslavsky, 1980) and then share their own finger-counting strategies. The class can discuss together the mathematical principles various strategies demonstrate.

3. How much experience do your children have with money? You might invite them to devise some trading games that require players to exchange play money: pennies to dimes to dollars (base ten), or pennies to nickels to quarters (base five). Board games that use play money, like Monopoly, also provide opportunities to manipulate this numeration system.

4. The photography books *Count and See* (Hoban, 1972) and *Counting the Wildflowers* (McMillan, 1986) might be used as models for students' own books, which they can illustrate with drawings or photographs. A nature walk can become a counting walk; bring a Polaroid camera to document the numbers the children see. The resulting photographs can be turned into a book, perhaps focusing entirely on numbers greater than ten in order to emphasize place value. This activity would interest younger children beginning to learn about place value; older children might enjoy making books for a lower-grade classroom.

5. How do your students think numbers began? You might read them some books on this topic and then invite them to create their own numeration system. How would a system based on five (the fingers of one hand) work? How about adding toes to establish a base twenty system? What are the pros and cons of these as compared to base ten?

6. Students who are interested in computers might like to explore the role of base two as the foundation of the electronic manipulation of numbers. *Binary Numbers* (Watson, 1977) is one helpful source of information.

7. Students may be interested in learning about the Dozenal Society, an organization that advocates the use of base twelve. This group has created symbols for ten and eleven and even devised an inexpensive slide rule. Their address is: Dozenal Society, c/o Mathematics Department, Nassau Community College, Garden City, NY 11530.

8. Students who are interested in a bit of mathematical magic might want to try the card-guessing trick described by Marilyn Burns in *The I Hate Mathematics! Book* (1975). The numbers 1 through 35 are written on several cards in a special way that reflects their composition in base two. This hidden relationship enables the magician to identify the mystery number every time.

Children's books

Adler, David. 1975. *Base five*. New York: Crowell.
——— . 1977. *Roman numerals*. New York: Crowell.
Anno, Mitsumasa. 1977. *Anno's counting book*. New York: Harper and Row.
——— . 1989. *Anno's math games II*. New York: Philomel.
Burns, Marilyn. 1975. *The I hate mathematics! book*. Boston: Little, Brown.
Dilson, Jesse. 1968. *The abacus*. New York: St. Martin's.
Hoban, Tana. 1972. *Count and see*. New York: Macmillan.
——— . 1981. *More than one*. New York: Greenwillow.
Martin, Bill, Jr., and John Archambault. 1987. *Knots on a counting rope*. New York: Henry Holt.
McMillan, Bruce. 1986. *Counting wildflowers*. New York: Lothrop, Lee, and Shepard.
Morrison, Philip, Phylis Morrison, and the Office of Charles and Ray Eames. 1982. *Powers of ten*. New York: Scientific American.
Russell, Solveig P. 1970. *One, two, three and many: A first look at numbers*. New York: H. Z. Walck.
St. John, Glory. 1975. *How to count like a Martian*. New York: H. Z. Walck.
Silverstein, Shel. 1974. Smart. In *Where the sidewalk ends*. New York: Harper and Row.
Simon, Leonard. 1972. Counting lightly. In Bill Martin, Jr., ed., *Sounds of the storyteller*. New York: Holt, Rinehart and Winston.
——— . 1963. *The day the numbers disappeared*. New York: McGraw-Hill.
Sitomer, Mindel, and Harry Sitomer. 1976. *How did numbers begin?* New York: Crowell.
———. 1978. *Zero is not nothing*. New York: Crowell.
Watson, Clyde. 1977. *Binary numbers*. New York: Crowell.
Zaslavsky, Claudia. 1980. *Count on your fingers African style*. New York: Crowell.
———. 1989. *Zero: Is it something? Is it nothing?* New York: Franklin Watts.

Teacher resources

Ascher, Marcia, and Robert Ascher. 1981. *Code of the Quipu*. Ann Arbor, MI: University of Michigan Press.
Hardin, Daniel. 1979. Teaching base three? In a pig's ear! *Arithmetic Teacher*, 25, 48–49.
Zaslavsky, Claudia. 1973. *Africa counts: Number and pattern in African culture*. Boston: Prindle, Weber, and Schmidt.

Children's first introduction to numbers, even before they start school, is often through counting books. From counting books they move quite naturally to books involving addition, many of which can also be used with older children. In this chapter we will look at both counting books and books that help young learners pose and solve their own addition problems.

Numeration counting books

Many counting books simply present a sequence of specific sets of objects. *The Balancing Act* (Peek, 1987), for example, shows a series of elephants on a high wire. Each number is matched with a distinct set of animals. Good counting books like this one have large, clear illustrations and tend to arrange the numbers from six to ten in smaller sets of two, three, or four. In *The Balancing Act*, the number seven is represented by seven elephants depicted as two sets of three and one set of one. *One Bear All Alone* (Bucknall, 1989) also does a good job of showing the nature of the larger numbers: for the number ten, there are three sets of bears asleep in three beds. The reader can clearly see that the number ten is made up of sets of four, three, and three.

The bold and simple illustrations in *Ten Black Dots* (Crews, 1986) emphasize the distinctness of each set of objects. The five portholes of a boat are clearly depicted as sets of two and three, six marbles as a set of three black dots in two open hands (reflecting the symmetry of even numbers), and the eight wheels of a train as sets of four, two, and two. Although the text has no story line, and there is thus no inherent relationship between one set of objects and the next, the illustration at the end of the book shows horizontal bands of black dots in the natural counting sequence. This pattern demonstrates the step sequence of the natural numbers and highlights the sub-base of five—the larger numbers are represented as $5 + 1$, $5 + 2$, and so on.

Another simple counting book, this one depicting this numerical sequence in reverse, is *Ten, Nine, Eight* (Bang, 1983). It is also one of the few counting books to portray African-Americans. As a father helps his daughter get ready for bed, they count different objects in her bedroom. Again, some of

4

counting and
addition

the larger even numbers are represented by the symmetry of two smaller sets: ten as the five toes on each foot, for example, or eight as two sets of four windowpanes. (Other books involving a descending sequence of numbers are included in Chapter 5 on subtraction.)

Many good counting books have a predictable story structure. In *I Can't Get My Turtle To Move* (O'Donnell, 1989), a little girl tries to persuade a sleepy turtle to move about, but it remains quiet. She urges two fish to swim, three kittens to purr, and eventually ten rabbits to hop, but her repeated requests to the turtle are to no avail until she entices it with some food. *The Midnight Farm* (Lindbergh, 1987) is another good counting book with a predictable text. Repetition and the rhythm and rhyme of the language enable children to predict the next set of farm animals they will encounter. The animal illustrations are also carefully arranged, so that a set of eight chicks clustered around a hen is clearly seen as sets of four, two, and two.

Some counting books contain more than one set of objects to count. One of the more amusing books in this category is *Willy Can Count* (Rockwell, 1989), in which Willy and his mother set off on a walk . When Willy's mother spies three large haystacks, she urges Willy to find three things to count. On turning the page, however, the reader discovers that Willy has found his own set of three: three chicks following a hen. While the mother focuses on towering trees, large stones, and distant stars, her son Willy notices small wonders of his own, such as leaping frogs, crawling ants, and bright ladybugs. *Anno's Counting Book* (1977) also depicts multiple sets of a given number. On the page representing the number two, the reader can look closely at the outdoor scene and find two children, two houses, two roads, and so on. The open-ended nature of these illustrations invites repeated readings and continual discoveries.

One last book worthy of mention in this particular category is *Numblers* (MacDonald and Oakes, 1988), a unique representation of numbers (concepts) through numerals (characters). Each numeral from 1 to 10 is magically transformed into the appropriate number of shapes. A 1 shimmers and becomes a seal; a 2 bends and stretches into two 2s to become an elegant swan; a 4 twists backward to become a triangular shape that is repeated four times to create a sailboat. This interplay between number and numeral makes this counting book a most unusual one.

Counting books as story and pattern

Some counting books go beyond representing sets of objects; they not only tell a story but also highlight a particular numerical pattern. One of the most common numerical patterns is the ascending sequence of adding on by one, also known as counting on: $1 + 1 = 2, 2 + 1 = 3, 3 + 1 = 4$; and so on. (Counting books for developing addition concepts appear in a separate list at the end of the chapter.) A humorous story depicting this pattern is *How Many Are In This Old Car?* (Hawkins and Hawkins, 1988). A bear goes for a drive in an old jalopy and is approached by a hippopotamus who wants a ride. Now there are two in the car $(1 + 1 = 2)$. Then a pelican asks for a ride $(2 + 1 = 3)$. One by one, other animals, including a crocodile, rhinoceros, and elephant, request a ride, and they too are permitted to climb aboard, despite the protests of those already in the car. Although all counting books are based on a sequence of adding on by one, a book like this makes the numerical pattern explicit through both story and illustration. By repeatedly portraying the original group in the car and setting off each new animal on the left hand side of the page, the authors help readers see the two distinct sets that join together to create the next larger set.

Other counting books depict this same ascending numerical sequence. In *Going Up!* (Sis, 1989), readers follow Mary on an elevator ride from the first to the twelfth floor. One by one, various people dressed in brightly colored costumes enter the elevator with Mary, all heading for a birthday surprise. Each time, readers see the original group on the elevator and the newcomer outside the door ready to join. Two books by John Burningham also illustrate this sequence of adding on by one. In *John Burningham's 1, 2, 3* (1985), a set of ten children clamber up into a big tree one at a time. In *Pigs Plus* (1983), a fold-out book, a single pig sets off for a ride in an old red car but encounters some difficulty driving through the mud. A second pig comes along to help (the text reads $1 + 1 = 2$). Each subsequent fold-out reveals another car problem and another pig on its way to assist the original group.

Several counting books incorporate both an ascending and a descending numeral sequence. In *Hippos Go Berserk!* (Boynton, 1977), consecutive sets of one to nine elephants arrive at a house for a party. The next day each set of elephants leaves, beginning with the largest set of nine. During the descending sequence, the consecutive sets of elephants are shown on opposite pages so that readers can observe the difference between them. Maurice Sendak also illustrates these counting sequences in *One Was Johnny* (1962). One by one a series of animals (and eventually a robber) come to visit Johnny. Then, one at a time, they leave. As each animal prepares to leave, it stands by the door while the rest of the animals remain inside the room. Readers can see the two distinct sets on each page and note the descending pattern of $9 - 1, 8 - 1, 7 - 1$, and so on.

Equivalence, an important mathematical concept, is incorporated into two counting books. In *Anno's Counting House* (1982), a set of ten children who live in one house (shown on the left-hand page) decide to move out, one after another, and live in another house (shown on the right-hand page). Children can watch the following number pattern emerge:

Number of Children in One House	Number of Children in the Other House
10	0
9	1
8	2
7	3
6	4
5	5
4	6
3	7
2	8
1	9
0	10

Such number combinations are often referred to as "names for a number," because they illustrate all the possible equivalent two-addend names for a particular number, in this case ten. This pattern also illustrates the mathematical law of compensation: if a certain quantity is subtracted from one addend and added to the other, the sum remains the same. At the end of the story, readers can look at the book from back to front and see the inverse relationship between addition and subtraction as the characters in the story reenter the original house.

Another counting book that addresses equivalence is *Annie's One to Ten* (Owen, 1988). Here, a variety of objects portray all the different two-addend combinations for ten. One of the strengths of this book is that it shows more than one representation for each combination—for instance, no carrots and ten rabbits and no bananas and ten monkeys both illustrate 0 + 10. Among the names for 1 + 9 are one rocket and nine planets, or one snowman and nine snowflakes. Unlike *Anno's Counting House,* there is no movement in this story. Instead, the concept of equivalence is conveyed through the classification of sets of objects. Reading and discussing both books would provide a good balance because of their different representations of the equivalence concept.

Counting books as sources of content-area knowledge

Obviously all counting books incorporate some knowledge about the world, whether it is what hippos look like in *Hippos Go Berserk!* (Boynton, 1977) or how to repair an automobile in Burningham's *Pigs Plus* (1983). But some books go further and make a concerted effort to focus on a certain area of study: a particular culture, a significant issue, or a highly specific topic.

Several counting books introduce features of a particular culture. Muriel Feelings acquaints readers with East African life in her Swahili counting book, *Moja Means One* (1971). Children learn about the one highest mountain,

Kilimanjaro, the game of mankala, which is played by two people, and other interesting facts about African food, clothing, customs, and musical instruments. The English equivalent of each Swahili word is highlighted in the accompanying sentence so that readers know what to look for.

A series of counting books by Jim Haskins introduces readers to many cultures. Among them are *Count Your Way Through Africa* (1989a) and *Count Your Way Through the Arab World* (1987a) (for other titles, see the reference list at the end of this chapter). These counting books are intended for older children, since some of the numbers are represented in an abstract way. For instance, in *Count Your Way Through China* (1987b), readers can see the two giant pandas that were given to the United States by the People's Republic of China in 1972, but they also learn about the seven different zones of vegetation in China and the ten major dynasties in Chinese history. Although these ideas are listed and discussed, there is no direct one-to-one correspondence between the numbers in the text and the illustrations. However, the books contain some fascinating information and are helpful in viewing a particular culture through a mathematical lens.

Another book that relates to a specific culture is *One Good Horse* (Scott, 1990). It is "a cowpuncher's counting book," which introduces readers to life on a cattle ranch. It tells about the people ("two buckaroos"), the vegetation ("eight clumps of sagebrush"), and the animals ("ten mountain quail") that are unique to this western landscape. The author also includes numbers beyond ten (such as fifty cedar fence posts and a hundred head of cattle). The last illustration in the book gives a panoramic view of the countryside so that readers can retrace the journey of the two buckaroos and review the other sets they have seen along the way. The outstanding watercolor illustrations by Lynn Sweat capture the rich beauty and deep textures of the American west.

A counting book that acquaints readers with the issue of endangered species is *Hey! Get Off Our Train* (Burningham, 1990). In this story, a boy and his stuffed dog climb aboard his toy train one night and embark on an imaginary journey around the world. Along the way they encounter representatives of endangered species, who want to join them: an elephant that is trying to save its tusks, a seal that wants to escape the polluted ocean, a crane whose marshland is being drained for development, and so on. As each newcomer asks to join the train ride, it is set off from the rest of the group; readers will soon discover a counting-on pattern. This counting book could easily be integrated into a larger study unit on environmental issues.

Two other counting books also provide information about animals. In *Deep Down Underground* (1989), Olivier Dunrea introduces readers to the world of animals that live in the earth. One by one, the reader meets sets of animals and insects busily engaged in their daily activities: one moudiewort (a Scottish word for "mole") digs and digs; two pink earthworms wriggle and wrangle; three black beetles scurry and scamper, and so forth. The numerical pattern is highlighted in the text by the numbers that run in a vertical column on each page. The cumulative nature of the story is reinforced through the illustrations: each page shows the previous sets of creatures as well as the new set. When readers finally reach the tenth picture they see a diverse world of twisting tunnels and energetic creatures. Dunrea's drawings include fascinating details of the underground world, such as a stony, earthy terrain and the egg sacs of red ants.

The other book that discusses animals is *Animal Numbers* (Kitchen, 1987). Each picture shows an animal and her offspring: a mother kangaroo and her single joey represent number one, a swan swims with two baby cygnets, and an Irish Setter sits beside her litter of ten pups. Except for a brief introduction, there are no words. Instead, each page contains a large numeral, and the mother and her babies crawl or swim around it. A short text at the back of the book describes why particular animals were chosen. In all cases, the number of offspring represented in the text is only an estimate or average. The number 4, for instance, is represented by four baby woodpeckers, but the text informs us that green woodpeckers can lay between four and seven eggs; the number 7 is represented by a Virginia opossum, but the text states that even though opossums often have more than seven offspring, only those who find a place on the mother's back will survive. Such use of estimates and indeterminate numbers makes this text an unusual counting book. It also represents a mathematician's perspective on the animal world, and could serve as a model for other quantitative explorations about animals.

Books in the classroom K-2

One of Cassandra Gary's favorite mathematical stories for young readers is Eric Carle's *The Very Hungry Caterpillar* (1969), a predictable story that follows a caterpillar's eating habits throughout the day. She read this story to Brandi, a first-grade student, and then invited her to create her own eating story. Brandi asked if she could use herself in the story instead of a caterpillar and was encouraged to do so. The first part of her story read:

On Monday I ate one pear.
On Tuesday I ate two cookies.
On Wednesday I ate three french fries.
On Thursday I ate four peaches.
On Friday I ate five cherries.
On Saturday I ate six ice cream cones.

Her last page appears in Figure 4–1. As Cassandra looked at Brandi's illustrations for seven she asked, "Can you think of another way to make seven?"

Brandi replied, "You could do four and three, or one and six."

"You know a lot about numbers," said Cassandra. "Do you see any other ways?"

FIGURE 4–1

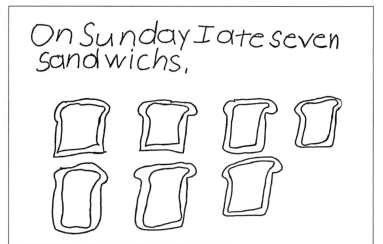

On Sunday I ate seven sandwichs.

FIGURE 4–2

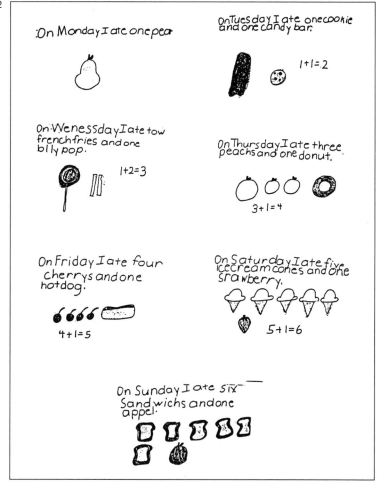

On Monday I ate one pear.

On Tuesday I ate one cookie and one candy bar.

1+1=2

On Wenessday I ate tow frenchfries and one billy pop.

1+2=3

On Thursday I ate three peachs and one donut.

3+1=4

On Friday I ate four cherrys and one hotdog.

4+1=5

On Saturday I ate five icecream cones and one srawberry.

5+1=6

On Sunday I ate six sandwichs and one appel.

Brandi didn't, but the question led her to think about her illustrations in another way: "I could eat two different things instead of one."

"That's a good idea," said Cassandra. "How would you do that?"

Brandi revised her text (Figure 4–2), so that each page showed two different kinds of food. Brandi's illustrations and corresponding number names demonstrate the adding-on pattern of one: $1 + 1 = 2$, $2 + 1 = 3$, $3 + 1 = 4$, and so on. As she began to write equations to accompany her text, she remarked, "You can use numbers to add." Thus *The Very Hungry Caterpillar* encouraged Brandi to explore the concept of equivalence and construct a pattern for addition.

Books in the classroom 3–4

An interesting text for third and fourth graders (discussed further in Chapter 10 on geometry) is *Round Trip* (Jonas, 1983). The reader journeys into the city, turns the book upside down, and then journeys into the country. The black-and-white illustrations are cleverly drawn to show different scenes from both perspectives. Although this book offers many possibilities for exploring shapes, fourth-grade teacher Sheila Hanley used it to start a discussion of trips in general. She asked her students to think of problems they might encounter on a trip. They generated the following list:

run out of gas	fuse blows out
car may break down	Dad eats last slice of pizza
lose luggage	lights burn out
need to use bathroom	become ill
forget games	flat tire
get stuck in traffic	get hungry
lock keys in the car	accident
read map wrong	get lost

Together the children brainstormed possible solutions for the problem of running out of gas: walk to find some gas, bring a gas container, push the car, get some money. Then Sheila challenged her students to select an idea from the list and write their own mathematical story. The children formed groups around the particular idea they wished to pursue. As they began to compose their stories, they used a variety of reference materials to help them, including maps, atlases, encyclopedias, dictionaries, library books, textbooks, and newspapers. Sheila found herself conducting impromptu mini-lessons on several mathematical questions, such as how to measure distance using a scale and how to calculate sales tax.

Many of the children wrote story problems that involved more than one step. Brad's group created a story about tires (Figure 4–3). Brad multiplied the cost of one new tire times four and then added the cost of the repair to determine the total cost. Many other children also based their story problems on

FIGURE 4–3

their own personal experience. Sean helped his group write about getting stuck in traffic (Figure 4–4) because it was a problem he knew about first-hand. Margy's family had set off on a long trip when she realized they had forgotten hairspray and nail polish. Her story (Figure 4–5) includes her inventive solution. Bryan described oil pumps and Julianne recommended ways to spend money allotted for food. Their stories reflect real-life contexts for addition and other

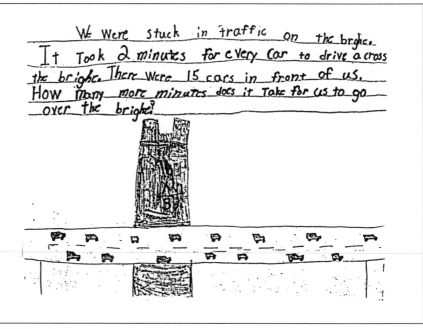

We Were stuck in traffic on the bridge. It Took 2 minutes for every Car to drive across the bridge. There Were 15 cars in front of us. How many more minutes does it Take for us to go over the bridge?

FIGURE 4-4

FIGURE 4-5

We were 50 miles from Irmo. We forgot our hair spray and nail polish. We could go back if our parents are in a good mood. But our Dad has to stop for gas in ten miles. We could buy the hair Spray and nail polish when Dad stops for gas. We have 5.00. The nail polish is $2.00 and the hair spray is $3.00. We would need tax to. Our sister has $20.00 Our Dad needs to borro $10.00 and We need 25¢ How much will our sister have left?

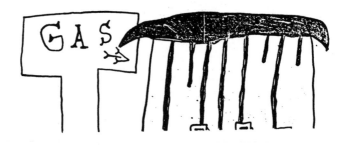

mathematical operations. Since Sheila kept the assignment open-ended and encouraged the children to make connections with their own lives, the stories that they created were rich in detail.

Children who are used to responding only to the story problems in textbooks do not always find the task of creating their own problems an easy one. One child commented to Sheila, "It's hard. Thinking is hard." Another child said, "I like to do a worksheet because I think it's better. It has the problems on there for you." But others recognized the challenge and felt it was more rewarding than the traditional textbook assignment: "I think it was easy because you had friends to help you." "It is fun writing your own problem because you get to write whatever you want to." "I think that a problem you make up has more creativity." "It was easy because we used the atlas." They enjoyed the opportunity to choose a story situation, relate it to their own lives, and use appropriate reference materials in a purposeful way to write about it.

Books in the classroom 5–6

Older students can use a variety of books to investigate topics that are interesting to them. Rick DuVall and his fifth-grade students began the year with a study unit on the environment. One of the books that helped to initiate classroom discussion was *50 Simple Things Kids Can Do to Save the Earth* (Earth-Works Group, 1990), which contains an assortment of statistical information about pollutants, recycling, and other environment-related issues. As the children became more knowledgeable about specific issues, they decided that they wanted to make changes in their own lives in order to help save the earth, a resolve that resulted directly from the mathematical computations they carried out in this unit.

During one investigation, the class learned that recycling one aluminum can rather than having to produce a new one from aluminum ore saves enough energy to run a television set for three hours. The children kept diaries for one week to tabulate the number of hours they spent watching television. Then they divided the total number of hours by three to determine the number of cans they would need to recycle in order to save the energy their television used on those programs.

The children also learned that the average American uses 1,500 cans per year. They converted this statistic to a more familiar grouping scheme: 125 twelve-pack cartons. Then they added this figure once for each member of their own family and graphed the number of cans their family would use in one year. When they added all the family totals together, they discovered to their amazement that just the families of the people in the class would probably use about 185,000 cans each year.

Another investigation involved plastic packaging. The children learned that each American throws away about sixty pounds of plastic packaging every year.

Armed with this figure, they calculated that their class must throw away about 1,560 pounds per year. Rick helped the children to personalize this statistic by having them stand together on a large packing scale owned by the school. They were shocked to discover that it took twenty-one of them to make up an approximate weight of 1,560 pounds. The successive addition of each person on the scale proved to be a dramatic portrayal of the recycling problem posed by plastic packaging.

The children extended this investigation in another way by seeing how much plastic packaging it took to weigh one pound. When they discovered that a tremendous amount of packaging is needed, they measured the physical dimensions of this one pound, multiplied it by 1,560, and discovered that just the plastic packaging the class might discard would fill a landfill area larger than their classroom. By personalizing statistics through comparisons with their own weights and classroom space, the children better understood the size of the recycling problem and realized what a difference individuals can make.

Another statistic the children learned was that the average American tosses out about 1,200 pounds of organic garbage every year. To make this statistic more comprehensible, the children calculated to see how that figure compared to their own body weight. One child was astonished to find out that she throws away approximately twenty-two times her own weight annually in organic garbage alone. A further extension of the soda can, plastic packaging, and organic garbage activities would have been for students to actually keep track of their own family's garbage, both at home and away. How many cans do they use every day? Does the amount of organic garbage thrown out vary from family to family? How much plastic is thrown away in the lunchroom and classroom every day? Do the figures in *50 Simple Things* seem reasonable, based on their own experiences? (The figures reveal a discrepancy between the figure of 1,500 cans per person per year given on one page and the figure of 65 billion cans a year for the whole country given on the previous page. If the figure for the whole country were calculated using the per person amount, the result would be about six times larger than 65 billion. In a case like this one, a data-gathering study can provide valuable experience in critical reading and thinking.)

Rick DuVall helped his students use the tools of mathematical computation to confront environmental issues and bring the large numbers down to the personal level. The investigations also helped to demonstrate that mathematics is not a value-free affair; it is used and manipulated by people to underscore problems and raise issues. Through their research the students experienced the power of mathematics as a tool for comparing, analyzing, and interpreting our world.

Further explorations

1. What are your students' interests? There are counting books for specific objects (*Trucks You Can Count On*, Magee, 1985), specific locales (*When*

We Went to the Park, Hughes, 1985), specific cultures (*Count Your Way Through Mexico,* Haskins, 1989c), and specific activities (*Scott Gustafson's Animal Orchestra,* Gustafson, 1988). You can invite your students to create their own counting books based on their specific interests, experiences, and cultures.

2. What environmental issues are your students most familiar with? You might read them *Hey! Get Off Our Train* (Burningham, 1990) and brainstorm ideas for writing other counting books, not only about endangered species but also about other related topics, such as recycling or energy consumption.

3. What animals are unique to your particular environment? What do your children know about these animals? After reading *Animal Numbers* (Kitchen, 1987), you might make a large chart of familiar animals and their estimated number of offspring. What conclusions can the children reach about animals that have many offspring? A few offspring? By analyzing the number of offspring of various creatures children will discover another way to view the differences between groups, such as mammals, reptiles, and insects. They might also want to list and explore other numerical characteristics, such as longevity, length of incubation period, weight, and so on.

4. What kind of things do your children tend to notice that other people often ignore? After reading *Willy Can Count* (Rockwell, 1989), your children might create a similar counting book by going on a class walk and being aware of what they see. Are they more drawn to large objects like trees or small ones like flowers?

5. How can you involve older children in creating counting books for younger children? You might read and display a wide range of counting books for them to analyze and discuss. You can help them develop a set of criteria that characterize good counting books and then invite them to use these guidelines in creating their own books for a primary grade class at your school.

6. Jim Haskin's *Count your way through . . .* series can be adapted for your own locale or one the class is studying. Students might research their own school, town, county, state, or province, then create a book or display incorporating the numbers one through ten.

Children's books

COUNTING

Anno, Mitsumasa. 1977. *Anno's counting book.* New York: Crowell.
———. 1982. *Anno's counting house.* New York: Philomel.
Archambault, John. 1989. *Counting sheep.* New York: Holt.
Aylesworth, Jim. 1988. *One crow: A counting rhyme.* New York: Lippincott.

Baker, Jeannie. 1982. *One hungry spider*. London: Andre Deutsch.

Bang, Molly. 1983. *Ten, nine, eight*. New York: Greenwillow.

Bennett, David. 1990. *One cow, moo, moo!* New York: Holt.

Blumenthal, Nancy. 1989. *Count-a-saurus*. New York: Macmillan.

Boon, Emilie. 1987. *1 2 3 How many animals can you see?* New York: Orchard.

Bridewell, Norman. 1985. *Count on Clifford*. New York: Scholasatic.

Brown, Marc. 1976. *One two three: An animal counting book*. Boston: Little, Brown.

Bucknall, Caroline. 1989. *One bear all alone*. New York: Dial.

Carle, Eric. 1968. *1, 2, 3 to the zoo*. Cleveland: World.

———— . 1969.*The very hungry caterpillar*. New York: Putnam.

———— . 1972. *Rooster's off to see the world*. Natick, MA: Picture Book Studio.

Cleveland, David. 1978. *The April rabbits*. New York: Coward, McCann, and Geoghegan.

Cole, Betsy. 1988. *Green creatures ten to one*. Martinsville, VA: Adventure Publishing.

Considine, Kate, and Ruby Schuler. 1963. *One two three four*. New York: Holt, Rinehart and Winston.

Crews, Donald. 1985. *The bicycle race*. New York: Greenwillow.

———— . 1986. *Ten black dots*. New York: Greenwillow.

Doolittle, Eileen. 1988. *World of wonders*. Boston: Houghton Mifflin.

Dunrea, Olivier. 1989. *Deep down underground*. New York: Macmillan.

EarthWorks Group. 1990. *50 simple things kids can do to save the earth*. Kansas City: Andrews and McMeel.

Ehlert, Lois. 1990. *Fish eyes: A book you can count on*. San Diego: Harcourt Brace Jovanovich.

Ernst, Lisa C. 1986. *Up to ten and down again*. New York: Lothrop, Lee and Shepard.

Feelings, Muriel. 1971. *Moja means one: A Swahili counting book*. New York: Dial.

Gardner, Beau. 1987. *Can you imagine . . . ? A counting book*. New York: Dodd, Mead.

Ginsburg, Mirra. 1982. *Across the stream*. New York: Greenwillow.

Gustafson, Scott. 1988. *Scott Gustafson's animal orchestra: A counting book*. Chicago: Contemporary Books.

Hagne, Kathleen. 1986. *Numbears: A counting book*. New York: Holt.

Hamm, Diane J. 1991. *How many feet in the bed?* New York: Simon and Schuster.

Hammond, Franklin. 1987. *Ten little ducks*. New York: Scholastic.

Haskins, Jim. 1987a. *Count your way through the Arab World*. Minneapolis, MN: Carolrhoda Books.

———— . 1987b. *Count your way through China*. Minneapolis, MN: Carolrhoda Books.

———— . 1987c. *Count your way through Japan*. Minneapolis, MN: Carolrhoda Books.

———— . 1987d. *Count your way through Russia*. Minneapolis, MN: Carolrhoda Books.

———— . 1989a. *Count your way through Africa*. Minneapolis, MN: Carolrhoda Books.

———— . 1989b. *Count your way through Canada*. Minneapolis, MN: Carolrhoda Books.

———— . 1989c. *Count your way through Mexico*. Minneapolis, MN: Carolrhoda Books.

———— . 1990a. *Count your way through Germany*. Minneapolis, MN: Carolrhoda Books.

———— . 1990b. *Count your way through Italy*. Minneapolis, MN: Carolrhoda Books.

Hawkins, Colin, and Jacqui Hawkins. 1990. *When I was one*. New York: Viking Penguin.

Hoban, Russell. 1974. *Ten what?* New York: Scribners.

Hoban, Tana. 1972. *Count and see*. New York: Macmillan.

———— . 1985. *1, 2, 3*. New York: Greenwillow.

Hughes, Shirley. 1985. *When we went to the park*. New York: Lothrop, Lee and Shepard.

Hutchins, Pat. 1982. *1 hunter*. New York: Greenwillow.

Inkpen, Mick. 1987. *One bear at bedtime: A counting book*. Boston: Little, Brown.

Jonas, Ann. 1983. *Round trip*. New York: Scholastic.

Johnston, Tony. 1987. *Whale song*. New York: Putnam.

Jones, Carol. 1990. *This old man*. Boston: Houghton Mifflin.

Keats, Ezra Jack. 1971. *Over in the meadow*. New York: Four Winds.

Kherdian, David, and Nonny Hogrogrian. 1990. *The cat's midsummer jamboree*. New York: Philomel.

Kitamura, Satashi. 1986. *When sheep cannot sleep: A counting book*. New York: Farrar, Straus and Giroux.

Kitchen, Bert. 1987. *Animal numbers*. New York: Dial.

Koch, Michelle. 1989. *Just one more*. New York: Greenwillow.

Leedy, Loreen. 1985. *A number of dragons*. New York: Holiday House.

Lewis, Paul. 1989. *P. Bear's new year's party*. Hillsboro, OR: Beyond Words.

Lindbergh, Reeve. 1987. *The midnight farm*. New York: Dial.

MacCarthy, Patricia. 1990. *Ocean parade: A counting book*. New York: Dial.

MacDonald, Elizabeth, and Annie Owen. 1985. *My aunt and the animals*. Woodbury, NY: Barron's.

MacDonald, Suse, and Bill Oakes. 1988. *Numblers*. New York: Dial.

Maestro, Betsy, and Giulio Maestro. 1977. *Harriet goes to the circus*. New York: Crown.

Magee, Doug. 1985. *Trucks you can count on*. New York: Dodd, Mead.

McMillan, Bruce. 1986. *Counting wildflowers*. New York: Lothrop, Lee and Shepard.

Miller, Jane. 1983. *Farm counting book*. Englewood Cliffs, NJ: Prentice-Hall.

Morgensen, Jan. 1990. *The 46 little men*. New York: Greenwillow.

Noll, Sally. 1984. *Off and counting*. New York: Greenwillow.

O'Donnell, Elizabeth. 1989. *I can't get my turtle to move*. New York: Morrow.

———. 1991. *The twelve days of summer*. New York: Morrow.

O'Neill, Mary. 1968. *Take a number*. Garden City, NY: Doubleday.

Oxenbury, Helen. 1968. *Numbers of things*. New York: Franklin Watts.

Peek, Merle. 1987. *The balancing act: A counting song*. New York: Clarion.

Rockwell, Anne F. 1989. *Willy can count*. New York: Arcade Publishing.

Scott, Ann. 1990. *One good horse: A cowpuncher's counting book*. New York: Greenwillow.

Sendak, Maurice. 1977. *Seven little monsters*. New York: Harper and Row.

Sheppard, Jeff. 1990. *The right number of elephants*. New York: Harper and Row.

Sis, Peter. 1988. *Waving: A counting book*. New York: Greenwillow.

Tafuri, Nancy. 1986. *Who's counting?* New York: Greenwillow.

Testa, Fulvio. 1982. *If you take a pencil*. New York: Dial.

Thomson, Ruth. 1987. *All about 1, 2, 3*. Milwaukee, WI: Gareth Stevens.

Tudor, Tasha. 1956. *1 is one*. New York: H. Z. Walck.

Unwin, Pippa. 1990. *The great zoo hunt*. New York: Doubleday.

Yolen, Jane. 1976. *An invitation to the butterfly ball: A counting rhyme*. New York: Parents Magazine Press.

ADDITION

Adams, Pam. 1973. *There was an old lady who swallowed a fly*. Sudbury, MA: Playspaces International.

Anno, Mitsumasa. 1977. *Anno's counting book*. New York: Crowell.

———. 1982. *Anno's counting house*. New York: Philomel.

Balin, Lorna. 1986. *Amelia's nine lives*. Nashville: Abingdon Press.

Bogart, JoEllen. 1989. *10 for dinner*. New York: Scholastic.

Boynton, Sandra. 1977. *Hippos go beserk!* Boston: Little, Brown.

Brandenberg, Franz. 1983. *Aunt Nina and her nephews and nieces*. New York: Greenwillow.

Brenner, Barbara. 1984. *The snow parade*. New York: Crown.

Burningham, John. 1983. *Pigs plus*. New York: Viking Press.

———. (1985). *John Burningham's 1, 2, 3*. New York: Crown.

———. 1990. *Hey! Get off our train*. New York: Crown.

Carle, Eric. 1984. *The very busy spider.* New York: Putnam.

——— . 1987. *A house for hermit crab.* Saxonville, MA: Picture Books Studio.

de Paola, Tomie. 1989. *Too many Hopkins.* New York: Putnam.

de Regniers, Beatrice S. 1985. *So many cats!* New York: Clarion.

Dubanevich, Arlene. 1983. *Pigs in hiding.* New York: Scholastic.

Ginsburg, Mirra. 1974. *Mushroom in the rain.* New York: Macmillan.

Gray, Catherine. 1988. *One, two, three, and four. No more?* Boston: Houghton Mifflin.

Hawkins, Colin, and Jacqui Hawkins. 1988. *How many are in this old car?* New York: Putnam.

Hellen, Nancy. 1988. *Bus stop.* New York: Orchard Books.

Hooper, Meredith. 1985. *Seven eggs.* New York: Harper and Row.

Kent, Jack. 1973. *Twelve days of Christmas.* New York: Scholastic.

Lewin, Betsy. 1981. *Cat count.* New York: Dodd, Mead.

MacDonald, Elizabeth. 1990. *Mike's Kite.* New York: Orchard.

Mathews, Louise. 1982. *Cluck one.* New York: Dodd, Mead.

Moore, Inga. 1991. *Six dinner Sid.* New York: Simon and Schuster.

Morgan, Pierr. 1990. *The turnip.* New York: Philomel.

Owen, Annie. 1988. *Annie's one to ten.* New York: Knopf.

Pomerantz, Charlotte. 1984. *One duck, another duck.* New York: Greenwillow.

Punnett, Dick. 1982. *Count the possums.* Chicago: Children's Press.

Russell, Sandra. 1982. *A farmer's dozen.* New York: Harper and Row.

Sendak, Maurice. 1962. *One was Johnny.* New York: Harper and Row.

Silverstein, Shel. 1974. Band-aids. In *Where the sidewalk ends.* New York: Harper and Row.

Sis, Peter. 1989. *Going up!: A color counting book.* New York: Greenwillow.

Trivas, Irene. 1988. *Emma's Christmas.* New York: Orchard.

Walsh, Ellen S. 1991. *Mouse count.* San Diego: Harcourt Brace Jovanovich.

Wood, Audrey. 1984. *The napping house.* San Diego: Harcourt Brace Jovanovich.

Although we most often think of subtracting as "taking away" part of a set, subtraction actually has four models, as illustrated in these four examples: twenty children were in a class but five went home at noon (take-away); fifteen children were in class, but because some regular members were absent, we didn't have our usual class of twenty (missing addend); our class has twenty children but the class next door has thirty (comparison); our class of twenty has eleven girls while the remainder are boys (set within a set). All four of these subtraction situations are represented in children's books.

Subtraction as take-away

The model that children are most familiar with is subtraction as take-away, and more books represent this model than the others. Children have had the experience of something getting lost or someone going away and can readily relate to this representation of subtraction. *Hello, Goodbye* (Lloyd, 1988) is a good illustration of the take-away process. A big brown bear says "hello" to the world and two bees say "hello" back. Groups of other creatures hidden in the leaves and among the tree roots echo this same "hello." However, when it begins to rain, all the "hellos" turn to "goodbyes" as the animals run away to hide. Although no number pattern is emphasized in the story, the coming and going of various forest creatures provides a good starting place for discussing take-away situations.

In *A Bag Full of Pups* (Gackenbach, 1981), Mr. Mullin's dog has a litter of twelve pups and he has to find homes for them. Throughout the story different people come by and take away a pup or two to help them perform a variety of chores, such as herding cows or assisting a magician. In *The Shopping Basket* (Burningham, 1980), a young boy buys groceries for his mother but keeps giving away food on the way home when he is pestered by a variety of hungry animals. In *Little Rabbit's Loose Tooth* (Bate, 1975), Little Rabbit endures the uncomfortable feeling of a wiggly tooth; he finally loses it in a bowl of chocolate ice cream and then must decide whether or not to give it away to the tooth fairy. These books can also be used to explore the reciprocal relationship between addition and subtraction in a variety of situations:

5

subtraction

coming and going (*Hello, Goodbye*); buying and selling (*The Shopping Basket*); finding and losing (*Little Rabbit's Loose Tooth*); and accumulating and giving away (*A Bag Full of Pups*).

Two authors have written spoofs of the take-away model of subtraction. The narrator of the poem "Using Subtraction" (Blair, 1971) claims that if subtraction really means "take-away" as his teacher tells him it does, then he would like to use it to remove a variety of unpleasant situations from his life, such as stomachaches, scoldings, and rainy Sundays. In *The Phantom Tollbooth* (Juster, 1961), the main character, Milo, discovers on his visit to the land of Digitopolis that things aren't what they seem. At one point he and two friends are quite hungry and are offered some stew by their helpful guide, the Mathemagician. As they finish their first bowls, however, they notice that they are hungrier than before they started. After consuming twenty-three bowls of stew they are starving! The Mathemagician informs them that this feeling is only natural since they were eating the specialty of the kingdom: subtraction stew! He explains, "Here in Digitopolis we have our meals when we're full and eat until we're hungry. That way, when you don't have anything at all, you have more than enough." The Dodecahedron tries to explain this economical system even further: "It's completely logical. The more you want, the less you get, and the less you get, the more you have. Simple arithmetic, that's all" (p. 186).

Several subtraction stories using the take-away model are based on familiar rhymes and songs. These include *Five Little Monkeys Jumping on the Bed* (Christelow, 1989), *Five Little Ducks* (Raffi, 1989), and various versions of the song "Roll Over" (e.g., Peek, 1981; Rees, 1988), which highlight patterns of consecutive numbers, an important aspect of mathematics for beginners. In each story there is a descending subtraction pattern of one each time a monkey jumps off a bed, a duck disappears, or a character rolls off a bed. The predictable nature of these stories is part of their appeal and provides a familiar structure children can use to create their own mathematical story pattern.

Subtraction as missing addend

Have You Seen My Duckling? (Tafuri, 1984) and *Little Rabbit's Loose Tooth* (Bate, 1975) use the missing-addend model of subtraction. In the first, a duck leads her brood of seven babies around the pond as she searches for one lost duckling. As she asks a variety of animals where her baby might be, the reader is able to see the lost baby hidden in the background of each illustration, and thus view the incidence of $7 + \square = 8$ from a problem-centered perspective. Stories in which an object is lost and there is an effort to find and restore it to the original group are an excellent context for exploring missing-addend subtraction. *Little Rabbit's Loose Tooth* (Bate, 1975) also represents the missing-addend model, and children might enjoy this opportunity to discuss their own tooth losses and gains. In fact, the gaps in their mouths are concrete representations of a missing-addend problem: "I used to have twenty teeth; I lost some, and now I have only seventeen. How many do I have to grow back so that I'll have twenty again?"

Subtraction as comparison

Comparison is another context for subtraction. In comparing two sets, a distinction can be made between discrete and continuous measures. Discrete materials are those that can be counted piece by piece, such as marbles, cookies, or children. What matters is the number of items in a set, not the size of individual items. Comparison on a continuous measure involves establishing a numerical value, as in comparing lengths of ribbon or the heights of individual children. Although none of the titles referred to in this chapter represents subtraction as a process that involves comparing discrete objects, some of the books discussed in Chapter 11 on measurement can be used to portray subtraction as the comparison of continuous sizes. Steven Kellogg's *Much Bigger Than Martin* (1976) and Pat Hutchins's two *Titch* books (1971, 1983) emphasize the varying heights of family members and could serve as a model for related classroom comparisons through measurement.

Subtraction as set-within-a-set

The set-within-a-set context is illustrated by two books in which subtraction is used to determine the size of a group within a larger set. In this case, there is no take-away action, nor is there any comparison or movement between different sets. *How Many Snails?* (Giganti, 1988) which we discussed in Chapter 2, is a predictable book that invites the reader to look at a variety of pictures and answer a series of three questions highlighting the set-within-a-set situation. For example, accompanying an illustration of a sky full of clouds are the questions: "How many clouds are there? How many clouds are big and fluffy? How many clouds are big and fluffy and gray?" *All About 1, 2, 3* (Thomson, 1987), a counting book, features similar classification questions that ask for help in finding one armadillo, two jaguars, and so on, counting from one to ten, and in identifying which animals are engaged in certain activities, such as swimming, sunbathing, or sticking their tongues out.

The inverse relationship between addition and subtraction

In some books, the illustrations themselves demonstrate the important inverse relationship between addition and subtraction. Because mathematics is often viewed as the study of relationships, it is important for children to understand addition and subtraction as interrelated and reciprocal processes. Two versions of the song "Roll Over" represent this inverse relationship. In *Ten in a Bed* (Rees, 1988), those children who remain in bed are shown on the left page and the increasing number of children who have fallen out of bed are pictured on the right page playing outside or in another room of the house. In *Roll Over!* (Peek, 1981), a little boy shares his bed with nine animals. One by one each animal falls out of bed and finds a resting place somewhere in the boy's room. In both stories the illustrations on each page show the number still left in the bed and the number who have rolled out, and the reader can add them together at any time in order to reconstruct the original set.

Anno's Counting House (Anno, 1982), which we have already discussed as a counting book, shows ten children moving one by one from their fully furnished home shown on the left-hand page to the empty house next door shown on the right-hand page. To reconstruct the total the reader can simply count the number of children in both houses. At the same time, turning the pages backward and forward enables readers to compare the two sets and demonstrates that addition and subtraction are inverse processes.

Books in the classroom K–2

Tim O'Keefe used *Ten in a Bed* (Rees, 1988) with his first-grade class. Since the children were already familiar with this counting song, they sang the song together as Tim read the story aloud. After singing the song a second time, the children were invited to create their own version of the story. Tray composed the variation seen in Figure 5–1, which reads "The baby said, 'Go cook breakfast.' And 3 babies in the bed." His story is interesting for several reasons. First, he highlighted the subtraction process by drawing a line down the bed itself to separate the three babies from the fourth one, who was being asked to leave and cook breakfast. The line thus divided the babies into two subsets of one potential cook and three sleepy babies. Then he drew the fourth baby again over in the kitchen standing by the stove, busily preparing breakfast for his friends. "He's cooking ham and eggs," said Tray, pointing to the ham bone boiling in a kettle on top of the stove. Tray thus used both space and line to designate the process of separation, thus demonstrating his understanding of the subtraction process.

His inclusion of the kitchen scene is important because it represents a dimension of mathematical stories rarely reflected in mathematical textbooks: there is life after subtraction! In most textbook problems students never learn what happens to the children or animals who are separated from the original group. They simply disappear. But where do they go, and what do they do? Traditional textbook publishers consider such details irrevelant, serving only to distract attention from the mathematical intent of the problem. However,

FIGURE 5–1

mathematics should not be separated from the rich details of its natural context. When we separate and oversimplify it, we distort its nature. The complexity of events in mathematical stories and problems can actually support understanding, as Tray demonstrates so well. Cooking ham and eggs in the kitchen may seem an irrelevant detail, but it was obviously quite important to Tray. The issue of relevancy is really a function of who 'owned' the problem in the first place.

While Tray relied on art to convey his mathematical message, Sheree also used the written language of mathematics. She drew a bed with six little ones lying on top, then turned her paper over and, singing the words aloud, wrote a sequence of subtraction problems corresponding to the number pattern in the song: "There were six in the bed and one fell off. There were five in the bed and one fell off . . . ." Sheree continued this pattern until all the little ones had met their fate (Figure 5–2). To complete her story, Sheree used both mathematics and written language. She wrote the numeral 0 to indicate that there were no more children left on the bed and then brought the sequence of events to a close by writing "And wasn't no children in the bed."

Although Sheree did not write complete equations for each step of her story, the answer to each subtraction problem is implied in the first number of the equation that follows. Sheree's strategy may not be conventional, yet it allowed her to communicate her ideas clearly and concisely. Uncovering patterns and discovering relationships is part of the order and structure of the mathematical system; Sheree latched on to this pattern and represented it in her own way.

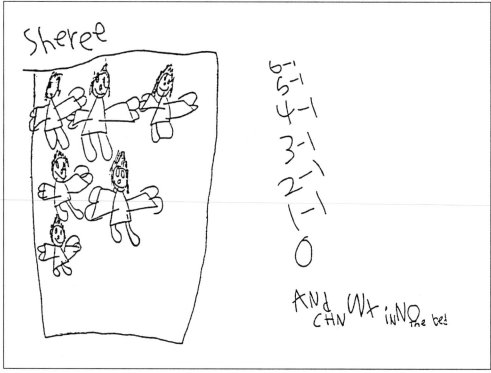

FIGURE 5–2

Books in the classroom 3–4

Teacher Julie Wyatt used *Alexander, Who Used to be Rich Last Sunday* (Viorst, 1978) with some of her fourth-grade students. In this story, a little boy named Alexander receives one dollar from his grandparents. Although he is determined to save his money, he finds the task too difficult and slowly squanders his fortune. When the children had heard the story read aloud, they recalled together how Alexander spent his money and recorded the list of events on the chalkboard:

1.00	
−.15	gum
−.15	bets
−.12	snake
−.10	bad names
−.03	down toilet
−.05	fell through crack
−.11	candy bar
−.04	magic trick

-.05   kicking
<u>−.20</u>   garage sale
.00

The story helped to highlight the take-away model in a financial context. When Julie invited the children to create their own spending story, they decided they needed more than a dollar! They felt that ten dollars was a fair amount and brainstormed some items they had bought in the past, such as slap bracelets, New Kids on the Block paraphernalia, and Teenage Mutant Ninja Turtle products (firmly grounding this anecdote in 1991!). In their own stories, some children purchased items similar to those Alexander spent his money on, such as bubble gum and candy bars. Others purchased very different things. Clayton used his money as shown in Figure 5–3. He knew that dots were used with numerals to represent money, so he used two dots (as in writing hours and minutes) to show the price of his purchases.

FIGURE 5–3

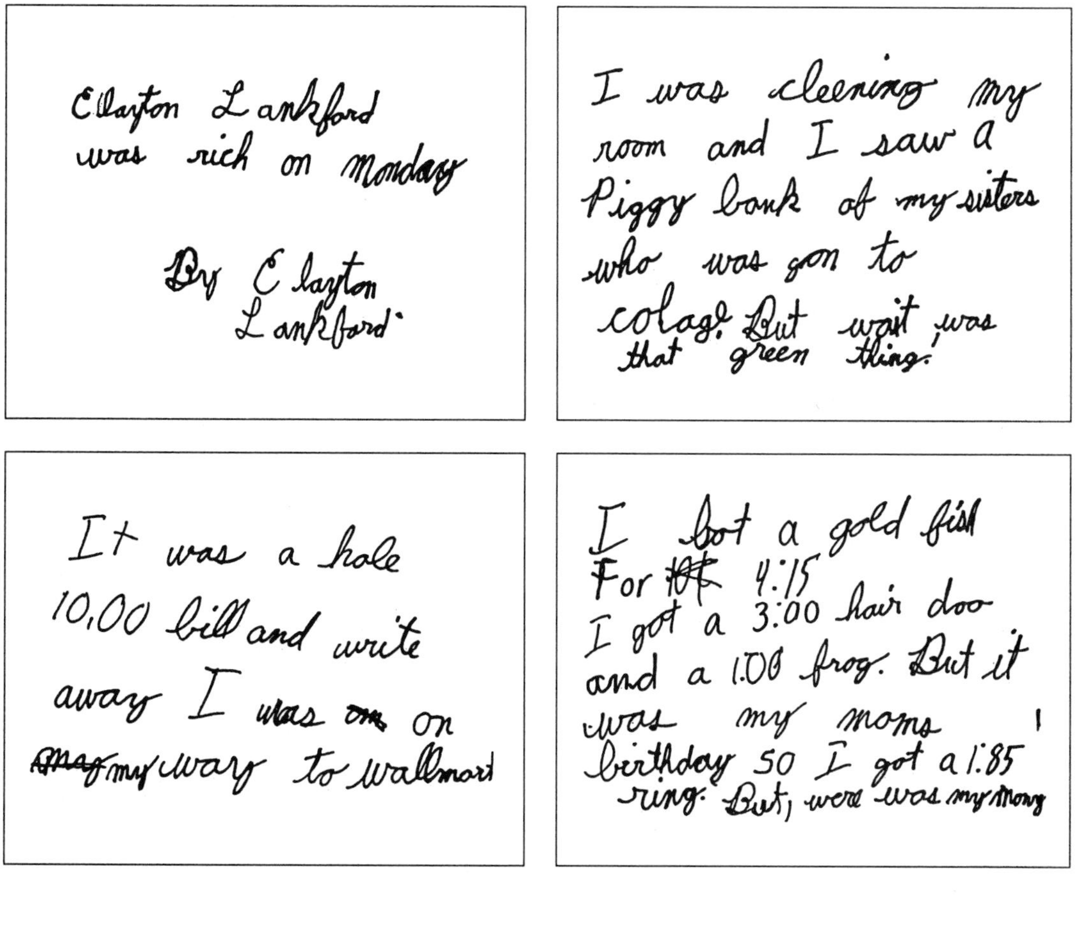

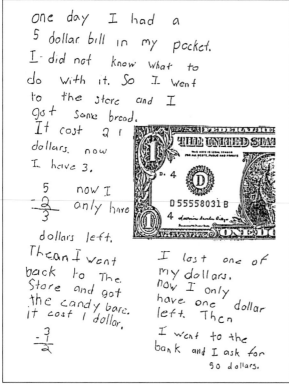

One day I had a
5 dollar bill in my pocket.
I did not know what to
do with it. So I went
to the store and I
got some bread.
It cost 2 r
dollars. now
I have 3.

 5   now I
-2   only have
—
 3

dollars left.
Then I went
back to the.
Store and got
the candy bare.
it cost 1 dollar.

 -3
 —
  2

I lost one of
my dollars.
now I only
have one dollar
left. Then
I went to the
bank and I ask for
50 dollars.

So I got 50 dollars.
Then I went to the
Store and got to lots of
bread and some milk.
Then I went back.
home. I found Three
more dollars at home.
So now I have 43 dollars.
left.

name
Tamara

FIGURE 5–4

JoAnn Reynolds introduced some third-grade students to the same book, also suggesting that they compose their own spending stories. Noting that the children represented their prices in various ways—35¢, thirty-five cents, 35 cents, and .35—she took the opportunity to discuss the monetary and decimal systems. One child created a subtraction story in which she alternated between written text and the subtraction algorithm, as shown in Figure 5–4. Her format contextualized subtraction facts, extending the meaning of the subtraction process through narrative and numerical representations. As her story demonstrates, when learners have the opportunity to create their own texts and tie their mathematical understanding to personal experiences, their stories are far more complex and richer in detail than those found in their mathematics textbook.

Books in the classroom 5–6

Sandra Medlin read the poem "Using Subtraction" (Blair, 1971) to her fifth-grade students. After reading it again several times, she asked her students to

list situations in which subtraction might be used. Some of their responses—
"When you buy stuff." "When you give things away." "When somebody
steals something from you."—highlighted a range of take-away situations. The
children then reviewed that section of the poem that listed the unpleasant circumstances on which the poet would like to use subtraction, and Sandra invited them to make their own list of things they would like "to take away." The
children kept the first and last stanzas of the poem intact but added their
own personal list of items in the middle stanza. Shelley created the variation
in Figure 5–5. The students' discussion helped to emphasize the contexts for
subtraction, while their poems gave them the opportunity to have fun with the
language of mathematics.

FIGURE 5–5

Further explorations

1. What objects do your students lose? Are they often looking for pencils, or marbles, or mittens? How might you use these situations to discuss subtraction?

2. Do your students know the familiar rhyme "Ten in a Bed"? You might want to share with them five illustrated versions of this rhyme (Dale, 1988; Gerstein, 1984; Mack, 1974; Peek, 1981; and Rees, 1988) and ask them to compare how each represented the subtraction process. Which version do they feel is most effective? Children might also create their own illustrated version of this story.

3. *Ten Little Elephants* (Leydenfrost, 1975) is an elimination rhyme in which ten elephants are gradually reduced to one ("Seven little elephants/In a sticky fix/The mud was really quicksand. . ./And then there were six!"). The children could try writing similar subtraction books on a variety of subjects: coins being spent, leaves falling off a tree, apples being eaten, and so on.

4. You can invite your students to collect and display data in different ways. As children interpret graphs together, they can apply different meanings of the subtraction process. For instance: How many more people voted for strawberry than vanilla? (comparison); How many more people are needed to vote for chocolate to tie strawberry for first place? (missing addend); If three fewer people voted for vanilla, what would the result be? (take-away); if five of the people who voted for chocolate are boys, how many are girls? (set-within-a-set).

Children's books

Anno, Mitsumasa. 1982. *Anno's counting house*. New York: Philomel.
Asch, Frank. 1980. *The last puppy*. Englewood Cliffs, NJ: Prentice-Hall.
Barrett, Judi. 1983. *What's left?* New York: Atheneum.
Bate, Lucy. 1975. *Little Rabbit's loose tooth*. New York: Crown.
Becker, John. 1973. *Seven little rabbits*. New York: Walker.
Blair, Lee. 1971. Using subtraction. In Alan and Leland Jacobs, eds., *Arithmetic in verse and rhyme*. Champagne, IL: Garrard.
Burningham, John. 1970. *Mr. Gumpy's outing*. New York: Penguin.
———. 1980. *The shopping basket*. New York: Crowell.
Christelow, Eileen. 1989. *Five little monkeys jumping on the bed*. New York: Clarion.
———. 1991. *Five little monkeys sitting in a tree*. New York: Clarion.
Coats, Laura. 1990. *Ten little animals*. New York: Macmillan.
Dale, Penny. 1988. *Ten in the bed*. Pleasant Hill, CA: Discovery Toys.
Dunbar, Joyce. 1990. *Ten little mice*. San Diego: Harcourt Brace Jovanovich.

Gackenbach, Dick. 1981. *A bag full of pups*. New York: Clarion.

Gerstein, Mordicai. 1984. *Roll over!* New York: Crown.

Giganti, Paul. 1988. *How many snails?: A counting book*. New York: Greenwillow.

Gray, Catherine. 1988. *One, two, three, and four. No more?* Boston: Houghton Mifflin.

Hawkins, Colin. 1984. *Take away monsters*. New York: Putnam.

Hayes, Sarah. 1990. *Nine ducks nine*. New York: Lothrop, Lee and Shepard.

Hindley, Judy. 1989. *Mrs. Mary Malarky's seven cats*. New York: Orchard.

Hooper, Meredith. 1985. *Seven eggs*. New York: Harper and Row.

Hutchins, Pat. 1971. *Titch*. New York: Macmillan.

———. 1983. *You'll soon grow into them, Titch*. New York: Greenwillow.

Juster, Norton. 1961. *The phantom tollbooth*. New York: Knopf.

Kellogg, Steven. 1976. *Much bigger than Martin*. New York: Dial.

Leydenfrost, Robert. 1975. *Ten little elephants*. Garden City, NY: Doubleday.

Lloyd, David. 1988. *Hello, goodbye*. New York: Lothrop, Lee and Shepard.

Mack, Stan. 1974. *10 bears in my bed: A goodnight countdown.*. New York: Pantheon.

Mathews, Louise. 1980. *The great take-away*. New York: Dodd, Mead.

Peek, Merle. 1981. *Roll over!* New York: Clarion.

Pomerantz, Charlotte. 1977. *The mango tooth*. New York: Greenwillow.

Raffi. 1989. *Five little ducks*. New York: Crown.

Rees, Mary. 1988. *Ten in a bed*. Boston: Little, Brown.

Ross, Pat. 1980. *Molly and the slow teeth*. New York: Lothrop, Lee and Shepard.

Silverstein, Shel. 1981. Eight balloons. In *A light in the attic*. New York: Harper and Row.

Tafuri, Nancy. 1984. *Have you seen my duckling?* New York: Greenwillow.

Thaler, Mike. 1991. *Seven little hippos*. New York: Simon and Schuster.

Thomson, Ruth. 1987. *All about 1, 2, 3*. Milwaukee, WI: Gareth Stevens.

Viorst, Judith. 1978. *Alexander, who used to be rich last Sunday*. New York: Atheneum.

Children's literature offers many contexts through which learners can explore the mathematical operations of multiplication and division. They come to see multiplication as a process of repeated addition of animals or people and division as a process of equal partitioning of cookies or money. Children's books can also give meaning to multiplication-related number theory topics like prime and composite numbers and factorials.

Multiplication as repeated addition

Learning is a process of making connections. Children often come to understand multiplication by relating it to the context of repeated addition. As children learn the basic addition facts they often find the "double" combinations of $3 + 3 = 6$, $4 + 4 = 8$, and so on to be especially easy to remember. They extend this understanding when they discover that multiplication is a way to add a particular set of objects a certain number of times. For instance, to determine the total number of marbles in three bags if each bag contains four marbles, learners can add $4 + 4 + 4$. They come to see that 3×4 is just another way to express an already familiar number. *Bunches and Bunches of Bunnies* (Mathews, 1978) is an excellent introduction to multiplication as repeated addition. Its rhyming format depicts groups of bunnies involved in various activities. On one page, two groups of two bunnies are "proudly beaming and gently dreaming" to show $2 \times 2 = 4$; on another page three groups of three bunnies are "planting seeds, pulling weeds, and watering gardens" to illustrate $3 \times 3 = 9$. The story continues with these double combinations up to 12×12. In all these examples, there are well-defined, discrete sets of rabbits performing a variety of actions. By successively counting the number of rabbits in each group the reader can view multiplication as a process of repeated addition. *Shoes in Twos* (Irons and Irons, 1987b) is another story that uses a repeated grouping of discrete objects. The illustrations show a variety of shoes with different attributes, such as leather straps and stick-down flaps. But each page also shows what all shoes have in common: they come in twos. The story invites children to examine their own shoes closely and then to look around them for other sets of objects that naturally occur in groups.

6

multiplication

and division

Multiplication as a process of repeated addition is an underlying idea in *Trucks You Can Count On* (Magee, 1985). Although this book is primarily a counting book, its pictures show various groups of objects: The reader counts by twos to determine the number of wheels on an eighteen-wheeler and by threes to find the two sets of three mirrors located on each side of the truck. The reader can also choose to count by sets of two or by sets of four to determine the number of lights on the front of a tractor. The book demonstrates the process of repeated addition using objects in a child's own environment.

Ruby Dee's *Two Ways to Count to Ten* (1988), mentioned in Chapter 1, incorporates a sequence of counting by multiples of two. The hyena becomes the new king of the jungle because it is the only animal that can count to ten before a javelin hits the ground (it counts by twos). The story invites children to skip count, using a variety of number sequences, and to represent these patterns on a number line. (The number line is a good repeated addition model for viewing multiplication, since, much like a ruler or yardstick, it can show a series of spaces or leaps of equal size.) A number of books about Noah's ark (for example, *Aardvarks Disembark* [Jonas, 1990] and *Noah's Ark* [Spier, 1977]), with their matched pairs of animals, are natural choices to help children practice counting by twos. *How Many Feet in the Bed?* (Hamm, 1991) also shows counting by twos, going both forward (2, 4, 6, 8, 10) and backward (10, 8, 6, 4, 2). Readers count the feet of five family members as they tumble in and out of bed on a Sunday morning. Dad begins the count with "two," and is joined successively by his daughter, son, infant, and wife. But a series of incidents, such as the ringing of the phone and the overflowing of the bathtub, force family members to leave the bed one by one (or two by two if you are counting by feet!).

Animals Galore (MacCarthy, 1989) explores the special terminology of grouping. The reader encounters some of the special terms that describe particular sets of animals, such as an army of ants, a school of fish, or a pod of whales. The black-and-white photographs of Tana Hoban's *More Than One* (1981) illustrate a variety of grouping words, such as a herd of elephants, a crowd of people, and a bundle of wood. Several are used more than once but in association with different objects (a pile of tires or leaves; a bundle of wood or newspapers), while words like *team* designate a specific (though perhaps varying) number of people. Both books emphasize the general concept of a group and introduce readers to specialized collective nouns.

Representing multiplication through arrays

An array is an arrangement of items in a number of rows, each row containing the same number of items. Classrooms often have many examples of array patterns (rows of ceiling or floor tiles, sets of lights, panes of window glass). This regular pattern of rows is often referred to as an area model for multiplication, since the area of a rectangle can be determined by multiplying the length

TABLE 6–1. *Sample array for multiplication*

by the width. By looking at an example of an array, such as a 3 × 5 pattern of squares (Table 6–1), it is easy to see the relationship between the lengths of the sides and the number of units it takes to cover the surface.

The array or area model is an extremely powerful one for learners and helps them move from the cumbersome and time-consuming strategy of repeated addition to the more efficient strategy of multiplication. The array or area model also provides the most effective way of demonstrating the principle of distributivity (for example, 3 × 5 = [3 × 4] + [3 x 1]), one of the most important principles in mathematics, and it can be used to demonstrate the multiplication of fractions and decimals.

Lucy and Tom's 1, 2, 3 (Hughes, 1987) introduces readers to the array model for multiplication. The illustrations show a variety of familiar objects, such as pairs of socks and plastic animals that march two by two, but the book also includes interesting pictures of food items often packaged in arrays at the supermarket: four muffins (2 × 2), a dozen eggs (2 × 6), six cartons of yogurt (2 × 3). These examples emphasize the widespread use of arrays in the commercial world. Another book that illustrates the array model for multiplication is *Number Families* (Srivastava, 1979). A series of large dots introduce special sets of numbers: odd, even, prime, square, and triangular. The dots are arranged in arrays to portray some of the special features of these numbers. Readers are encouraged to investigate the relationships between the number families along with the text, using a set of buttons or chips. For instance, they can see the distinction between prime and composite numbers when they try to devise all the possible arrays for each of the counting numbers:

2	3	4	5	6	7	8	9
1 × 2	1 × 3	1 × 4	1 × 5	1 × 6	1 × 7	1 × 8	1 × 9
		2 × 2		2 × 3		2 × 4	3 × 3

Some numbers, such as 2, 3, 5 and 7, have only one possible array. These are known as prime numbers (those having only 1 and themselves as factors). Numbers with more than one possible array configuration are called composite numbers (those having more than two factors, such as 8 with factors 1, 2, 4, and 8).

Another book that introduces both the process of grouping through multiplication and the number theory topic of prime and composite numbers is *I Can Count the Petals of a Flower* (Wahl and Wahl, 1976). (Multiplication is shown here as repeated addition rather than as arrays.) In this counting book, each number is illustrated by a color photograph of a flower: one petal of a lily flower, two petals of a crown of thorns, three petals of a snowdrop, four petals of a clematis, and so on. After one sequence of ten, the numbers are represented again in a second series of color photographs: numbers one, two, and three through a single example, as before, but number four as one Chinese dogwood with four petals (1 × 4) and as two crown of thorn flowers (2 × 2); and number six as one yellow day lily (1 × 6), two painted trillium (2 × 3), and three crown of thorns (3 × 2). In effect, prime numbers are represented through a single photograph and composite numbers through multiple photographs (and factors). The even numbers are represented consistently through the repetition of the two-petaled crown of thorns.

Multiplication patterns: factorials and doubling

Another multiplication pattern to explore with children is that of factorial numbers (products such as 1 × 2 × 3 × 4). A good example is *Anno's Mysterious Multiplying Jar* (1983), which we encountered in Chapter 1. This book portrays an expanding pattern of one jar times two islands times three mountains times four castles and so on. To reach the final total, the reader eventually multiplies the first ten counting numbers together. Parts of this factorial sequence are represented in the back of the book in a series of arrays of dots, which dramatically portray the explosive dimension of multiplication:

1 × 1 = 1	jar
1 × 2 = 2	islands
1 × 2 × 3 = 6	mountains
1 × 2 × 3 ×4 = 24	walled kingdoms
1 × 2 × 3 × 4 × 5 = 120	villages

A book like this one helps learners to visualize the abstract numerical pattern of factorials by illustrating numerical progressions through pictures, narrative, arrays, and numbers. This kind of multiple representation enables learners to deepen their understanding of how factorials operate.

Several stories incorporate a multiplication pattern called successive doubling. In *Mirror Mirror* (Irons and Irons, 1987a) the symmetry of even numbers is made clear when sets of hats, hands, and flowers are held before a mirror and thus doubled in appearance. A sequence of numbers in which each number is a fixed multiple of the previous one is called a geometric progression and the process is called an exponential increase. The most common real-life circumstance in which repeated doubling and exponential growth takes place is in biological reproduction. This pattern is known as the binomial (names of two) sequence, since its doubling represents the powers of two—$2^1 = 2$, $2^2 = 4$ $2^3 = 8$, and so on. Virginia Kahl's story, *The Habits of Rabbits* (1957), describes what happens when rabbits are allowed to continue to reproduce: two rabbits soon become four, four become eight, and the population of rabbits begins to rise at an exponential rate. *Germs Make Me Sick!* (Berger, 1985), represents the same numerical sequence in the continuous division of bacteria.

Two other stories that look at the sometimes surprising growth rate produced by doubling are *The King's Chessboard* (Birch, 1988) and *A Grain of Rice* (Pittman, 1986), both versions of an old tale found in Persia, India, and China. In the Birch version, the king wants to reward the grand vizier, his principal adviser, for his helpfulness. Although the king offers jewels, palaces, and many other wonderful prizes, the grand vizier only wishes for a humble reward: grains of rice. He asks that he be given a single grain of rice the first day, twice that on the second day, twice this amount on the third day, and so on, for a month's time. The king marvels at the unselfishness of his counselor and graciously consents to the proposal. But the king is in for a rude surprise. Although the number of grains of rice starts out small enough (1, 2, 4, 8, 16, 32, 64, 128, 256, 512, 1,024), by the time the thirtieth day rolls around the amount of rice is astronomical. Children who enjoy large numbers and like using the calculator may find it an interesting task to try to tabulate the final product!

The King's Chessboard and *A Grain of Rice* use discrete materials (the grains of rice) to demonstrate this doubling pattern. *Binary Numbers* (Watson, 1977) and *Melisande* (Nesbit, 1989) use continuous materials—a piece of string and a lock of hair—to represent the same geometric progression. *Binary Numbers* introduces the doubling sequence of the powers of two through a ball of string. Readers are asked to measure off a foot of string, then double the length of the string by folding it at the one foot mark, then double it again. How many times would one have to double its length before it went all the way around the earth? Amazingly it would take only twenty-seven doublings, and according to the author's calculations, after only thirty-one doublings the string would be long enough to reach to the moon and beyond! An interesting practical application of the binary sequence involves weights. Using a series of weights in the binary sequence (such as one ounce, two ounces, four ounces, and eight ounces), one can weigh all whole-ounce amounts from one to fifteen ounces on a balance scale. In fact, by using the first ten numbers of the binary sequence one can build all the whole numbers up to 1,023. (Your students might want to check this out by creating a table showing what combination of weights would be equal to each amount.)

Melisande (Nesbit, 1989) is a fairy tale about a princess who is cursed by an evil fairy at her christening and grows up beautiful but bald. When she is finally granted one wish, she asks for golden hair a yard long that grows an inch every day and twice as fast when it is cut. Naturally, problems of mathematical proportion begin to arise! At one point the family tries to reverse the wish but succeeds only in making Melisande herself grow at this alarming rate. With the help of a determined fairy godmother and a prince, order is finally restored. While Melisande's hair was growing, however, the full mathematical impact of her wish was revealed. Her hair grew an inch every night. When it was three yards long she cut off two yards, but of course it then grew back twice as fast, and in thirty-six days it was again as long as ever. She cut her hair again and felt better, but for a shorter time. Now her hair was growing four inches daily, and in eighteen days it was as long as before. At this point it was growing eight inches per day, and this rate would double as soon as she cut it again. Children could keep track of the pattern in this way:

Rate of Growth	Time Needed to Grow Back 2 Yards
2" per day	36 days
4" per day	18 days
8" per day	9 days
16" per day	4½ days
32" per day	2¼ days

This story not only demonstrates the binary sequence, it also shows an inverse relationship between length and time: as the amount of hair grown per day doubles, the amount of time needed to grow it halves.

Division

The most important mathematical concept involved in the operation of division (a concept also used in fractions and decimals) is partitioning, the dividing of discrete items or continuous quantities into groups of equal size. It might involve a set of baseball cards (discrete) or a length of cloth (continuous). It might use the entire quantity or it could use a remainder in some special way.

Two types of situations give rise to division: partitive and measurement scenarios. In a partitive situation, the size of the original set and the number of subsets are known, while the size of each subset is to be determined. Dealing out a deck of cards is a good example: If fifty-two cards are to be distributed equally among four people, one way to do so is by dealing or partitioning out the cards one at a time, giving one to each person until all of them are given out. The answer to the division problem is then the number of cards that each person has. In a measurement model of division, the size of the original set and the size of each subset are known, while the number of subsets is to be determined. For instance, if a group of twelve friends is going out for the evening and can fit no more than four people in a car, how many cars will they need? One way to determine the answer is by repeated subtraction $(12 - 4 = 8, 8 - 4 = 4, 4 - 4 = 0)$, for an answer of three cars. In this way learners can see division, represented by repeatedly removing equal-sized groups, as the opposite of multiplication, represented by repeatedly adding equal-sized groups.

A book that nicely demonstrates the partitive division model is *The Doorbell Rang* (Hutchins, 1986). Two children eager to share a dozen cookies think to themselves, "That's six each." But before they have the chance to eat a single cookie, the doorbell rings and two friends come in. "That's three each," they say to each other. Soon the doorbell rings again and two more friends come in. The problem is soon resolved when the doorbell rings one last time and Grandma arrives with a large batch of cookies. The separation of the original set of twelve into a changing number of subsets is illustrated through a series of events:

Original Set	Number of Divisors	Size of Each Subset
12 cookies	2 children	6 cookies
12 cookies	4 children	3 cookies
12 cookies	6 children	2 cookies
12 cookies	12 children	1 cookie

Children can be invited to act out this story. They might use a different number of cookies and explore the results when one variable is changed. For instance, if two children must share nine cookies, how will they be able to divide them? Some children suggest giving each child four cookies and leaving the last one in the cookie jar. Others recommend that the last cookie be broken in half and divided, which leads to a discussion of fractional parts. If the children were sharing marbles, baseball cards, or other nonedible materials, however, such division into fractional parts would not be possible. It is important for them to see that the fate of the remainder depends on the context of the story situation.

The Country Bunny (Heyward, 1939) demonstrates the measurement model of division. It tells the story of Mother Cottontail, who attains the special position of Easter Bunny despite her already overwhelming responsibilities in caring for her twenty-one children. At one point she engages pairs of her children in various tasks around the house: two sweep out the cottage, two make the beds, two cook dinner, two wash the dishes, and so on. After she has designated a job for each pair of rabbits, Mother Cottontail notices that one sad and lonely bunny is left. She grants him the singular responsibility of "keeper of my chair" and instructs him to seat her politely every time she comes to the table. This story highlights the grouping of twos up to twenty and illustrates the measurement model (determining the number of equal-sized subsets in a given set, as Mother Cottontail does when she doles out two responsibilities to each of ten pairs of rabbits). Children might act out this story and similar division stories or make a series of drawings to show division as a process of repeated subtraction: two bunnies sweep the cottage and there are eighteen left (20 – 2 = 18), then two more make the beds and there are sixteen left (18 – 2 = 16), and so on.

Another important issue raised by this story and others like it is the handling of remainders. There is no universal rule for treating remainders; the context of the situation determines the appropriate choice. Several different kinds of remainder situations have been identified (Kennedy and Tipps, 1991). In some cases the remainder does not get divided up to become part of the quotient. *The Country Bunny* illustrates this situation. If one asked, "To how many pairs of bunnies could Mother Cottontail give jobs?" the answer would be ten pairs. Even though the remaining bunny is not really a part of the answer, leftover bunnies in stories are always given some kind of responsibility. The problem that Mother Cottontail encountered can be related to similar remainder situations: "There are thirty-two children in our class. If we play a game that requires three equal-sized teams, how many players will there be on each team?" Although some children agree that there ought to be ten on each team, they devise elaborate schemes to involve the remaining two children, in some cases designating them as rotating substitutes or scorekeepers. Children may also solve the problem by dividing the teacher along with the two extra children among the three teams. Choosing teams is a familiar context for children, and they feel it only fair to help any leftover players by treating them in an equitable fashion. This kind of problem has an ethical dimension that children can explore in some of their mathematical problem solving.

Another book that focuses on remainders in different contexts is *The Greatest Guessing Game: A Book about Dividing* (Froman, 1978). A variety of situations are discussed. In some situations involving money, there must be some kind of exchange before the partitioning can continue; for instance, when six dollars are divided among four people, the last two dollars must be changed into half dollars or quarters. In another case, when $8.27 is divided among five people, there are two cents left over. The book urges the reader to consider how that money ought to be used. Perhaps the group could draw straws for it, or they could buy a piece of candy and split it five ways. Then there is the situation of eleven club members who owned 237 books but had only one small bookshelf in their clubhouse. After taking out two sets of 10 books for each person there were only 17 books left. Since club members wanted more books to remain in the clubhouse, they each returned one book, producing a total of 28. The rest would be stored at the homes of club members until more bookshelves could be built. This story helps to highlight the point that it is sometimes beneficial to have a remainder that is not divided up completely.

Once children are familiar with the division situations found in *The Doorbell Rang, The Country Bunny* and *The Greatest Guessing Game*, it would be valuable to discuss other contexts for remainders (Kennedy and Tipps, 1991). For instance, the following problem addresses the economics of shopping: "It costs seventy-nine cents to buy three packs of baseball cards. If I buy only one pack, how much do I have to pay for it?" In this case, division yields a whole-number quotient of twenty-six with a remainder of one. Children will see that the store is not likely to sell one pack for twenty-six cents because such a policy would change the price of three packs to seventy-eight cents. In situations such as these, no matter what the remainder is, the quotient is always rounded up, contradicting the common rule of rounding up only if the quotient ends in .5 or above.

A similar situation, only in a nonmonetary context, involves a problem like this: "A group of fifty-three children is riding to camp in cars. If each car can carry six children, how many cars are needed?" Here, the quotient is eight with a remainder of five children, and again, no matter what the size of the remainder, the quotient must be increased by one to accommodate the extra children. In other situations ("How many change would you get if you bought as many four-cent pencils as you could and gave the clerk fifteen cents?"), the remainder is viewed as a whole number and not discarded but presented as the answer.

Books in the classroom K–2

Second-grade teacher Julie Robinson used the story *Germs Make Me Sick!* (Berger, 1985) to introduce her students to the growth of bacteria as part of their class study on health. Since the children had discussed viruses and bacteria but seemed confused about the difference, the teacher asked the children to look again at pictures of bacteria similar to Table 6–2.

"What do you notice happening?" she asked.

"The bacteria are growing," Sean replied.

"Yeah, and one, two, four, eight, sixteen . . . they're all even numbers except the first," said David.

"Yes, they're doubling," observed Vincent.

TABLE 6–2. *Model of bacteria growth*

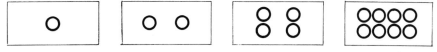

In order to provide another context for the doubling pattern, the teacher invited the children to create their own family tree. Jennifer traced successive generations in her family from herself to two parents to four grandparents (Figure 6–1). Because there were still a few children who did not seem to understand the concept of doubling, the teacher reflected on this problem and planned to revise the lesson to capitalize on her students' interests. She wrote, "There are other ways of introducing doubling. Maybe one way that could have worked was telling a secret to two people, and their [each] telling two people, and so on, and so on. Maybe next time I will use the idea of telling a secret. It may have more [of an impact] on all the children since keeping a secret is a big deal among friends in second grade." Good teachers connect mathematical investigations to the experiences and interests of their students.

When first-grade teacher Timothy O'Keefe read aloud *Two Ways to Count to Ten* (Dee, 1988), the class discussed the special sequence of the even numbers two, four, six, eight, and ten. But it wasn't until a few days later that six-year-old Veronica noticed that she could represent the evenness of these numbers with fingers: she held up two fingers on each hand to represent $2 + 2 = 4$, and so forth, and in this way nicely conveyed the symmetry of even numbers. Children can also represent this sequence of numbers on a hundred square sheet (Figure 6–2). When Tim asked the class to describe the patterns they noticed on the chart, the children made these observations: "They go in rows down." "They go every other one." "All the numbers that end in two are in the same line." "Yeah, and it's the same for four, six, eight, and zero." "We didn't circle the one, three, five, seven, and nine." Their comments emphasize the potential of exploring patterns through repeated addition.

FIGURE 6–1

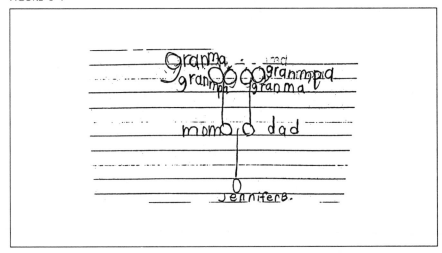

FIGURE 6–2

1	(2)	3	(4)	5	(6)	7	(8)	9	(10)
11	(12)	13	(14)	15	(16)	17	(18)	19	(20)
21	(22)	23	(24)	25	(26)	27	(28)	29	(30)
31	(32)	33	(34)	35	(36)	37	(38)	39	(40)
41	(42)	43	(44)	45	(46)	47	(48)	49	(50)
51	(52)	53	(54)	55	(56)	57	(58)	59	(60)
61	(62)	63	(64)	65	(66)	67	(68)	69	(70)
71	(72)	73	(74)	75	(76)	77	(78)	79	(80)
81	(82)	83	(84)	85	(86)	87	(88)	89	(90)
91	(92)	93	(94)	95	(96)	97	(98)	99	(100)

Teachers can use this same book to address the general purposes of number lines. Where do the children notice number lines and why do people use them? The children might list such contexts as thermometers, height charts, or even mile markers along the roadside, which assist people in calculating temperature, height, and distance.

Books in the classroom 3–4

Fourth-grade teacher Nancy Wallace used *Anno's Mysterious Multiplying Jar* (Anno, 1983) to discuss situations that used factorial numbers, such as the number of seating possibilities at a table or the number of possible arrangements for three crayons. When Nancy invited the children to write a letter about factorials to their parents, Brandon used the example of four different crayons to communicate his understanding (Figure 6–3). Although his letter is not reproduced in color here, it has strips of color that match the pattern of letters. In part of Matt's letter to his parents (Figure 6–4), he described what factorials enable you to determine as well as what they do not.

Writing for a real audience can support learners as they represent their current understanding of mathematical ideas. The enthusiasm generated in this fourth-grade class by factorials was demonstrated in other ways as well. Scott and Jennifer insisted on determining the number of possibilities for arranging twenty-eight students in desks. Their teacher provided them extra time in class to calculate the total. After an hour or more of diligent work they informed the class that there were 305,465,559,986,570,052,501,504,000,000 seating possibilities! The teacher observed that if she had given these children an hour's worth of multiplication problems from their textbook they would

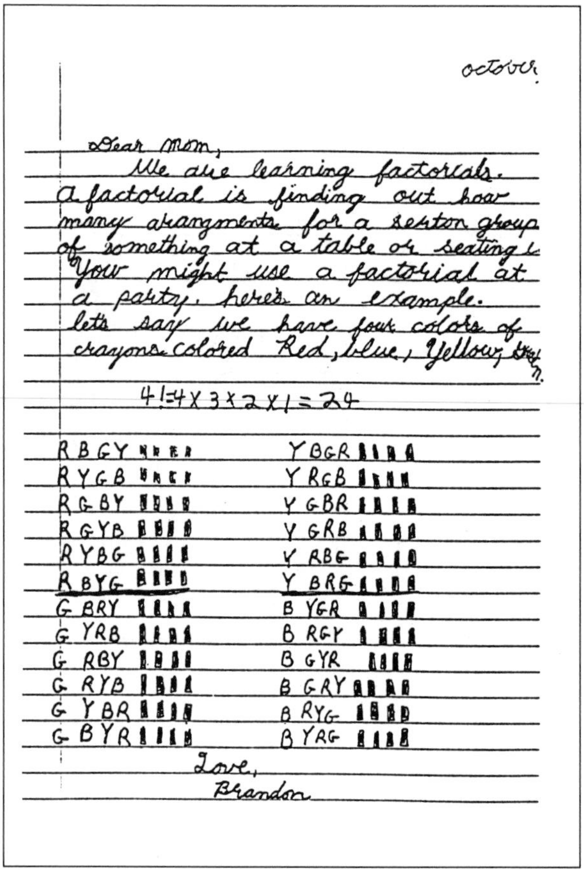

october

Dear mom,
     We are learning factorials.
A factorial is finding out how
many arangments for a seston group
of something at a table or seating
Your might use a factorial at
a party. heres an example.
lets say we have four colors of
crayons. colored Red, blue, Yellow, th

$4! = 4 \times 3 \times 2 \times 1 = 24$

R B GY	Y BGR
R Y G B	Y R G B
R G BY	Y G BR
R GYB	Y GRB
R YBG	Y RBG
R BYG	Y BRG
G BRY	B YGR
G YRB	B RGY
G RBY	B GYR
G RYB	B GRY
G YBR	B RYG
G BYR	B YRG

Love,
Brandon

FIGURE 6–3

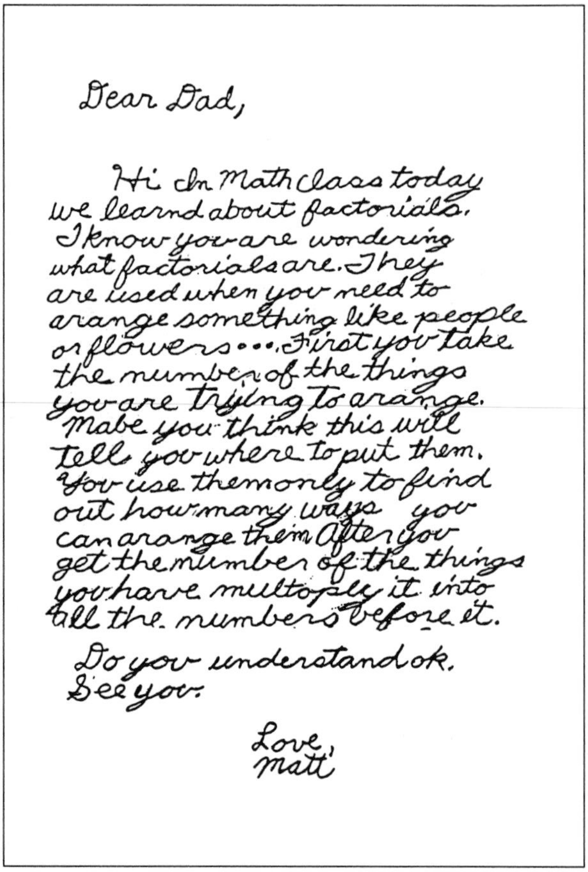

Dear Dad,

     Hi In Math class today
we learnd about factorials.
I know you are wondering
what factorials are. They
are used when you need to
arange something like people
or flowers.... First you take
the number of the things
you are trying to arange.
Mabe you think this will
tell you where to put them.
You use them only to find
out how many ways   you
can arange them After you
get the number of the things
you have multoply it into
all the numbers before it.

Do you understand ok.
See you.

Love,
matt

FIGURE 6–4

have balked immediately; but because this multiplication was in the context of a purposeful, self-initiated challenge, the children were eager to complete the calculations.

Nancy also noticed that her children's interest in factorials became part of playground conversation. She saw several of her students drawing diagrams in the sand, proudly explaining the meaning of factorials to their friends. Inside the classroom, there was even one ambitious student who was determined to figure out how many ways all the paperback books on the reading shelf couldbe arranged! Children's literature helped to provide the spark for these enthusiastic demonstrations.

In another fourth-grade class, teacher Joe Duprey invited his children to create their own factorial story. Van used a limousine to begin his story (Figure 6–5). Renee used some pictures to help her readers actually see the details she was tabulating (Figure 6–6). Other children also created familiar contexts for this mathematical concept.

FIGURE 6-5

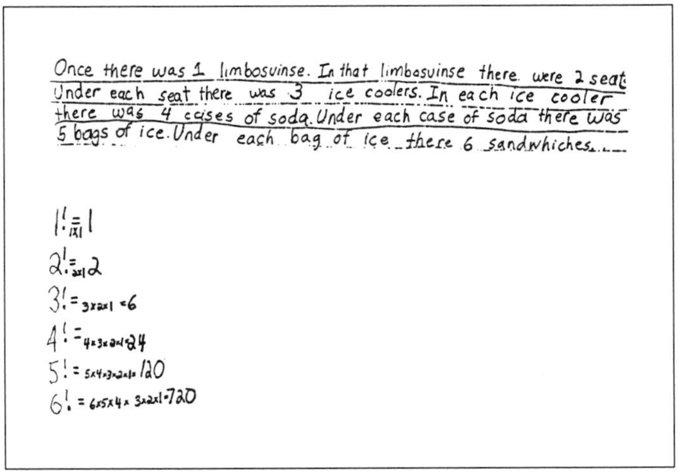

Once there was 1 limbosuinse. In that limbosuinse there were 2 seat
Under each seat there was 3 ice coolers. In each ice cooler
there was 4 cases of soda. Under each case of soda there was
5 bags of ice. Under each bag of ice there 6 sandwhiches.

$1! = \frac{1}{1 \times 1} 1$

$2! = 2 \times 1 \; 2$

$3! = 3 \times 2 \times 1 = 6$

$4! = 4 \times 3 \times 2 \times 1 \; 24$

$5! = 5 \times 4 \times 3 \times 2 \times 1 \; 120$

$6! = 6 \times 5 \times 4 \times 3 \times 2 \times 1 = 720$

FIGURE 6-6

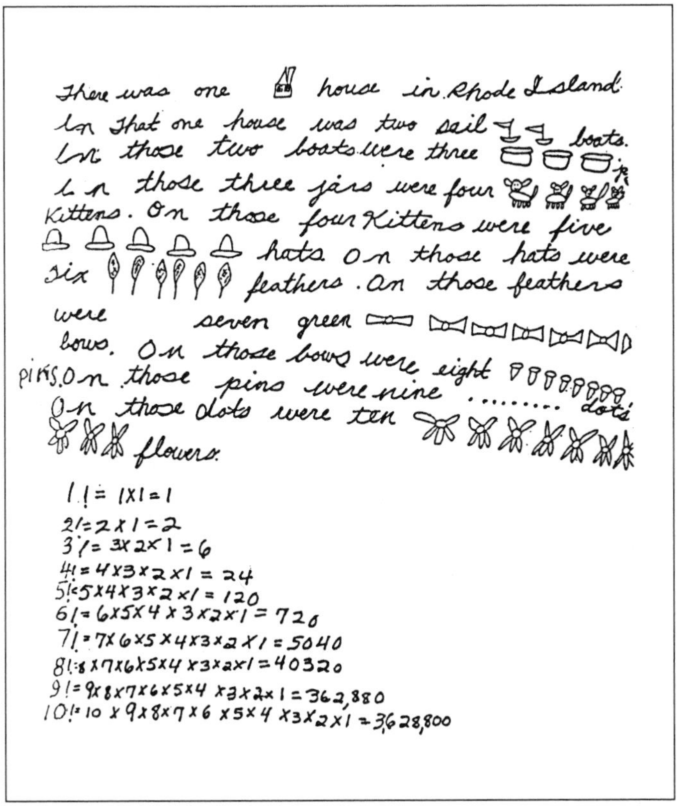

There was one 🏠 house in Rhode Island.
In that one house was two sail ⛵⛵ boats.
In those two boats were three 🏺🏺🏺 jars.
In those three jars were four 🐱🐱🐱🐱
Kittens. On those four Kittens were five
🎩🎩🎩🎩🎩 hats On those hats were
six 🪶🪶🪶🪶🪶🪶 feathers. An those feathers
were seven green 🎀🎀🎀🎀🎀🎀🎀
bows. On those bows were eight 📌📌📌📌📌📌📌📌
pins. On those pins were nine .... dots
On those dots were ten 🌸🌸🌸🌸🌸🌸🌸🌸🌸🌸
flowers.

$1! = 1 \times 1 = 1$

$2! = 2 \times 1 = 2$

$3! = 3 \times 2 \times 1 = 6$

$4! = 4 \times 3 \times 2 \times 1 = 24$

$5! = 5 \times 4 \times 3 \times 2 \times 1 = 120$

$6! = 6 \times 5 \times 4 \times 3 \times 2 \times 1 = 720$

$7! = 7 \times 6 \times 5 \times 4 \times 3 \times 2 \times 1 = 5040$

$8! = 8 \times 7 \times 6 \times 5 \times 4 \times 3 \times 2 \times 1 = 40320$

$9! = 9 \times 8 \times 7 \times 6 \times 5 \times 4 \times 3 \times 2 \times 1 = 362{,}880$

$10! = 10 \times 9 \times 8 \times 7 \times 6 \times 5 \times 4 \times 3 \times 2 \times 1 = 3{,}628{,}800$

Books in the classroom 5–6

Fifth-grade teacher Evelina Montgomery read *Bunches and Bunches of Bunnies* (Mathews, 1978) and asked her students to write stories that used repeated addition in a rhyming format. One child wrote the piece seen in Figures 6–7 and 6–8. The two illustrations, which were incorporated into a class book on multiplication, show two different arrangements for four: the first picture illustrates two sets of two, or 2 × 2 = 4; the second shows the nerds together in a

FIGURE 6–7

FIGURE 6–8

single line, or 1 × 4 = 4. Thus the factors of four (1, 2, and 4) are all appropriately represented.

Another child used five discrete sets of baby chicks to represent multiplication as repeated addition (Figures 6–9 and 6–10). Each subset of the total is involved in a different activity, such as shopping, eating, and resting. Even though there is a diversity of activity within the larger set, the story can still be viewed as a context for multiplication. As these figures show, children discover variations in problem generation when they are given the opportunity to create their own contexts for mathematical ideas.

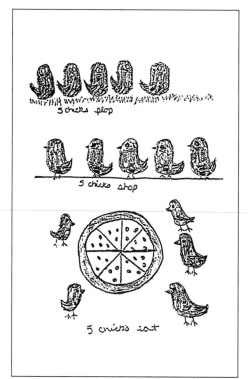

FIGURE 6–9

FIGURE 6–10

Further explorations

1. What objects can your students think of that are packaged or named as
   groups in unique ways? After reading *Lucy and Tom's 1, 2, 3* (Hughes,
   1987), brainstorm a list of words that describe groups of objects:

Group Word	Context	Approximate or Exact Number
pack	soda	6
carton	eggs	12
bevy	geese	15
bag	marbles	20
herd	cattle	50
set	baseball cards	750

   Some words may designate a specific number, such as the number of eggs
   in a carton, while others may be more variable, like the number of cattle in

a herd. These groupings can start the class on further work with multiplication and division. For instance, how many cartons of eggs are needed to make deviled eggs for a crowd of fifty?

2. You might read *What Comes in 2's, 3's and 4's?* (Aker, 1990) and begin a list of common sets of objects that the children find in their environment. Some of the fourth-grade students in Sandra Medlin's class composed the list seen in Figure 6–11.

3. What associations do your children have with the term *bunch*? You might read them *Bunches and Bunches of Bunnies* (Mathews, 1978) and ask them to describe other objects that can be grouped into bunches, such as a bunch of flowers or a bunch of baseball cards. How many flowers typically form a bunch? Is the number different for baseball cards? The students might enjoy writing stories that emphasize a variety of bunches.

FIGURE 6–11

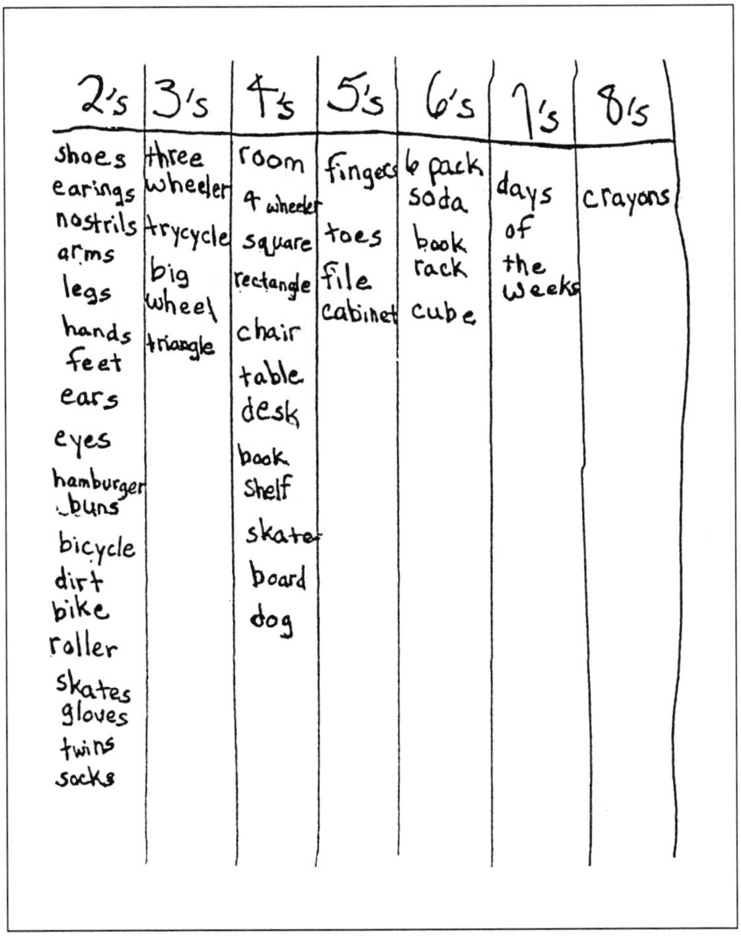

2's	3's	4's	5's	6's	7's	8's
shoes	three wheeler	room	fingers	6 pack soda	days of the weeks	crayons
earings		4 wheeler				
nostrils	trycycle	square	toes	book rack		
arms						
legs	big wheel	rectange	file cabinet	cube		
hands	triangle	chair				
feet		table				
ears		desk				
eyes		book shelf				
hamburger buns		skate board				
bicycle		dog				
dirt bike						
roller skates						
gloves						
twins						
socks						

4. What rhymes or chants do your children know that include a skip counting sequence for multiplication? You might read *Two Ways to Count to Ten* (Dee, 1978) and then create a class book of rhymes students know, with representations of these counting sequences using number lines and hundred square charts.

5. In what situations do you find your children sharing? Is it out on the playground, at lunch, or in the library? Do they share crayons, books, or apples? You can use these situations to discuss division.

6. How do your students treat remainders in their own lives? If they have leftover food, money, playing cards, or people, how do they partition out the remainder? What is the influence of context? You might read aloud some of the books in this chapter and then invite your students to write and classify their own stories about remainders.

Children's books

Aker, Suzanne. 1990. *What comes in 2's, 3's, and 4's?* New York: Simon and Schuster.

Anno, Mitsumasa. 1983. *Anno's mysterious multiplying jar*. New York: Philomel.

Berger, Melvin. 1985. *Germs make me sick!* New York: Crowell.

Birch, David. 1988. *The king's chessboard*. New York: Dial.

Brown, Margaret Wise. 1961. *Four fur feet*. Columbiana, AL: Hopscotch Books.

Dee, Ruby. 1988. *Two ways to count to ten*. New York: Holt.

Emberley, Barbara. 1966. *One wide river to cross*. Englewood Cliffs, NJ: Prentice-Hall.

Froman, Robert. 1978. *The greatest guessing game: A book about dividing*. New York: Crowell.

Hamm, Diane J. 1991. *How many feet in the bed?* New York: Simon and Schuster.

Heller, Ruth. 1987. *A cache of jewels: And other collective nouns*. New York: Grosset and Dunlap.

Heyward, DuBose. 1939. *The country bunny and the little gold shoes*. Boston: Houghton Mifflin.

Hoban, Tana. 1981. *More than one*. New York: Greenwillow.

Hughes, Shirley. 1987. *Lucy and Tom's 1, 2, 3*. New York: Viking Kestrel.

Hutchins, Pat. 1986. *The doorbell rang*. New York: Greenwillow.

Irons, Rosemary, and Calvin Irons. 1987a. *Mirror mirror*. Crystal Lake, IL: Rigby Education.

———. 1987b. *Shoes in twos*. Crystal Lake, IL: Rigby Education.

Jonas, Ann. 1990. *Aardvarks disembark*. New York: Greenwillow.

Kahl, Virginia. 1957. *The habits of rabbits*. New York: Scribner.

Low, Joseph. 1980. *Mice twice*. New York: Atheneum.

MacCarthy, Patricia. 1989. *Animals galore*. New York: Dial.

——— . 1991. *Herds of words*. New York: Dial.

Magee, Doug. 1985. *Trucks you can count on*. New York: Dodd, Mead.

Mathews, Louise. 1978. *Bunches and bunches of bunnies*. New York: Dodd, Mead.

McMillan, Bruce. 1991. *One, two, one pair!* New York: Scholastic.

Merriam, Eve. 1964. Gazinta. In *It doesn't always have to rhyme*. New York: Atheneum.

Nesbit, E. 1989. *Melisande*. San Diego: Harcourt Brace Jovanovich.

Pittman, Helena C. 1986. *A grain of rice*. New York: Hastings House.

Silverstein, Shel. 1974. Lester. In *Where the sidewalk ends*. New York: Harper and Row.

Spier, Peter. 1977. *Noah's ark*. Garden City, NY: Doubleday.

Srivastava, Jane. 1979. *Number families*. New York: Crowell.

Trivett, John. 1975. *Building tables in tables: A book about multiplication*. New York: Crowell.

Wahl, John, and Stacy Wahl. 1976. *I can count the petals of a flower*. Reston, VA: National Council of Teachers of Mathematics.

Watson, Clyde. 1977. *Binary numbers*. New York: Crowell.

Teacher resource

Kennedy, Leonard, and Steve Tipps. 1991. *Guiding children's learning of mathematics*. Belmont, CA: Wadsworth.

Fractions have often been a difficult learning experience, since students may be pushed into manipulating symbols and solving equations before they understand what they are doing. To reverse this early rush toward symbolic manipulation, it is important for teachers to encourage children to focus on the functional use of fractions. Children need to see how other people use fractions in real-life situations and to recognize how they themselves put fractions to use in their own lives. Children's literature can help to establish this conceptual base.

Models of fractions

The part-whole relationship in a fraction can be represented in several ways. The two most important are the set model and the region model. In a set model, a set of objects is subdivided into smaller groups of equal size. For instance, when a set of twelve pennies is subdivided into two equal-sized subsets, the expression $\frac{1}{2}$ of $12 = 6$ describes it. Children can build an understanding of this set model by using egg cartons to subdivide sets of twelve objects in various ways. The region model does not involve the use of individual, discrete objects but subdivides a particular area into parts of the same size. Folding regular polygons (such as squares, hexagons, and equilateral triangles) along their axes of symmetry so that both sides match is an excellent way to demonstrate the equal partitioning of an area. Children can also use wooden pattern blocks (a set model), to create a region model of fractions; for instance, they can discover that six small equilateral triangles cover the same area as one large hexagon.

Two books that portray fractions through a set model are *The Doorbell Rang* (Hutchins, 1986) and *The Half-Birthday Party* (Pomerantz, 1984). Although less common than a region model, this is an important representation of the part-whole relationship. If children only view fractions in regional terms, as in the typical pizza or pie analogy, they sometimes think that fractions always deal with numbers less than one. In *The Doorbell Rang*, mentioned as a book about division in Chapter 6, two children are eager to share a batch of cookies and figure out that they are entitled to six apiece. Although no mathematical equations appear in the story, readers can discover that a set of twelve objects is subdivided into two

7

fractions

equal-sized groups and that the mathematical sentence of 12 ÷ 2 = 6 repre-sents this situation. Since the six in the sentence represents one half of the orig-inal set of twelve, the expression ½ of 12 = 6 also describes the situation. As the story progresses, a series of children come to the door and are invited into the house to share the same set of twelve cookies. A list of parallel divisions and fractions can be used to describe this chronology of events:

2 children in all	12 ÷ 2 = 6	½ of 12 = 6
4 children in all	12 ÷ 4 = 3	¼ of 12 = 3
6 children in all	12 ÷ 6 = 2	⅙ of 12 = 2
12 children in all	12 ÷ 12 = 1	¹⁄₁₂ of 12 = 1

The Doorbell Rang is a story that teachers of all grade levels can use to explore the concept of equivalence through partitioning. The three classroom scenar-ios at the end of this chapter illustrate several inventive ideas.

The *Half-Birthday Party* also views fractions through a set model. Older brother Daniel becomes so excited when his six-month-old sister Katie stands up for the first time that he decides to organize a half-birthday party for her. He invites Mom, Dad, Grandma, and the neighbors and urges them to bring half a present. A neighbor brings one slipper (half a pair), since her dog has chewed apart the other one (Katie enjoys chewing on the remaining slipper!). Mom brings one gold earring, having lost the other one many years ago. She shows it to Katie but puts it aside for her to enjoy when she is a bit older. Grandma adds to the celebration by bringing half a birthday cake lit by half a candle to the party. Daniel himself waits until it gets dark and then asks every-one to look outside, for his gift is a half-moon. The story uses both the set model for fractions (the slippers and earrings) and the region model (the cake, candle, and moon).

The part-whole relationship can also be shown through a region model. *Tom Fox and the Apple Pie* (Watson, 1972) and *Gator Pie* (Mathews, 1979) present a circular region model. The first story introduces a family of sixteen foxes. Tom Fox, the youngest, sneaks off to the country fair, buys an apple pie, and starts to head home so he can share it with the rest of the family. During his journey homeward, however, he imagines his mother slicing the pie into sixteen pieces and becomes concerned that the pieces will be so small he won't taste the apple part at all. He thinks he solves the problem by deciding to wait until eight of his brothers and sisters go out to see the stars; when the remaining eight eat the pie, the pieces will be much bigger. Yet he is still con-cerned about the size of the pieces and imagines the pie being divided into fourths and then halves. In the end, of course, he eats the whole pie himself! The illustrator, Wendy Watson, nicely depicts the partitioned pie so that the reader can see the difference each time. The story not only demonstrates the important concept of equivalence (by partitioning a region into equal-sized pieces), it also shows the inverse relationship between the size of the piece and the number of pieces. Children often find it difficult to understand that ½ is larger than ⅛, since they know from their work with whole numbers that the number 2 is smaller than the number 8. However, this story helps to demonstrate that fewer parts mean bigger pieces. This insight enables learners to compare fractions, such as ½ > ¼ > ⅛ > 1/16, and to be better estimators of quantities that involve fractional parts.

Gator Pie also uses a circular region. Alice and Alvin are two alligators who intend to share a pie equally until the other alligators hear about the dessert and begin to clamor for a piece. As each new set of alligators arrives, the size of each potential piece is shown to be smaller and smaller. Here again, the inverse relationship between the size of the piece and the number of pieces is illustrated. Finally, one hundred alligators are each demanding a piece of pie when an argument over the concept of equivalence erupts. One alligator claims, "Hey, your piece is bigger than my piece," and a free-for-all ensues. When the dust clears only Alvin and Alice remain, and they divide the pie between themselves as they had first intended. The complaint about unequal pieces is one that children can relate to, and the story nicely highlights the important mathematical concept of the equal partitioning of a whole. When children have to share a treat equally, such as a cookie, a pie, or a candy bar, they often raise the cry, "Hey, your half is bigger than my half!" Sometimes they are aware of the difficulty of dividing something into equal pieces and use or reinvent the rule "One cuts and the other chooses." Their sensitivity to the issue of equality is an important one in both mathematical and human terms. Perhaps *Gator Pie* will inspire a more detailed discussion.

Pezzettino (Lionni, 1975) is another story that demonstrates the region model for fractions but uses a square rather than a circle. It is important for children to have experience in partitioning a variety of shapes so that they do not think of a fraction as always being "part of a pie." Pezzettino, a small square, sees himself as so small compared to his larger friends that he is convinced he must be a piece of somebody else and sets off to try to find out where he fits in. The animals he encounters, such as fish, birds, and giraffes, are all composed of many equal-sized squares but they insist that Pezzettino is not a part of them. He finally stumbles on a rock and breaks himself into many smaller squares. As he puts himself back together, he realizes happily that he really is like all the rest of his friends, composed of many equal-sized pieces, thus highlighting the concept of equal-size partitioning.

Equivalence

Some books also demonstrate the important mathematical concept of equivalent fractions. At the end of *Gator Pie*, Alvin and Alice divide the pie in half so that each receives fifty slices. This partitioning helps to show that 50/100 is the same as ½. Children could also figure out how the two alligators could have shared the pie when it was partitioned into $\frac{1}{4}$'s, $\frac{1}{8}$'s, $\frac{1}{16}$'s, and so forth. In this way learners come to see that any given fraction has an infinite number of equivalent names. *Ed Emberley's Picture Pie* (Emberley, 1984) is a nonfiction book that also highlights the concept of equivalence. Here children learn to cut paper into halves, quarters, and eighths to make a variety of animals, flowers, designs, and patterns. As learners use these basic fractional pieces to create pictures, they begin to see the equivalent relationship between the pieces, for instance, that $\frac{1}{2} = \frac{2}{4} = \frac{4}{8}$.

Another aspect of equivalence is the notion that $\frac{n}{n} = 1$. *Gator Pie, Tom Fox and the Apple Pie*, and the poem "Little Bits" (Ciardi, 1962) all illustrate this concept. The two stories show the main characters partitioning a pie into equal pieces and eventually eating the entire pie themselves. Both illustrate the idea that a whole is equal to the sum of its partitioned parts ($\frac{2}{2} = \frac{3}{3} = \frac{4}{4} = \frac{5}{5} = \ldots = 1$). The poem "Little Bits" reiterates this idea. A pie is eventually consumed in a series of little bites. If we assume that the bites are the same size, then the total number of equal-sized bites is equivalent to a whole pie.

Equivalence is an important concept for learners because it helps them to be more flexible problem solvers. For instance, renaming is an essential skill in adding or subtracting unlike fractions: $\frac{1}{2} + \frac{1}{6}$ can be renamed as $\frac{3}{6} + \frac{1}{6}$. When learners understand that a given fraction has an infinite number of names, they can then devise appropriate names to fit various problem situations.

Fractions and decimals

Decimals, also known as decimal fractions, are simply another way to represent fractional numbers. A decimal fraction is a special kind of common fraction that has a power of ten as its denominator. Children need opportunities to discuss situations that involve decimal fractions, such as gas pumps, car odometers, or the number of pennies in a dollar, and they need to use common fractions and decimal fractions simultaneously so they can see the relationship between the two. Norton Juster highlights this relationship in his classic novel *The Phantom Tollbooth* (1961). Milo is wandering around the land of Digitopolis when he meets half a child. (The illustration in the book shows a child who is neatly divided in half from top to bottom.) Milo apologizes for staring, but he has never seen half a child before. The child responds (replying through the left and only side of his mouth) by telling Milo that he is actually .58, to be exact. When Milo does not hear him correctly, he repeats his size, claiming he really is a bit more than one half. Milo goes on to learn that this child is .58 because the average family has 2.58 children and someone has to be the .58! However, being .58 has its advantages because the average family has 1.3 automobiles and .58 is the only person capable of driving three tenths of a car.

Books in the classroom K–2

First-grade teacher Cassandra Gary read *The Doorbell Rang* (Hutchins, 1986) to her class and invited them to act out the events of the story. Two children volunteered to come to the front of the room and divide a set of twelve cookies. They placed their cookies in clear plastic bags for their classmates to see. As the story progressed, more children joined the drama. At one point, there were four children who had just shared their cookies and then two more children arrived. Cassandra asked the class, "What can we do now?"

Tejal responded, pointing to the four kids who already had cookies, "You need to take one away from each of them, and that will give you four; so then you can give two to each of the kids who came in." Thus Tejal did not add together the total number of children and then divide but figured out a way to redistribute the cookies from the existing set of four to accommodate the additional two children.

As the children finished acting out the story, Cassandra told them, "Think of a food or something else that you would like to share and write about it. Try to make your story into a math word problem." Cole wrote a story about people sharing bananas: "There were 6 bananas. 2 people came along. 4 more came along" (Figure 7–1). He drew the two people first and showed each one clasping three bananas. He then drew four other people and cleverly used arrows to show how the bananas were equally distributed. Cassandra marveled at his inventiveness and in a written conversation challenged him to alter his problem slightly: "What would happen if 6 more people came along?" Cole responded by writing "12 people." Cassandra wanted him to consider the implications of this decision to include six other children and asked, "Would there be enough bananas for everyone?" Again Cole answered the question directly by writing "No." Cassandra realized that she needed to make her question more open-ended, so she continued by asking, "How could the bananas be shared among 12 people?"

Adrienne, who was sitting next to Cole, had overheard them discussing this last question and suggested, "You could cut them in half." Cole thought about it for a minute in silence. He then drew lines across the bananas at the top of his paper and counted the halves. Once he had verified this solution and saw that it made sense, he wrote a response to Cassandra's question by saying, "Cut them in half," thus extending his notion of fractions to incorporate not only parts of a set but parts of a whole within that set.

Ahmed wrote quite a different story: "There were 100 cupcakes. Josh and Cindy were eating them but before they did James came. They shared 20 each. There was 40 left" (Figure 7–2). At first Ahmed had written his last sentence as "There were 10 left." When Cassandra asked him to explain how he got ten, he reasoned, "Well, I had a hundred. After the first one there was eighty, and after the second one there was sixty, and after the next one there was forty. Oh, it must be forty." Counting backward helped Ahmed revise his initial

FIGURE 7-1

There wor 6 Bnans.
2 PePl kam a log.
+ Mr kam a log.

2
+4
___
6

What would happen if 6 more people came along? If people would there be enough ~~bananas~~ bananas & for everyone? No How could the bananas be shared between in Haf 12 people? kut Them in Haf

FIGURE 7-2

there wer 100 cupcakes. Josh and Cindy when eating them but befar they did James came they shared 20 eoch, their was 40 'left' They must have been hungry! What happened to the other cupcakes? ther going to eat them but not yet.

calculation. He was asked to extend his problem further: "What if these three kids got hungry again? How would they share those forty cupcakes that are left over?" He thought for a few seconds and then wrote on another piece of paper, "10 each and 10 left."

"Then what would happen if they got hungry and wanted to eat the ten?"

"That's a hard question," he admitted. He drew a picture of ten cupcakes and then explained, "They could have two each and then four left."

"And then what would happen if they got hungry again?"

"That's another hard question," he replied. He thought again for a moment and then said, "Then they'd get one each." Predicting what the next question was going to be, he tried to explain how the last cupcake was to be shared. "Then they could break the last one in half, and then break it again so they each get a part." Although he used the word "half" to describe these partitions, when he drew his subdivision lines on another piece of paper he showed a cupcake divided into three equal pieces. Ahmed's story helped him see the process of division as repeated subtraction:

$$
\begin{array}{r}
\frac{1}{3} \\
3 \\
10 \\
\underline{20} \\
3 \;\overline{\big)\; 100} \\
\underline{60} \quad (20 \times 3) \\
40 \\
\underline{30} \quad (10 \times 3) \\
10 \\
\underline{9} \quad\;\; (3 \times 3) \\
1 \\
\underline{1} \quad\;\; (\tfrac{1}{3} \times 3) \\
0
\end{array}
$$

Books in the classroom 3–4

Fourth-grade teacher Cherie Larson used *The Doorbell Rang* (Hutchins, 1986) with her students to explore the concept of equivalence through partitioning. After reading the story once, Cherie read it again and stopped at the point when Joy and Simon arrived.

"Let's imagine that this time Joy and Simon arrived *without* their four cousins. How many children and cookies would there be in the story right now?" Cherie asked.

"Just eight kids and twelve cookies," one student answered.

"That's right," said Cherie. "Now, what would happen if Grandma didn't arrive with those extra cookies? How could eight kids share twelve cookies?"

The children worked in groups of four using paper cookies to try to solve the problem. As they shared their solutions later on, three main strategies emerged:

1. Some children distributed one whole cookie to each of the eight kids and then divided the remaining four cookies in half and distributed those half pieces. They described their result as "one whole cookie and a half of a cookie." Cherie wrote "1½ cookies" on the board.

2. Other children divided all the cookies in half and distributed them in that way. They found that each child would receive three half-pieces. Cherie wrote "³⁄₂ cookies" on the board.

3. Another group of children gave one whole cookie to each of the eight kids and then cut the remaining four cookies into quarters. In this way each of the eight kids received one whole cookie and two quarter pieces. Cherie wrote "1²⁄₄ cookies" on the board.

As the children shared their unique solutions, Cherie was able to point out the relationship between mixed numbers and improper fractions.

The next day Cherie reformulated the problem again. "Suppose Mom looks out the window and sees six kids knocking on the door and she has only four cookies to offer them. How could she solve that problem?" Cherie was interested in how the children might approach a problem that involved more children than cookies. Again the children worked in groups of four, but before they began their work in small groups, they brainstormed some possible strategies.

"Hey, let's cut the cookies into sixths," suggested one.

"Or maybe cut them into thirds," said another.

Each group followed one or the other of these suggestions. Cherie said she would cut some of the cookies into halves and then fourths to see what would happen if that route were followed. In this way she contributed to the investigation as a fellow learner and problem poser.

The group that divided the cookies into thirds made this discovery:

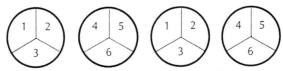

So, each person gets two thirds:

The group that divided cookies into sixths shared these results:

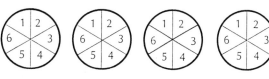

So, each person gets four sixths, or one piece from each cookie.

Cherie displayed her own results using halves and fourths. If she divided the first three cookies in half, each person could get a ½ piece and a ⅙ piece.

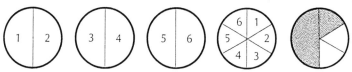

Alternatively, each person could get two quarter pieces and a ⅙ piece.

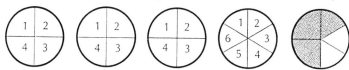

As the children looked at the size of the piece that each group offered as its solution, one child remarked, "Hey, look, they're all the same!" Many of the children seemed surprised at this observation. They thought that cutting cookies into all these different-sized pieces should have yielded different results, but their visual representations clearly showed that all four areas were congruent. Cherie asked the children why all the answers were the same, and their explanations underscored the concept of equivalency of fractions. The children became intrigued by this concept and suggested other possible scenarios with different numbers of children and cookies.

Books in the classroom 5–6

Earlier in the week, fifth-grade teacher Robin Cox had read her children *Gator Pie* (Matthews, 1979). A few days later she wanted to discuss the story in more detail and asked her children what they remembered about the story.

"It was about some alligators who cut a pie," said Courtney.

"It was a hundred slices, a hundred slices!" commented Chantell.

"And they were fighting about even pieces," remarked Damian. Robin extended this observation by asking, "How do you suppose they could get one hundred slices even?"

"Well, you can cut it in half, then half again, and then half again," suggested one student.

"How would you describe what you're doing?" asked Robin.

"You're dividing it by two each time," responded the child. His comment described the numerical pattern $\frac{1}{2}$, $\frac{1}{4}$, $\frac{1}{8}$, $\frac{1}{16}$, and so on that is found in this particular partitioning strategy.

"Yes, and finally those alligators had a pie divided into one hundred slices," continued Robin. (She chose not to point out that repeated halvings cannot produce exactly one hundred pieces.) "So how would you describe one of those slices?" Ricky hesitated as he began to share his observation: "One . . . one . . . one . . . one one-hundredth?" Robin realized that Ricky knew from the story that $\frac{1}{100}$ made sense, but he hesitated, partly because he was used to discussing more commonplace fractions such as $\frac{1}{2}$ or $\frac{1}{4}$. The story helped confirm for him that fractions can be of any size as long as the whole is partitioned equally.

"What did those two alligators do with the pie at the end of the story?" asked Robin.

"They divided it up," the children chimed in together.

"So how much did they each get?" continued Robin.

"They each got half of it," said Chantell.

"So how many pieces did they each get?"

"Fifty," said Chantell again. Robin noticed that Carleton seemed a bit puzzled by that response and so she asked him, "Carleton, why do you think each alligator might have received fifty slices?"

"Cause fifty is half of one hundred?" he suggested.

"Good," said Robin. At this point the class spent some time talking about how the concept of equivalence applies to fractional parts, such as $\frac{1}{2} = \frac{50}{100}$. As their discussion concluded, Robin wanted to show how impressed she was with the children's responses to the story: "You all have learned so much about fractions today."

"This seems like play," said Pamela.

"Yeah," continued Carleton, "we get to learn all kinds of ways in this class." Robin commented, "It's interesting that you said that, Carleton. You know, the author of *Gator Pie* isn't the only author out there. All of you have your own information to share about these mathematical ideas."

"We can make our *own* stories," suggested Carleton. "And could we read them to each other in class?"

"Of course you can," said Robin.

"That's good," said Liz. "That way we get to learn from each other rather than a worksheet."

The children spent several days writing and revising their stories. When they eventually shared them with each other, Robin noticed that many of the stories provided new contexts for exploring the concept of equivalence through partitioning. Marvin's story "The Candy Bar" (Figure 7–3) was one such example because it invited the reader to think about partitioning a candy bar in different ways. (Note his original "going to halfin it up" terminology.)

Robin changed some of the variables in Marvin's story and posed some additional questions. "What would happen if you had already divided the candy bar in half and this third person came to join you. How could you divide the candy bar equally among these three people?"

Marvin did not feel that a solution was possible. "If you halfed it," he said, "you couldn't split it up into thirds. My piece would have to be bigger." He was insistent that his half would remain as a half, but that the other half piece should be divided between the two other people. He knew it was not equal partitioning, but at least it was an attempt at giving some candy to everyone.

Amber had a different strategy. "At first I would take my candy bar and cut it in half like this," she said, showing how she would cut her bar lengthwise.

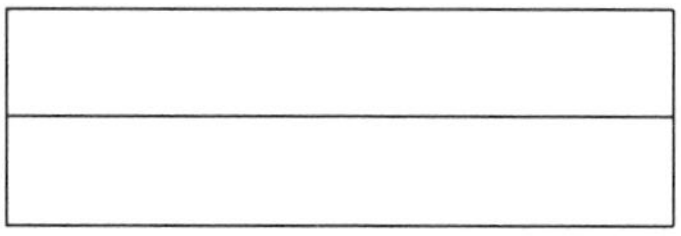

"Then I would just cut it the other way into three parts,

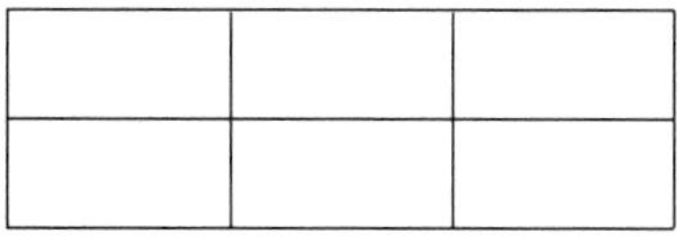

so everyone would get two pieces each." Her strategy demonstrated the multiplication of fractions through an area model. She showed that a rectangular region that is partitioned into horizontal sections of $\frac{1}{2}$ and vertical sections of $\frac{1}{3}$ created equal-sized pieces that are $\frac{1}{6}$ of the whole:

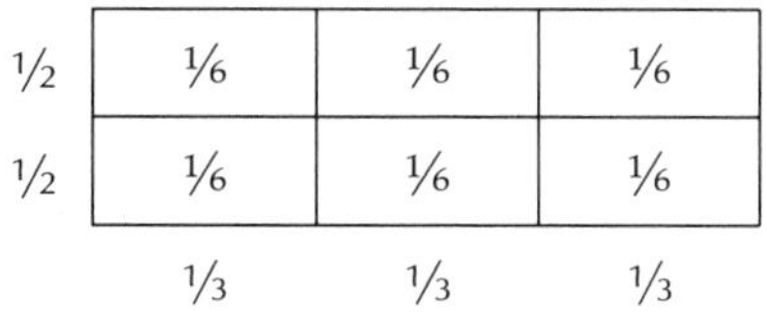
½
½
⅙ ⅙ ⅙
⅙ ⅙ ⅙
⅓ ⅓ ⅓

$\frac{1}{2} \times \frac{1}{3} = \frac{1}{6}$

Stephanie devised another unique strategy. "If you had already broken the candy bar in half, you just put it back together and cut it again":

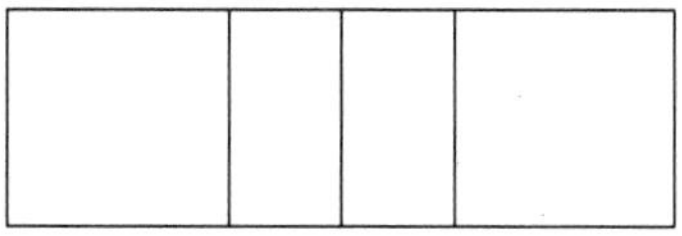

The Candy Bar

BABY RUTH

One day me and my friend Chris went to the store. I brought a candy bar and was going to halfin it up with Chris. When we was going home, Hakeem came out of know where. "Can I have some." Sure, good thing I haven't halfin it up yet. Now each off us get $\frac{1}{3}$ of a candy bar.

When I was about to halfin it up here comes my older brother "If you don't give me piece, I'm gonna beat you up" he said "O.k. I'll give you piece" I said, Now each of us get $\frac{1}{4}$ of a candy bar

"Can I have some" said a voice. It was Dewayne "Ya, I guess so" I said. "I better get mine first" my brother said. "No you ain't, I am" said Hakeem. "Both of ya'll wrong, I'm getting mine first" said Chris. Then they all started fighting and I ate the candy bar by myself.

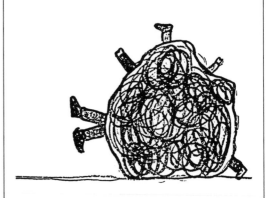

FIGURE 7–3

In this way, she reasoned, each person would receive one-third of the candy bar, but one person would get a third that was divided into two equal pieces. Stephanie's solution indirectly focused on equivalent fractions; she partitioned off $1/3$ of each of the one-half pieces, to create two new pieces that were each $1/6$ of the whole candy bar (multiplying $1/3 \times 1/2$ to create $1/6$). The pieces that each of the three children got can be seen as $1/3$ or $2/6$.

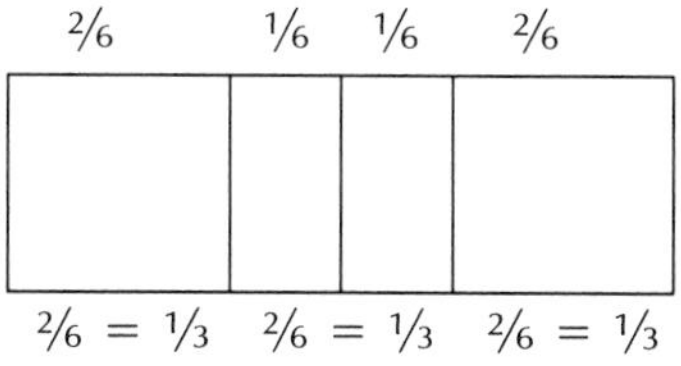
2/6
1/6
1/6
2/6
2/6 = 1/3
2/6 = 1/3
2/6 = 1/3

Further explorations

1. Have your students used fractions to describe events in their own lives? Some situations might include time, such as half past two; cooking, such as one third of a cup of flour; or sales, such as one third off the regular price. They might like to create "day in the life" fraction stories.
2. The use of fractions in everyday life can be highlighted by asking when and why it is important to make pieces the same size. Is it ever appropriate to divide a set or an object into *un*equal pieces? Have your students ever heard the familiar complaint, "Hey, your half is bigger than my half!"? What do they think this means? Invite students to share their personal experiences, which can then be related to situations in the books they have read.
3. Have your children used parts of things to create artistic representations? Based on *Ed Emberley's Picture Pie* (Emberley, 1984) and *Pezzettino* (Lionni, 1975), invite them to create their own designs using fractional parts of basic geometric shapes.
4. When your students eat a whole candy bar, a whole apple or a whole sandwich, how many equal-sized bites does it take to consume the "whole"? You might read aloud John Ciardi's poem "Little Bits" and discuss the concept that a whole can be described by an infinite number of equivalent names, such as $2/2$ (a few bites) or $50/50$ (many bites).
5. When we eat more than one whole apple, sandwich, or candy bar yet less than enough to make up another whole one, how do we describe the amount eaten? You might read Shel Silverstein's *A Giraffe and a Half* (1964) and ask students to compare their own stories of mixed fractions with this one.
6. *Fractions are Parts of Things* (Dennis, 1971) includes pictures of fractions in the real world—half a glass of water, a windowshade pulled a third of the

way down, and a set of children, half of whom have black hair. Students could do a fraction hunt in their environment in and out of school, perhaps creating a class book out of what they find.

Children's books

Ciardi, John. 1962. Little bits. In *You read to me, I'll read to you*. New York: Lippincott.

Dennis, J. Richard. 1971. *Fractions are parts of things*. New York: Crowell.

Emberley, Ed. 1984. *Ed Emberley's picture pie: A circle drawing book*. Boston: Little, Brown.

Hutchins, Pat. 1986. *The doorbell rang*. New York: Greenwillow.

Juster, Norton. 1961. *The phantom tollbooth*. New York: Random House.

Lionni, Leo. 1975. *Pezzettino*. New York: Pantheon.

Mathews, Louise. 1979. *Gator pie*. New York: Dodd, Mead.

Pomerantz, Charlotte. 1984. *The half-birthday party*. New York: Clarion.

Silverstein, Shel. 1964. *A giraffe and a half*. New York: Harper and Row.

Watson, Clyde. 1972. *Tom Fox and the apple pie*. New York: Crowell.

Estimation is one of the most important strategies in mathematics. With the increasing use of calculators and computers, the National Council of Teachers of Mathematics (1989) recommends that students spend less time on computational practice, particularly on long multiplication and division problems, and more time on using estimation to see if their answers make sense. It is important that children be aware of their own personal uses of estimation and view it as a strand that runs throughout mathematics. Indeed, NCTM recommends that the practice of estimation be included in all of young learners' mathematical experiences.

There are several reasons for placing a greater emphasis on this important strategy (Reys, Suydam, and Lindquist, 1984). Studies show that 80 percent of the real-world applications of mathematics involve estimation or mental computation. In our everyday lives, we ask ourselves questions like: Do I have enough gas in the car to get home? What time do I need to leave to get to the 7:00 meeting? How many calories are in this meal? Can we afford a vacation this year? Estimation is also an important sense-making strategy. With the increasing use of calculators and computers, learners must be able to look at the solution being displayed and ask themselves, Is this a reasonable answer? Estimation is also an important consumer tool. Comparison shopping involves a lot of estimating to determine the best buy, and consumers are best served if they know a variety of estimation strategies. Estimation also helps people make choices about the level of accuracy required to solve a real-life mathematical problem. Should I estimate or use mental computation? Should I use a calculator, a computer, or paper and pencil? It is disconcerting to see students solve problems such as $275 + 125$ by using a calculator, or a store clerk use pencil and paper to determine the tax on a purchase costing exactly $10, when mental computation is obviously the most efficient choice. Ignoring estimation gives learners a distorted view of mathematics. A preoccupation with the exact right answer often compels learners to perform unnecessary calculations and prevents them from gaining experience in devising appropriate estimates to fit a variety of circumstances.

Why do people estimate?

Developing good estimation strategies should be an integral part of the classroom curriculum. Through a variety of

8

estimation

situations and problem-solving experiences, children become flexible thinkers. Children's literature can demonstrate why people use estimation in the first place.

First, people may estimate because they find themselves in a situation where an exact answer is simply unobtainable and they have no other choice (Usiskin, 1986). *Estimation* (Linn, 1970) gives several examples. For instance, builders must estimate the amount of money needed to build a house; since their projected cost is based on the estimates of other workers, including electricians, plumbers, and landscapers, a builder's total cost as well as the anticipated profit can only be approximated before the job is actually done. Another example, easily understood by children, is that of cafeteria personnel who must estimate the amount of food to prepare at school. Although a lunch count is taken, children sometimes come to school late or go home sick, and it is impossible to serve exact portions. Estimating what might be needed is the only choice.

In a series of questions that can only be answered conditionally, Shel Silverstein's poem "How Many, How Much" (1981) takes a metaphorical look at estimating. The number of slices in a loaf of bread depends on how thin you slice it and the number of slams in an old screen door depends on how loud you shut it. The value varies, depending on who is doing the slicing or the slamming.

Cooking is another context that requires estimates, because the definition of a serving varies. How much spaghetti should be cooked for a family of four? It depends. How much do they like spaghetti? How hungry are they? Did they eat a big lunch? Are the children preschoolers or teenagers? Two books that address the problem of feeding a large number of people are *Moira's Birthday* (Munsch, 1987) and "The Doughnuts" in *Homer Price* (McCloskey, 1943). In the first story, Moira invites her whole school to her sixth birthday party and looks for a way to feed them all. In "The Doughnuts," Homer must estimate how much batter he will need to cook enough doughnuts to sell to customers after the evening movie. Both stories could lead to cooking experiences in school involving estimating quantities and amounts.

A second reason people estimate is that estimates increase ease of understanding (Usiskin, 1986). An excellent teacher resource book that touches on this aspect of estimation is *In One Day* (Parker, 1984), a compendium of 365 bits of statistical information that describe what Americans do in one day: what they eat, what they buy, what they build, and what they make a mess of. For instance, Americans buy 2,900 tons of chocolate each day, jog 28 million miles, and use 550,000 pounds of toothpaste. They spend $2.5 million washing their cars every day and buy 4 million eraser-tipped wooden pencils. In these examples, the estimate is easier to grasp, and therefore clearer, than the more precise actual figure. Estimates used to increase clarity are almost always calculated by rounding, which underscores an interesting irony in mathematics: clarity and precision are often in conflict with one another. If someone is involved in an environmental debate over the number of trees needed annually for the production of pencils, using an estimate of four million pencils rather than the exact figure 3,958,241 makes it easier for the audience to understand the argument and remember the statistical reasoning. Sacrificing precision for clarity is a beneficial strategy. *In One Day* is an excellent place to start a discussion about this kind of estimation strategy with students. (Be aware, though, that because the book is aimed at an adult audience, it includes a few statistics inappropriate for elementary school children, such as the amount spent on pornography and prostitutes each day.)

A third reason for estimating is that estimates are easier to use (Usiskin, 1986). Estimating for a purpose focuses on operating with numbers rather than merely understanding them, since learners actually use their estimates to solve a problem or make a decision more efficiently. Many good examples of this active use of estimation can be found in Tom Parker's two *Rules of Thumb* resource books (1983; 1987). Parker describes "rules of thumb" as homemade recipes that fall somewhere between a mathematical formula and a shot in the dark. These personal estimates have been honed, revised, and refined through hours of personal experience in diverse contexts and enable people to make things work out most of the time. Here are some examples the author solicited from people in all walks of life: one acre will park a hundred cars; you need a half-ton of hay per cow per month, or six tons per cow per year; it takes about four pounds of fresh herbs to make one pound of dry herbs; it takes about forty gallons of maple sap to make one gallon of maple syrup; no sizable apiary (bee farm) should be placed within two miles of another.

Estimation strategies

Several children's books address estimation strategies. In *The Jelly Bean Contest* (Darling, 1972), a candy store is promoting the familiar challenge of guessing the number of jelly beans in a jar. The children who enter the contest devise some good strategies. One child uses the strategy of averaging by counting the number of beans of one color (black) and then multiplying that number by the total number of colors (assuming equal distribution). Another child uses the strategy of *comparison* by filling a similar size jar with rocks the size of jelly beans. A third child uses the strategy of sampling by trying to count the number of beans that were needed to fill a jar one inch high and then multiplying that figure by the ten inches of the contest jar's height.

People become good estimators when they have certain benchmarks or reference points upon which to base their estimates. If they know that the height of a door frame is about six-and-a-half feet, for example, they can better estimate the height of individuals who walk through the door. In our Chapter 11 on measurement, the books listed under the subheading "Comparisons" focus on comparisons of people, animals, and buildings in terms of their size and weight. An excellent book that uses this comparison strategy is *The Dinosaur Who Lived in My Backyard* (Hennessey, 1988). Children understand some aspects of dinosaur life better through estimates that compare dinosaurs to objects they are familiar with. Here, for instance, one particular dinosaur hatches from an egg as big as a basketball. As it grows, one of its footprints becomes so large it won't fit into a child's sandbox. The dinosaur weighs as much as twenty pickup trucks. These estimates of comparison help readers to grasp the size of dinosaurs, and suggest strategies for communicating their own estimates of real-life sizes and quantities.

Books in the classroom K–2

First-grade teacher Margaret Tuten used the book *Many is How Many* (Podendorf, 1970) to explore this strategy of estimation. The book contrasts various comparison words, such as *a lot* and *a few, big* and *small,* and *long* and *short,* used to estimate the size of objects. Their meaning is not absolute but depends on each particular situation.

After reading the story aloud, Margaret asked the children to list what they considered to be a "few" versus "many" pieces of candy. Some of their responses included:

Few	Many
3	100
4	50
8	51
2	1,000
5	100

They reached general agreement that five pieces of candy would be considered "few." But when Margaret asked them if they would view five spoonfuls of yucky-tasting medicine as "few," the children clamored "No" in unison. They felt that five spoonfuls of medicine would be considered "many." Margaret's question helped the children see that estimating words like "few" and "many" are dependent on the context in which they appear. The same point was underscored when the children discussed temperature: 60° F seemed cool in the summer but warm in the winter.

Margaret also posed a question about the local shopping mall because she knew all the children had been there and had ridden the elevator. "If all the children in our class and the other first-grade class got on that elevator, would there be 'few' or 'many' people on the elevator?" The children felt the elevator would be quite crowded and agreed that there would be "many" riders. When Margaret asked if they would consider the theater at the mall crowded if it held that same group of children, however, her first graders just laughed and said there would be plenty of room in the theater, and that the children would be "few" in number.

"But how can you call this same group of kids 'many' on one occasion and 'few' a little later on?" Margaret asked. Some children were not sure, but others felt the amount of space made the difference in whether the group should be called "few" or "many." Margaret then asked the children if they could think of other examples in which the same number of people seemed like a small number in one place and a lot in another. They noted that their class seemed like a lot of people when they had to crowd into the bathroom area during tornado drills, but Monica recalled another time when their class seemed much smaller: "On the playground at second recess there's not anybody out there except our little ol' class."

The children were coming to see how mathematical language ("few" and "many") was used to estimate the size of a group and that this language could be used and interpreted in different ways depending upon the situation. One child realized that estimates provided a numerical range and wished that her mom would allow her to have a "few" cookies, rather than just two, so that she could eat perhaps three or four.

Books in the classroom 3–4

JoAnn Reynolds used *The Jelly Bean Contest* (Darling, 1972) with some of her third-grade students. Before reading the story she asked if anyone had ever entered a contest. Some children said they had entered contests by writing their name on a slip of paper and putting it in a box, while others had entered events that asked them to estimate the number of objects in a container. They noted that the first kind took only luck to win, but the second required some skill.

As JoAnn read the story aloud, the children were intrigued by the strategies the characters used to determine the number of jelly beans in the jar. Some students shook their heads in disapproval as one character tried to count a jelly bean more than once. Others mumbled, "Hey, that's not going to work, they're all different," when other children in the story tried to put rocks of different sizes in a similar jar. JoAnn brought her own jar of jelly beans to school and invited the children to estimate the total and then record the strategy they used to determine that total. Tim used an interesting strategy when he compared the size of JoAnn's jar with a penny jar he had at home (Figure 8–1).

Good estimators often used familiar benchmarks or reference points as a basis for estimating an unknown amount. Tim drew on his own personal experience with a penny jar to make a very good estimate.

Dione tried another strategy when he wrote the piece in Figure 8–2. Good estimators also set parameters on their estimates. By establishing a high and low range, as Dione was trying to do, learners can determine what answers seem most reasonable.

FIGURE 8-1

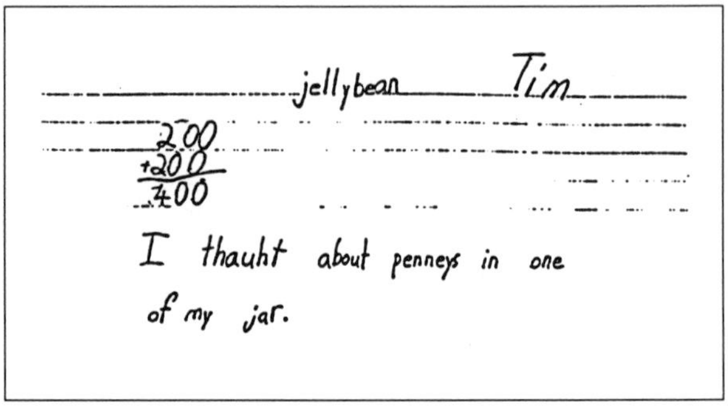

jellybean   Tim

$$\begin{array}{r} 200 \\ +200 \\ \hline 400 \end{array}$$

I thauht about penneys in one
of my jar.

FIGURE 8-2

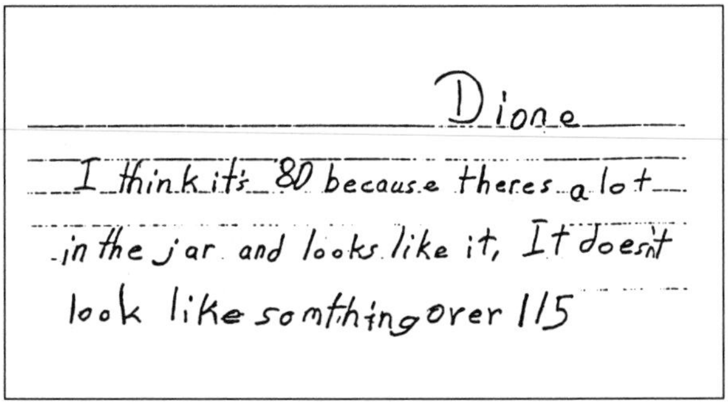

Dione

I think it's 80 because theres a lot
in the jar and looks like it, It doesnt
look like somthing orer 115

FIGURE 8-3

malted milk balls
24

I think it would be 24
because they are big.

FIGURE 8-4

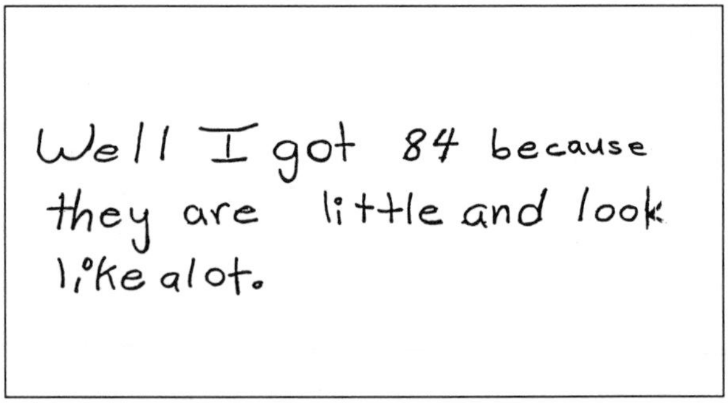

Well I got 84 because
they are little and look
like alot.

Later in the morning JoAnn filled the same jar with malted milk balls and invited the children to estimate the total again. Deidra noticed the size difference between a jelly bean and a malted milk ball and justified her estimate by writing the piece seen in Figure 8–3. When she made her estimate for the jelly beans she had also incorporated the attribute of size in her reasoning (Figure 8–4). Deidra's thinking reflects an important insight: there is an inverse relationship between the size, or volume, of an object and the total number of objects in the jar. Other children agreed as they discussed this strategy together: the larger the object, the fewer the number of pieces, and the smaller the object, the greater the number of pieces. Such a sense of quantitative relationships is at the heart of mathematical thinking. The inverse relationship Deidra discovered is similar to a concept discussed in Chapter 7. Children sometimes find it difficult to understand that ½ is larger than ⅕ because in using whole numbers 5 is always more than 2. But when a whole is partitioned into different arrangements of equal-sized pieces (*Gator Pie*, Mathews, 1979), learners come to see the inverse relationship between the number of pieces and the size of each piece.

Books in the classroom 5–6

Kathryn McColskey shared Shel Silverstein's poem "How Many, How Much" (1981) and Tom Parker's *Rules of Thumb* (1983) with her fifth- and sixth-grade students. She then invited the students to write their own variations on these texts. In response to the Silverstein poem the children created the following problems:

How much water in the bathtub?	Depends on who is in it.
How many freckles on a freckle face?	It depends on whose face it is.
How much hair spray do you use?	It depends on how many times your boyfriend comes over.
How long does it take to take a test?	It depends on how long you study.
How much time does it take to get dressed?	Depends on what you wear.
How long does it take your pimples to go away?	Depends on if you use OXY 5.

The answers to these questions will vary from person to person; they can only be estimates because they are influenced by so many different factors. Whether one is trying to determine the amount of water, the number of freckles, or the duration of dressing time, the answers will reflect the natural diversity of individual life-styles, habits, and interests. As the children's personal examples show, estimates are always context dependent.

The children also wrote their own rules of thumb based on Tom Parker's books. Kathryn asked them to record the rules of thumb they used in their own lives. Some of their responses, which they illustrated and bound into a class book, included these entries:

If you spend more than ten minutes on homework you have too much.
Never go outside in 100° F weather.
Always bring at least $600.00 on vacations.
If you have more than two pimples, use Stridex.
Never wear make-up until you are thirteen years old.
You should never have homework higher than one inch.

The last rule of thumb refers to the height of homework books when stacked up and measured. The child who suggested $600.00 for vacations actually went on a vacation with his family and helped them decide how to spend their fixed amount of money wisely. By sharing their rules of thumb, the children began to recognize the important role that estimation plays in their daily lives.

Further explorations

1. What language do your students use to describe their estimates? To introduce the language of estimation, you might read aloud some estimation stories and then invite children to find other examples in their reading. One class found a variety of examples in the newspaper (the words that indicate estimates are highlighted):

   At least 27 deaths were attributed to the fire.
   Nearly 50 percent of the building was damaged.
   Up to 19,000 cars were being shipped into the country.
   She received *more than* $550 in winnings.
   In the *late 1930s* he began his political career.

   Why were estimates rather than exact numbers used in these cases? What examples of the language of estimation can your children find?

2. What decisions at your school are based on estimates? Students might find out how your cafeteria personnel estimate the amount of food to prepare. What other decisions, such as making up class schedules, ordering supplies, or organizing bus transportation routes, involve estimates? They might interview a variety of school employees and record their discoveries. This could be extended to interviewees from other work sites.

3. When do your children's parents estimate? You might ask your students to interview their parents. How are their estimates related to their occupations? When do they estimate around the house?

4. How does the language of cooking reflect the language of estimation? You might read some cooking stories that involve estimation and the invite students to look through new and old cookbooks and interview parents and grandparents to find words that relate to estimating amounts. Here is a partial list: a smidgen, a tad, a pinch, a dash, a pat, a dab, a dollop, a scant cup, a heaping cup, a rounded cup, a level cup, a scoop. When do exact amounts matter (for example, in baking), and when can measurements be less precise? Old cookbooks often contain other kinds of estimation terms: a cool oven, a hot oven, a quick oven, 10¢ worth of citron, butter the size of an egg, and two good-sized handfuls of cracker crumbs.

5. What statistical information can children gather about their own school activities? After reading some of *In One Day* (Parker, 1984), they might brainstorm a list of questions about the daily occurrences at school: How much milk is drunk in one day at our school? How many people use the swings each day? How many kids go home sick? The children might compile their own book of estimates.

6. *Estimation* (Linn, 1970) talks about how to practice estimation. This could be the basis for a series of activities such as estimating distances in a schoolyard, grains of rice in a box, or the number of words on a page.

Children's books

Darling, Kathy. 1972. *The jelly bean contest.* Champaign, IL: Garrard.
Hennessy, B. G. 1988. *The dinosaur who lived in my backyard.* New York: Viking Kestrel.
Hoban, Tana. 1981. *More than one.* New York: Greenwillow.
Linn, Charles F. 1970. *Estimation.* New York: Crowell.
Mathews, Louise. 1979. *Gator pie.* New York: Dodd, Mead.
McCloskey, Robert. 1943. *Homer Price.* New York: Viking.
Munsch, Robert. 1987. *Moira's birthday.* Toronto: Annick.
Podendorf, Illa. 1970. *Many is how many?* Chicago: Children's Press.
Silverstein, Shel. 1974. Invention. In *Where the sidewalk ends.* New York: Harper and Row.
———. 1981. How many, how much. In *A light in the attic.* New York: Harper and Row.

Teacher resources

National Council of Teachers of Mathematics (NCTM). 1989. *Curriculum and evaluation standards for school mathematics.* Reston, VA: National Council of Teachers of Mathematics.

Parker, Tom. 1983. *Rules of thumb*. Boston: Houghton Mifflin.

———. 1984. *In one day*. Boston: Houghton Mifflin.

———. 1987. *Rules of thumb #2*. Boston: Houghton Mifflin.

Reys, Robert, Marilyn Suydam, and Mary Lindquist. 1984. *Helping children learn mathematics*. Englewood Cliffs, NJ: Prentice-Hall.

Usiskin, Zalman. 1986. Reasons for estimating. In Harold Schoen, ed., *Estimation and Mental Calculation* (1986 Yearbook). Reston, VA: National Council of Teachers of Mathematics.

Although elementary school children are often taught how to read large numbers, they are seldom encouraged to use them or work with them, nor are topics such as exponents and factorials, which often involve *very* big numbers, usually part of the elementary school mathematics curriculum. Yet children are fascinated by big numbers, and children's literature can be a provocative way for them to explore this area of mathematical knowledge.

Stories involving big numbers

For young children who are still trying their wings with counting, *One Watermelon Seed* (Lottridge, 1986) provides a gentle introduction to big numbers. Two children plant a small number of seeds (from one watermelon seed to ten corn seeds) and, as seeds will, they grow. The children are able to pick ten watermelons, twenty pumpkins, and so on, up to a hundred ears of corn—which on the last page turn into "hundreds and thousands of big white crunchy puffs because that corn was POPCORN!" A classic Dr. Seuss story, *The 500 Hats of Bartholomew Cubbins* (1938), tells the story of a boy who tries to take off his hat to show respect for the king but finds another one underneath it, and another and another. As the story progresses, Bartholomew keeps counting. Although the reader may start feeling that the number of hats is going to be infinite, the five-hundredth one is the last, to everyone's relief. Another story about a set of big numbers that threatens to become infinite is "The Doughnuts," from *Homer Price* (McCloskey, 1943). This update of "The Sorcerer's Apprentice" is about a machine that just wouldn't stop making doughnuts and how Homer Price finally got rid of them all. Students might enjoy estimating, then counting, the number of doughnuts in the two illustrations in which they are piled high on the diner counters. *Millions of Cats* (Gág, 1928), the classic introduction to really big numbers for young children, is a tale of "hundreds of cats, thousands of cats, millions and billions and trillions of cats" that a man brings home to his very surprised wife. This is also a good introduction to the poetry of the words used for big numbers. Children could write their own adaptations, and even parodies, using other big number words (for example, "googols of geese").

big numbers

Learning how big numbers work

There are many excellent books available to help children understand what numbers like a million, a billion, and a trillion *really* mean (beyond their literary use in a book like *Millions of Cats*). In a world where population, federal budgets, and similar statistics are rapidly climbing beyond intuitively understandable figures, students will be better informed as future citizens if they have a good grounding in how to interpret them. Teachers might want to look at *Innumeracy* (Paulos, 1988), an entertaining way to build their own background knowledge. *How Much Is a Million* (Schwartz, 1985), discussed in Chapter 1, is probably the best known of the children's books on this topic (along with its companion book, *If You Made a Million*, [Schwartz, 1989], which is discussed in Chapter 11). *How Much Is a Million?* is probably the best single introduction to big numbers and to developing an intuitive sense of their magnitude. Even most adults don't really understand how big the leap from a million to a billion to a trillion is; this book makes the orders of magnitude involved clear and unmistakable (to count to a million would take twenty-three days; to count to a trillion would take 200,000 years). The book relates big numbers to measurement by using units of length (kids standing on each other's shoulders), volume (goldfish bowls), area (tiny stars laid out in arrays), and time (counting to a million and more). The afterword provides enough information for weeks of activities to translate big numbers into units of time, height, area, and volume.

Big numbers are often produced through multiplying numbers by themselves (powers) or by other numbers (factorials). Two books in particular deal with powers of two and how rapidly—and how large—numbers grow through doubling. *A Grain of Rice* (Pittman, 1986), set in fifteenth-century China, tells the story of a peasant and a princess who are in love with each other but not allowed to marry. When Pong Lo, the peasant, cures the dying princess and is offered any reward he wants, he asks for a grain of rice, to be doubled in amount every day for a hundred days. As the days go by, the emperor realizes that he will soon be bankrupt, leading to the predictable happy ending for Pong Lo and the princess. Students might enjoy comparing this book with *The King's Chessboard* (Birch, 1988), another version of the same story (discussed earlier in Chapter 6). Powers of ten are even bigger numbers. Burns, in the "How Big Is Big?" section of *Math for Smarty Pants* (1982, pp. 119–123), supplies a brief but fascinating discussion of powers of ten, including the names of numbers from 10^3 (a thousand) to 10^{100} (a googol) and what they're used for. This is a good introduction to scientific notation (the scientific notation for a number expresses it as a power of ten; for instance, the sun is 93,000,000, or 9.3×10^7, miles from the earth). Students could use reference books such as the *Guinness Book of World Records* to find interesting statistics to chart in scientific notation. *Cosmic View: The Universe in 40 Jumps* (Boeke, 1957) is worth trying to hunt down at a library. It makes a journey from the edges of the universe to the inside of an atom, jumping by a factor of ten each time. This journey was the inspiration for the film and adult book *Powers of Ten* (Morrison, Morrison, and Eames, 1982), discussed in one of the classroom scenarios in this chapter. Although *Cosmic View* is less elaborate and up-to-date than *Powers of Ten*, it was written for children and can therefore be read by them in its entirety. Children might enjoy making their own book about powers of ten (or powers of five or two) with their own illustrations of life in "40 jumps."

Anno's Mysterious Multiplying Jar (Anno, 1983), which illustrates factorial numbers, can be used, as we have seen, in different ways with students of different ages. First graders can enjoy the story in the first half of the book and write their own stories of magical jars and what can be found inside them, while sixth graders can examine the detailed description of factorials that makes up the second half of the book, and, with adult help, extend them into applications. For instance, the factorial 52! tells how many possible ways there are to arrange a deck of playing cards.

Using and enjoying big numbers

Once students understand big numbers, they can come to appreciate how they are used in the world around them. Part of the fun of big numbers is in enjoying them. The poem "Ten Billion, Ten Million, Ten Thousand, Ten" (Keils, 1973) is about what a great number this number is; four of the eight lines of the poem consist solely of the number itself or a variation, written in numeral form (10,010,010,010). *Reading the Numbers: A Survival Guide to the Measurements, Numbers, and Sizes Encountered in Everyday Life* (Blocksma, 1989) is an encyclopedia of how people use numbers in many branches of science, technology, and business. Big numbers are scattered throughout: for instance, the binary numbers used in computers, the Richter scale used for earthquakes, and the astronomical prefixes mega-, giga-, and tera- used to describe really great distances. Students will love browsing in this book, and it is also a valuable reference tool and source of inspiration for activities. *The Guinness Book of World Records* (McFarlan, 1991, with annual editions), with its exhaustive listings of the biggest, hottest, richest, and longest of everything imaginable, provides many opportunities for students to discover big numbers and work with them in various ways. They might want to develop a chart showing what orders of magnitude occur with various superlatives. The longest word in English uses fewer than a hundred letters, the longest river is measured in thousands of miles, but the farthest star is tens of thousands of light-years away. *In One Day* (Parker, 1984), also discussed in Chapter 8, focuses on statistics, many of them involving big numbers, about what Americans do every day. We gain more than 5,000 people a day (births and immigration minus deaths and emigration) and spend $12,000 on dental floss. *Counting*

America: The Story of the United States Census (Ashabranner and Ashabran-ner, 1989) is a fascinating book that shows how we actually find out what some of those big numbers are. Students might use it to plan a local census project.

Big numbers, explored through literature, are wonderfully exciting for elementary school children. They can experience some of the exhilaration of mathematics by going beyond everyday numbers into the realm of the colossal. Experiential exposure to concepts like factorials and exponents, particularly if hands-on activities and active thinking are involved, can provide an early foundation for more sophisticated applications later on.

Books in the classroom K–2

First-grade teacher Pammy Wills read *What Is Beyond the Hill?* (Ekker, 1985) to her class. The story focuses on a series of questions that ask what is beyond the next hill, the next mountain, and the next star. As Pammy finished the story, the children talked about the continuity of the world and space. "Outer space never ends," remarked one child, and he then used the globe to help explain his reasoning.

As the classroom discussion progressed, the children and the teacher explored a variety of interesting interpretations of the concept of the infinite. In contrast to this distance model of space as never-ending, another child shared her understanding by noting that the oceans also represented the concept of infinity because "all the oceans join together." She used the globe to show her classmates that as one ocean flowed into the next, there was a continual flowing and mixing that had no beginning or ending point but seemed to go on forever.

Pammy shared another interpretation of the infinite by using the context of ordering and inclusion. She used the globe to explain to her students that their school is located in the Spring Valley area; Spring Valley is part of Columbia; Columbia is part of Richland County; Richland County is part of South Carolina; South Carolina is part of the United States; the United States is part of North America; North America is part of the earth; the earth is part of our solar system; and so on, and so on.

Janet Fickling, the student teacher who was working in Pammy's room, decided to bring this book home and share it with her two sons, ages four and six, because the word "infinity" was used often in their household. Her four-year-old son Eddie had apparently heard "infinity" used at his daycare center and had since used it during disagreements with his six-year-old brother Ryan. Sometimes when they argued over the amount of something, Ryan would say, "I'm going to have a million of those," but Eddie would top his boast with the reply, "Well, I want infinity of that!"

After Janet read *What Is Beyond the Hill?* to the boys, she asked them to explain what infinity meant to them. Eddie's reply was, "Like, you can keep counting apples and never stop. You just have to know the names of all the numbers. If you told me the names I could do it." Eddie might have used apples as an example since he had eaten some sliced apple at dinner that night. He used a set of discrete objects (apples) to represent his current understanding; he was also beginning to tie together concepts of place value and the infinite.

When Janet asked Ryan to explain his understanding of the infinite, he shared a different kind of relationship: "Time keeps going on. We have a clock. And sometimes the clock stops when the electricity goes off, but time just keeps going." Ryan was quite familiar with the electricity stopping; Hurricane Hugo had caused his family to lose their electricity for some time. More recently the electrical lines in front of his house were taken down for repairs and Ryan had witnessed the work from inside the house. He seemed to note from these experiences that the day passed by as it had always done, despite the fact that the clocks were not running. Thus Ryan realized that time itself is independent of our timepieces and tied the concepts of time and infinity together.

The concept of infinity can be an abstract idea for learners, but children's literature can make the concept less abstract by embedding it in a story and thereby giving learners the impetus to tell their own stories.

Books in the classroom 3–4

Annie and Heather were two third graders in a small group that had just read *The King's Chessboard* (Birch, 1988). The book tells the old folktale of a wise man who, in return for doing a favor for the king, asked for a grain of rice for the first square of a chessboard, two grains of rice for the second, four grains of rice for the third, and so on, doubling the number of grains of rice each time. Through pictures and text, the book amusingly illustrates how the amount of rice rapidly increased. On the eighth day, a servant carried 128 grains of rice in a small pouch. By the twenty-fifth day, four men each carried a heavy sack weighing over a hundred pounds. By the thirty-first day, sixteen wagons that could each hold a ton of rice were needed. Finally, the royal mathematicians discovered that there was not enough rice in the world to carry out the wise man's request and finish out the chessboard. Heather and Annie were intrigued by the large numbers involved. Annie decided to use a calculator to actually determine the number of grains of rice involved at each stage (Figure 9–1), and was able to get as far as the twenty-seventh number (67,108,864) before the calculator's display capacities were overloaded.

In the meantime, Heather divided a sheet of paper into sixty-four squares and began to write in the numbers as Annie calculated them (Figure 9–2). With adult help, Annie figured out a few more numbers, but the task was becoming frustrating. Sandra Wilde, who was working with the students, realized that they could move up to a more sophisticated calculating tool and invited them to her office, where they used a spreadsheet program to generate quickly the number of grains of rice corresponding to the sixty-fourth square (2^{63}). Heather decided to work backward on her chessboard for a while, adding the sixty-third and sixty-fourth numbers. (Her numbers are not precise because of the computer's rounding error.) Then the two girls decided that it would be interesting to find out how many grains of rice the one-hundredth, or two-hundredth, square of a giant chessboard would hold. Sandra typed in the formulas that would calculate the results, and the children vied for the honor of pressing the key that would cause a new series of numbers to appear as if by magic. They discovered that 2^{236} was the largest number that could be displayed as a whole number (rather than in scientific notation) in the largest column width that the computer could use. (Figure 9–3 shows a portion of the computer display.)

Students can also explore alternatives to the wise man's request. Would there have been more or fewer grains of rice if the chessboard's squares had contained 1!, 2!, 3!, 4! grains of rice and so on, rather than 2^0, 2^1, 2^2, 2^3?

FIGURE 9–1

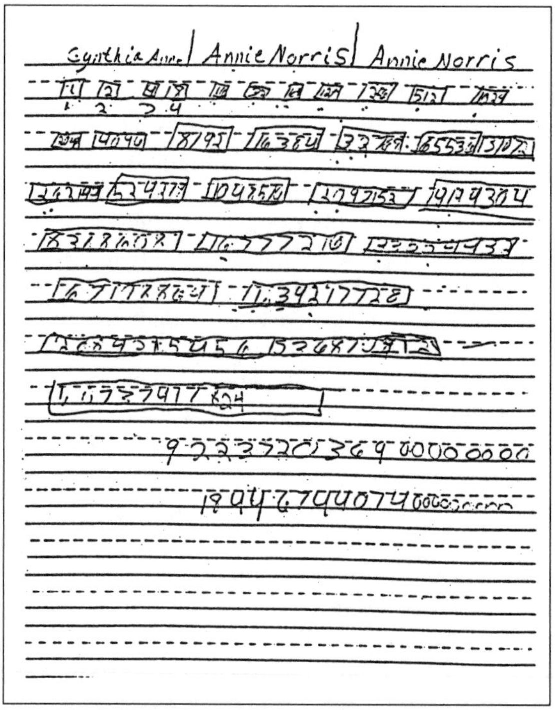

FIGURE 9–2

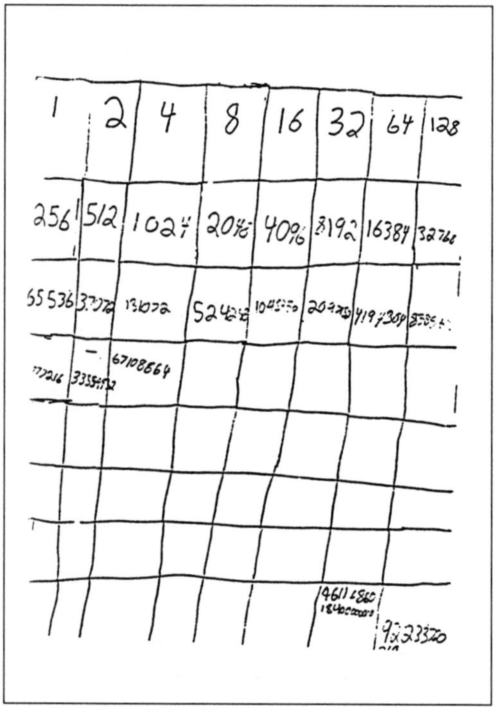

FIGURE 9–3

1	1
2	2
3	4
4	8
5	16
6	32
7	64
8	128
9	256
10	512
11	1024
..	....
58	144115188080000000
59	288230376150000000
60	576460752300000000
61	1152921504600000000
62	2305843009200000000
63	4611686018400000000
64	9223372036900000000
..	....
95	6044629098100000000000
96	12089258196000000000000
97	24178516392000000000000
98	48357032785000000000000
99	96714065570000000000000
100	193428131140000000000000

Books in the classroom 5–6

Anno's Mysterious Multiplying Jar (Anno, 1983) is a lesson in factorial numbers for children of all ages told in story form. The book begins, "This story is about one jar and what was inside it," and continues by showing that inside the jar there was one ocean, which held two islands, each of which had three mountains, and so on until the final revelation that each of nine boxes (in cupboards in rooms in houses in villages in kingdoms on those mountains) held ten jars just like the original. After sharing this book with a small group of fifth and sixth graders, Sandra Wilde helped them figure out, with the use of a calculator, that there were 3,268,800 jars in all. The next day the class had a hands-on lesson on factorial numbers, in which the students were asked to arrange five blocks in as many ways as possible. They explored the 5 factorial (5!) pattern (5 × 4 × 3 × 2 × 1) and related it back to Anno's book, discovering that the total number of jars amounted to 10!. On both days, they wrote something about what they'd done and what they'd learned, and their writing ranged from Samari's straightforward description of the book (Figure 9–4) to Jen's explication of how factorials work (Figure 9–5). This kind of exploration should be done in heterogeneous groups. Samari, for example, who was not a particularly strong mathematics student and was not able to express himself

FIGURE 9-4

Samari

We read a book call
ANNO'S MYSterionus
Multiplying Jar and it
Was good We figured
out how many Jars
there were and how
many country there were
and how many Kingdoms.
there were and how
many Villages there were.
there were lots of
country and lots of
rooms and lots of
cupboards.

FIGURE 9-5

March 1   Jen.

I learned how to play
a fun game. I will probally
play it a lot. I learned
that a factorial is an
easy way to say __x__x__ ext.
I learnd that there are many
ways to make a 5! pattern
120 to be exact. I figured that
out by doing this 5X4X3X2X1=120.
It was an eady way. I wonder
how many dots it would take
to make 120! I'm going to count
the dots on the ceiling
one of these days.

as articulately about factorials as some of the other students were, benefited from sharing in the activity and from exposure to the other children's ideas.

Books about large numbers for classroom use need not be limited to children's books. Adult books are helpful, but they need to be used somewhat differently. Although children won't usually read them all the way through, they can serve as inspiration for activites or for selective browsing. A group of fifth and sixth graders had an opportunity to explore both very large and very small numbers using an adult science book. Sandra Wilde began by showing the group a meter stick and did a quick introduction to powers of ten, including the information that an exponent of ten can be translated into zeroes following a one (for example, 10^5 = one followed by five zeroes, or 100,000) and that a negative exponent signifies the inverse of the original number (for example, 10^{-5} = 1/100,000). They then visually estimated what some powers of ten would look like if 10^0 = 1 meter and then chose other exponents to estimate and illustrate (Figures 9–6, 9–7, and 9–8).

At this point, Sandra introduced the book *Powers of Ten* (Morrison, Morrison, and Eames, 1982), which also uses 1 meter (10^0) as a base and provides a visual tour from 10^{25} meters (empty space on the edge of the universe) to

FIGURE 9–6

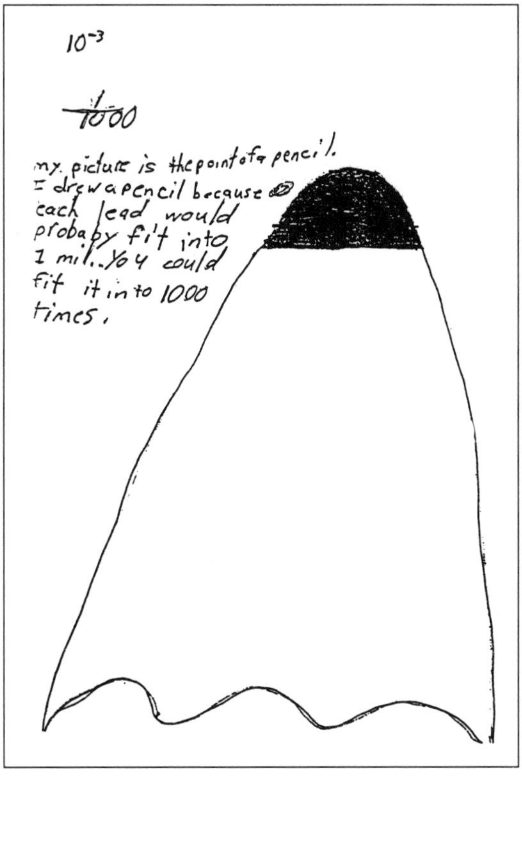

FIGURE 9–7

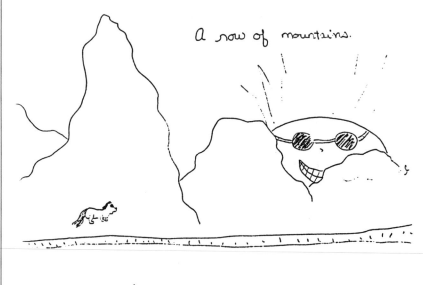

a row of mountains.

Mountains are pretty I chose this because it is long long. An ocean might be 10⁵ too, but I thought an mountain would be I think it would take about 2 I draw. mountains to make 10⁵. If I was 10⁵ power -I would be very tall!

100,000

FIGURE 9–8

10^{-80}

I chose negative 80 because I'm cross also because I didn't know what we were doing. 10^{-80} power would be a microscopic dot. like a microscopic animal. I imagine if a person whas that small. I wonder what they would eat and how.

10^{-16} meters (inside the proton), the upper and lower dimensional limits of what science has been able to study. The students loved browsing through the illustrations of relative size in our universe, and were amazed to see how quickly the sizes represented by powers of ten "jump." Of course, they were also fascinated to see how close their estimations came to the real thing. (Of the three student estimations shown here, only 10^{-80} [Figure 9–8] was significantly inaccurate.)

Further explorations

The book *50 Simple Things Kids Can Do to Save the Earth* (EarthWorks Group, 1990) offers many opportunities for exploring large numbers. The ideas suggested here might also be adapted for use with other books that provide information about big numbers in the real world, such as the *Guinness Book of World Records* (McFarlan, 1991) and *In One Day* (Parker, 1984).

1. Students can confirm or disconfirm the book's calculations. The younger students described in Chapter 1 did this with simple numbers, while older students can manipulate larger numbers (usually using a calculator). For instance, the book states that "a leak that fills up a coffee cup in ten minutes will waste over 3,000 gallons of water in a year" (p. 42). This can be used to create the following equation:

$$\frac{8 \text{ oz.}}{\text{cup}} \times \frac{6 \text{ cups}}{\text{hour}} \times \frac{24 \text{ hours}}{\text{day}} \times \frac{365 \text{ days}}{\text{year}} = \frac{420{,}480 \text{ oz.}}{\text{year}}$$

   Dividing by 128 ounces in a gallon indeed equals 3,285 gallons a year.

2. Similarly, you can also check the reasonableness of the book's figures. For instance, the statement that Americans use 2.5 million plastic bottles every hour (p. 29) can be multiplied by 24 hours per day and 365 days per year, then divided by the roughly 250 million people in the United States, for a total of about 90 bottles per person per year, or about two a week, which seems well within reason.

3. Based on the information in the book and figures they gather on their own, students can make comparisons of energy-saving strategies. For instance, they could compare the cost of standard and rechargeable batteries for operating a portable tape recorder over the course of a year.

Children's books

Anno, Mitsumasa. 1983. *Anno's mysterious multiplying jar*. New York: Philomel.

Ashabranner, Melissa, and Brent Ashabranner. 1989. *Counting America: The study of the United States census*. New York: Putnam.

Birch, David. 1988. *The king's chessboard*. New York: Dial.

Boeke, Kees. 1957. *Cosmic view: The universe in 40 jumps*. New York: John Dax.

Burns, Marilyn. 1982. *Math for Smarty Pants*. Boston: Little, Brown.

Chalmers, Mary. 1986. *Six dogs, twenty-three cats, forty-five mice, and one hundred sixteen spiders*. New York: Harper and Row.

EarthWorks Group. 1990. *50 simple things kids can do to save the earth*. Kansas City: Andrews and McMeel.

Ekker, Ernest. 1985. *What is beyond the hill?* New York: Lippincott.

Gág, Wanda. 1928. *Millions of cats*. New York: Coward, McCann, and Geoghegan.

Keils, Phil. 1973. Ten billion, ten million, ten thousand and ten. In Bill Martin, ed., *Sounds of freedomring*, pp. 278–279. New York: Holt, Rinehart and Winston.

Lottridge, Celia B. 1986. *One watermelon seed*. Toronto: Oxford.

McCloskey, Robert. 1943. *Homer Price*. New York: Viking.

Petie, Haris. 1975. *Billions of bugs*. Englewood Cliffs, NJ: Prentice-Hall.

Pittman, Helena C. 1986. *A grain of rice*. New York: Hastings House.

Schwartz, David. 1985. *How much is a million?* New York: Lothrop, Lee and Shepard.

————. 1989. *If you made a million*. New York: Lothrop, Lee and Shepard.

Seuss, Dr. 1938. *The 500 hats of Bartholomew Cubbins*. New York: Vanguard.

Siegel, Alice, and Margo McLoone-Basta. 1985. *The kids' world almanac*. New York: Pharos Books.

Teacher resources

Blocksma, Mary. 1989. *Reading the numbers: A survival guide to the measurements, numbers, and sizes encountered in everyday life*. New York: Viking Penguin.

Hertzberg, Hendrik. 1970. *One million*. New York: Simon and Schuster.

Heymann, Tom. 1989. *On an average day*. New York: Fawcett Columbine.

McFarlan, Donald, ed. 1991. *1990 Guinness book of world records*. New York: Bantam.

Morrison, Philip, Phylis Morrison, and the office of Charles and Roy Eames. 1982. *Powers of ten*. New York: Scientific American Library.

Parker, Tom. 1984. *In one day*. Boston: Houghton Mifflin.

Paulos, John. 1988. *Innumeracy*. New York: Hill and Wang.

Weiss, Daniel. 1988. *100% American*. New York: Poseidon.

Tana Hoban's photographic concept books illuminate the world in fresh, yet analytical ways. As these books remind us, we are surrounded by shapes, sizes, colors, and patterns, which we can abstract from our visual environment. Teachers can assist children in beginning to learn about geometry by encouraging them to explore their own perceptions of the world and give names to the shapes they see all around them. Children can also learn more about how geometry works as they cut, fold, combine, and manipulate shapes and as they consider the role these shapes play in practical applications such as architecture. An important aspect of teaching children about geometry is conveying an appreciation of the power of shapes to delight and awe us. Picture books like Hoban's introduce children to all of these forms of learning.

Early geometric explorations

An exploration of geometry might begin with an author/illustrator study of Tana Hoban. Even a handful of her books can serve as a children's-book collection on geometry for beginners. Teachers might want to start with *Shadows and Reflections* (1990), one of Hoban's newer books. Each of its striking color photographs illustrates the idea of a "double," the shadow or reflection of an object or objects. The pictures vary in many ways; some show only the shadow or reflection itself, while others also reveal its source. Some reflections are clear, while others are distorted (a musician reflected in his tuba). Some shadows fall on smooth water, others on ripply water. After spending time with the book, a class might like to go out for a shadow and reflection walk, perhaps after a rain when there are puddles all around. *Shapes and Things* (1970) offers a chance to examine pure shapes, with no other visual information. Its pictures were made without a camera through direct exposure of photographic paper with objects placed on it. These witty outline collages include silverware, buttons, and even a fish skeleton. *Take Another Look* (1981) and *Look! Look! Look!* (1988), the first in black and white and the second in color, use abstract shapes that are then recontextualized. In each book, cut-out squares on every other page allow a peek at just a small part of an object. The fun is in trying to guess what the larger picture will turn out to be and often being surprised. Mixing natural and human-made objects, Hoban highlights shapes like a tightly packed collection

10
geometry

of circles that turn out to be a sunflower's center and some odd cylindrical shapes that are the spokes of a Ferris wheel.

Two of Hoban's books help introduce the terminology of physical relationships, which will be useful to children in learning about geometry: *Over, Under, and Through and Other Spatial Concepts* (1973) illustrates such related concepts as *in, on, across, between, behind* (a bear behind bars in a zoo), and *against* (shovels leaning against a wall), and *Push-Pull, Empty-Full* (1972) deals with pairs of opposites like *front/back* (two sides of a clock) and *thick/thin* (elephants and flamingos).

Several of Hoban's other books can help children learn the conventional names of shapes. *Round and Round and Round* (1983a) is a circle book that shows hollow circles (wheels, holes in a drain, Swiss cheese), solid ones (peas, the ends of a stack of logs), and concentric ones (ripples on a pond). Children might also use this book to reflect on why so many things in the world are round and how they got that way. The pictures in *Circles, Triangles, and Squares* (1974), an earlier, (black-and-white) book, include different shapes the reader can look for, a format that Hoban developed even further in *Shapes, Shapes, Shapes* (1986). This book begins with the outlines of many shapes, not only the basic ones but also arches, trapezoids, and stars, which children can find in the photo illustrations. These are especially exciting because they include so many shapes combined in such creative ways: a lunchbox with a sandwich cut into two triangles, a rectangular thermos, a round orange, an oval hard-boiled egg, and cookies in the shape of a star and a heart. This is one of Hoban's best books. It inspired Tyler, a first grader, to create a "How many shapes can you find?" picture (Figure 10–1). *Dots, Spots, Speckles, and Stripes* (1987) is a playful book in which the title shapes appear as (or on) freckles, dalmatians, and confetti as well as zebras, giraffes, and Adidas sneakers. In *I Read Symbols* (1983b), Hoban expands into another whole set of shapes: those used as ideographic symbols. The photographs include wordless signs for restrooms, bus stops, playgrounds, and many others. (These are unlabeled in the body of the book, but there is a glossary at the end.) Children might find it interesting to take this book on a "sign walk" in the school neighborhood, perhaps with a camera along.

Other geometric explorations

A variety of picture books by other illustrators fall into the same general categories as Hoban's: open-ended exploration of shapes, relational terminology (like *over* and *under*), and conventional names of shapes. *It Looked Like Spilt Milk* (Shaw, 1947) uses white letters and outline shapes on a deep blue background to present a predictable text that follows the same pattern on every page ("Sometimes it looked like Spilt Milk. / But it wasn't Spilt Milk.") until on the final page we learn that what looked at times like a flower or an angel

FIGURE 10–1

"was just a Cloud in the Sky." Children can, of course, be taken outside to discover their own shapes in the clouds. The little girl in *Holes and Peeks* (Jonas, 1984) has divided many similar shapes into two mutually exclusive categories: scary holes like the one on the bottom of the bathtub or in the toilet, and fun peeks, like the one she can make from rolled-up paper. She feels better when she learns that holes can be fixed, plugged, or made smaller so they're not scary anymore. A good companion book is *Holes* (Rahn, 1984), which uses photographs to look at many kinds of holes in the everyday world and the purposes they serve: passageways, screens, water-holders (as in sponges), and holes that help us hold things (like the eye of a needle).

Bruce McMillan, like Tana Hoban, creates photo-illustrated concept books. One of his most charming is *Becca Backward, Becca Frontward* (1986), which uses a little girl to illustrate the terminology of spatial relationships: Becca is above her bed when she bounces on it and below it when she hides; a whole round cracker is big enough to cover her face but is reduced to half when she bites into it. Many books name basic geometric shapes and show them used in functional ways. *The Wing on a Flea* (Emberley, 1961) is a good introduction, because its single-color shapes stand out clearly on monochrome pages. Emberley's cartoonlike drawings are a good setting for his abstract representations of the shapes found in everyday objects, so that the beak of a bird and the tail of a fish become triangles and squares appear in confetti and in a hopscotch game. *Shapes* (Reiss, 1974) introduces each of several shapes abstractly, then as objects, then assembled into three-dimensional forms, so that circles appear as buttons and in a spinning wheel and then expand into spheres. Most of the book is about triangles, squares, and circles, but ovals, pentagons, hexagons, and octagons also make brief appearances. *Color Farm* (Ehlert, 1990), like *Color Zoo* (Ehlert, 1989), uses cleverly overlapping cut-out pages to create strongly geometrical pictures of animals. A picture of a sheep with a diamond cut-out for its nose is overlapped by a heart that, covering part of the earlier picture and adding a new outline, becomes a goose. A circle overlapping both turns the picture into a dog. The back of each cut-out page names the shape. *Changes, Changes* (Hutchins, 1971) is a wordless book that shows dolls using blocks to build a house, which then turns, according to the demands of the crisis-laden plot, into a fire truck, boat, truck, train, and a house again. The shapes, which include cubes, cylinders, arches, hemispheres, and others, can be discussed in their two-dimensional form as the squares, triangles, and so on seen on the page, and also related to the three-dimensional forms children use in their own block play. Tangrams are another good avenue for learning about basic shapes. These seven pieces (five triangles, a square, and a parallelogram) can be arranged to form a square and many other shapes. A book like *Sam Loyd's Book of Tangram Puzzles* (Van Note, 1968), formerly known as *The Eighth Book of Tan,* can provide students with hours of pleasure as they attempt to create the shapes.

Symmetry and related topics

Picture books are an ideal way to explore symmetry, reflection (as in a mirror), and other variations in shape. Beau Gardner's *The Turn About, Think About, Look About Book* (1980), *The Look Again . . . and Again, and Again, and Again Book* (1984), and *What Is It?* (1989) are fascinating books of strongly drawn two-color abstract shapes. Rotating each book allows different ways of seeing: The shape shown here, for instance, gray on a green background, is, as you turn the page clockwise, the number four, a road intersection, a chair, and a capital "J."

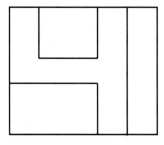

The labels are printed in pale gray type so that children can look at the pictures from a bit of a distance and invent their own descriptions without inadvertently reading the ones on the page. Marion Walter has created puzzle books using geometric figures and mirrors (included in a pocket in the book). *The Mirror Puzzle Book* (1985) presents a series of abstract geometric shapes. Using a master shape and a mirror, children can create other shapes in a related set. One of the book's challenges is that it is not possible to make all of the shapes with the mirror, and students might enjoy predicting which ones will work before they test their predictions. (Teachers might want to help them discover one necessary condition: the target pattern has to be symmetrical.) Students who enjoy these puzzles may want to create some of their own. Two other books by Walter, *Make a Bigger Puddle, Make a Smaller Worm* (1971a), and *Another, Another, Another, and More* (1975), use single and hinged mirrors to further explore symmetrical shapes. The hinged mirror puzzles are especially enjoyable because they produce aesthetically pleasing shapes with several axes of symmetry (similar to snowflakes or kaleidoscope figures). Ann Jonas has created two justifiably acclaimed books that present a picture story whose first half is read normally, and whose second half is read from back to front using the same pictures upside down. *Round Trip* (1983), the earlier (black-and-white) book, shows a journey from the country into the city and back again. The whitecaps seen on the water on the inbound trip become birds in the sky on the way home. The road into the city, shown in vanishing-point perspective, becomes searchlights spread across the sky as the traveler heads out of the city. Readers are fascinated when they get to what appears to be the end of the book and discover that they are to flip it over and continue. Even on a first reading they are likely to clamor to see what the picture on each page had been before it was turned upside down. *Reflections* (1987) is even more of a tour de force for being in full color. Its setting by the sea gives Jonas the opportunity to play around with horizon lines and reflections. Amazingly, the pictures in *Reflections* are less abstract than those in *Round Trip,* despite the additional constraint of color. Children will enjoy the transformation of sailboats and storm clouds into people flying kites when turned upside down and, even more miraculously, the way that birchbark turns into frogs floating in a pond. *What Is Symmetry?* (Sitomer and Sitomer, 1970) discusses symmetry in a more systematic way and would be a good complement to all the other, more exploratory books. It clearly develops the concepts of line, point, and plane symmetry, with varied examples of each.

Geometry through paper folding

Two books by Jo Phillips focus on helping children learn about geometry by folding paper. *Right Angles* (1972) shows the reader how to make a right angle by folding a piece of scrap paper twice, then using it to find angles in the environment that are larger than, smaller than, and equal to right angles. Extensions of this initial activity involve folding paper into rectangles, congruent halves of a rectangle, and a square. The reader who does the activities in this book should end up with a good sense of both right angles and the quadrilaterals that contain them. The companion book *Exploring Triangles* (Phillips, 1975), which is more difficult, uses folding to create the bisectors of the angles of triangles and the perpendicular bisector and median of each side. In a brief space it manages to present a comprehensive set of terms and concepts related to triangles and, more important, to ground them in experience. Both of these books should be used in a hands-on way.

Origami, the classic Japanese art of paper folding, is another good way to explore shapes. Its benefits come not through any explicit geometrical pedagogy but through children's direct experience of spatial relationships as they manipulate paper. *The ABC's of Origami* (Sarasas, 1964) offers a nice collection of figures that would fit in well with a class's study of animals. Every page has an origami animal figure (from albatross to zebra), its name in English, French, and Japanese, and a diagram of how to make it. *Sadako and the Thousand Paper Cranes* (Coerr, 1977) puts origami in its cultural context in a fictionalized but true story about a young girl in Hiroshima who tried to fold a thousand paper cranes as she was dying of leukemia brought on by radiation. This moving story is another example of how books that contain mathematical elements can be related to more human themes.

Learning more about geometry

Fun with Figures (Freeman and Freeman, 1946), although an older book, is still a classic introduction for students who are ready to learn more about the definitions of different shapes and how to make them. Readers are shown simple ways to make precise straight and parallel lines, spirals, Möbius strips, and other shapes. There are also suggestions about noticing shapes in the world around us: an ellipse formed by the water in a tilted glass; a parabola in the water coming out of a hose and in a suspension bridge.

The excellent titles in the Young Math Book series published by Crowell include quite a few that focus on geometry. There are enough of them that a teacher could make them the centerpiece of a lengthy class exploration of the topic, checking them out from the library and encouraging students to read as many as possible, perhaps working in groups to carry out activities. These books can be divided into those that focus on lines (the geometry of one dimension) and those that focus on shapes (geometry in two or three dimensions).

Lines, Segments, Polygons (Sitomer and Sitomer, 1972) begins with the concept of an infinite straight line and explores the way segments can be defined and then combined into angles and polygons. The reader is encouraged to use not only pencil and paper but also toothpicks and geoboards to make a variety of polygons. These activities are very well suited for small-group exploration. *Straight Lines, Parallel Lines, Perpendicular Lines* (Charosh, 1970) shows how to use string to determine whether a line is straight and suggests a series of checkerboard activities for making parallel and perpendicular lines with checkers. (Although all the patterns described are illustrated, students' understanding of these concepts will be more deeply grounded if they actually make the patterns themselves rather than simply read about them.) *Angles Are Easy as Pie* (Froman, 1975) looks at how angles are formed from two lines that meet, and includes lengthy demonstrations of how the angles in a triangle always add up to 180° (conceptualized here as "half a pie"), while a quadrilateral adds up to 360°. Students can test this out for themselves by tearing paper polygons into pieces and lining up their angles. The book also talks about angles in the world around us. Because of angles we are able to determine the steepness of a hill, the time on a clock, and directions in space. These books explore straight lines, while *Spirals* (Sitomer and Sitomer, 1974) looks at a special kind of curved line, which appears in real life as the grooves in phonograph records, the springs in watches, and (as three-dimensional helixes) the threads in screws and the stripes in barber poles. Spirals also occur in the natural world in shells, tornadoes, and galaxies. Although the book focuses primarily on becoming aware of spirals in the world around us, a few pages show how to use graph paper to make patterns of dots that can be connected into spirals.

    Circles (Sitomer and Sitomer, 1971) and *The Ellipse* (Charosh, 1971) deal with two different enclosed shapes. *Circles* begins with a discussion of why circles are the best shape for many purposes (pots and pans are easier to clean with no corners, for example, and wheels need to have spokes of equal length). But the bulk of the book is a series of exercises, done mostly with paper, pencil, and compass, that help readers to explore the properties of circles and to inscribe other figures within them, the latter offering many opportunities to create aesthetically pleasing designs. *The Ellipse* builds on students' knowledge of circles by introducing ellipses as "tipped circles" and the circle as a special case of the ellipse. The book also shows how to draw ellipses using tacks and string and demonstrates that the parabola and hyperbola are members of the same family of shapes. *Rubber Bands, Baseballs and Doughnuts: A Book about Topology* (Froman, 1972) looks at shapes from a higher-level perspective in its discussion of topology, the study of what doesn't change when lines and shapes are distorted. Students might be intrigued to find out that to a topologist, a circle, a square, and a triangle all fall into the same category, since they are simple closed curves (defined as a line that separates a plane into two regions, one inside it and the other outside). A person's face reflected in the curved side of a toaster is another example of a distortion that doesn't produce a topological change (this could be related back to the reflections in Hoban's *Shadows and Reflections*, [1990]). This book includes a surprising amount of information about topology, given its short length and simplicity; much of it is likely to be new even to teachers. Although some teachers may feel that topics like topology are unnecessary in elementary school, since they're not part of the usual curriculum, it is exactly this kind of enrichment topic that is likely to spark a continuing interest in mathematics among children.

Geometric extensions: architecture and art

One of the most important and visible uses of geometry in the world around us is in architecture. The buildings we see every day and the famous ones around the world are designed the way they are because of the structural and decorative properties of shape. Roxie Munro's *Inside-Outside Book of New York City* (1985)—there is also a companion book for Washington, D.C.—looks at famous and ordinary buildings from both the outside and the inside, in most cases providing enough structural detail to help learners think about why different shapes—the tall rectangles of the skyscrapers of the stock exchange, the pillars holding up the roof of the subway, and the arches of a cathedral, inside and out—are used in architecture. The famous Flatiron Building is seen from outside; a view from its windows shows the sharply angled converging streets that made its odd shape necessary. The views from inside buildings sometimes have a surprising twist: the beauty of the Statue of Liberty perhaps gains a new depth when we are inside seeing the beams that hold up the crown, and the bars of the zoo take on a new perspective when we're behind them looking out at our own species!

Round Buildings, Square Building, and Buildings That Wiggle Like a Fish (Isaacson, 1988) is a young reader's introduction to the question of why buildings use the shapes they do and deals with both the practicalities and the aesthetics of form. A chapter on shapes talks about why lighthouses and windmills look alike all over the world, while skyscrapers are designed as an efficient arrangement of boxlike offices, and other buildings reflect the attitudes of their designers that architecture should be serious or playful or something else altogether.

David Macaulay is an author-illustrator best known for his large-format architectural books for children. In black-and-white, pen-and-ink illustrations, he documents the construction of several, mostly ancient structures: a medieval cathedral (1973), an Egyptian pyramid (1975), a Welsh castle (1977), a Roman city (1974), and the structures beneath a modern city (1976). The books are based on extensive research and executed with tremendous detail and authenticity. Each is filled with a wealth of detail about how, in building design, shapes are chosen to serve many different functions. Students can try out some of these same principles for themselves through *Architecture: A Book of*

Projects for Young Adults (Wilson, 1968), which helps students understand how structures like arches and cantilevers work by building models out of simple materials like sugar cubes. Macaulay also explores architecture-in-reverse in *Unbuilding* (1980), in which he uses an imaginary plot about a plan to transport the Empire State Building to the Arabian desert as a pretext for "unbuilding" it from the top down to the ground. (He has suggested that readers who find this plot too upsetting read the book from back to front!)

One further way to explore geometry through children's books is to look at the work of illustrators who have used shapes to go off on playful flights of imagination and fantasy. *Thirteen* (Charlip and Joyner, 1975) is a series of thirteen two-page spreads on which thirteen picture stories unfold simultaneously, several involving shape transformations. In "The Mystery of the Pyramid," a scene of a pyramid develops into a man with an hourglass whose grains of sand turn into another pyramid. In "Swans Becoming Water," a series of soft-edged shapes turn into one another in surprising ways, as a tree becomes a lobster that in turn becomes an angel. This is a book that rewards long and detailed attention.

Some of Mitsumasa Anno's books also explore shapes in new ways. *Topsy-Turvies: Pictures to Stretch the Imagination* (1970) is a collection of illustrations that seem increasingly strange the longer the viewer looks at them. Large numbers of tiny people are found in, on, and around buildings, sometimes upside-down yet looking oddly normal, sometimes on staircases that appear to be going up and down simultaneously. *In Shadowland* (1988) tells two stories at the same time on facing pages. One takes place in a regular town, the other in Shadowland, which is populated only in the "dark winter season," when the shadows are no longer needed in the outside world. The pictures of Shadowland are pure shape: made of cut paper silhouettes, they have no color or internal definition. Students might enjoy comparing this book with the silhouette photographs of Hoban's *Shapes and Things* (1970), and making their own silhouettes.

Graham Oakley's *Magical Changes* (1979) is one of the most fascinating explorations of shape available. It is a split-page book whose halves can be recombined to make new combinations, with unusually imaginative scenes and anomalies of scale producing truly bizarre results. An unsplit picture of men carrying black umbrellas looks relatively normal until the pages are flipped to reveal the men carrying huge lollipops licked by a giant tongue and the umbrellas growing out of a garden plot. These are shapes taken to the far reaches of surrealism!

Books in the classroom K–2

First-grade teacher Cassandra Gary read *The Boy with Square Eyes* (Snape and Snape, 1987) to Maria, one of her former students. Maria had just finished the

Maria's  Book

Chapter I
Things that are
Square

How many things can you think of that are square? I can think of lots. Do you know how many things I can think of? Here are some: Books, bread, and Blocks and many more.

If you have a computer in your house, look and see if the screen is square. My computer is square.

At my house we have books. Books are square. Books have 4 sides

A house has 4 sides like a square. A square has 4 equal sides.

FIGURE 10–2

Look at your TV. and see if it is
square

At my house we have a fruit basket.
A fruit basket is a square basket with
fruit in it.

Chapter 2
Making things out
of Squares

This is a
flower made
out of squares.

There is 7
petles.

There is 4 squar
on the stem.

Here are some patterns made
out of squares.

square
head

This is a person.
It is a girl.

FIGURE 10–2 (CONTINUED)

second grade, and Cassandra wanted to enlist her help during the summer. After reading the story aloud, Cassandra invited Maria to create a book about squares that could be used with first graders the next fall. Maria gladly accepted the invitation and set to work on a first draft of her book. Before sharing it with Cassandra, Maria read it aloud to several children in the neighborhood. Following a suggestion from one of them, Maria made some changes that included providing quite a complete list of square things—books, a house, a television, a computer, and a fruit basket. Cassandra encouraged Maria to look her story over again to see whether she wanted to make any other changes. When she looked at her sketch of a table on the first page, Maria remarked, "This looks more like a rectangle than a square because two of the sides are longer than the other two," thus revising with a mathematician's eye. Her completed book appears in Figure 10–2.

As she looked at her book with Cassandra, Maria pointed out that "two or three squares make a rectangle." She used the stem of a flower and the body of a girl as examples from her book. Maria had not noticed the relationship between squares and rectangles until she began to manipulate square pieces herself. She felt that it was an important observation and told Cassandra, "You need to be sure you explain about the squares making rectangles when you read this book to others, especially the first graders." Maria also noted the concept of equivalence when she was making the stem for her flower. As she was placing four squares on the paper, she observed that she could arrange them in different ways and remarked, "There are lots of ways you can make four: one plus three, or two plus two, or four plus zero."

Books in the classroom 3–4

Fourth-grade teacher Sheila Hanley noticed that her children did not have a sound understanding of the concepts of area and perimeter. She decided to use *Grandfather Tang's Story* (Tombert, 1990) to explore these concepts further. It tells a Chinese fairy tale about two animals who take turns trying to catch each other but escape each time by transforming themselves into other creatures. The author uses a set of seven geometric pieces (tangrams) to represent each animal and its subsequent transformation.

After reading the story aloud, Sheila gave each child a set of tangram pieces to use. When her students had had the opportunity to create some of their own animals, Sheila showed them two tangram patterns on the overhead projector. Each pattern used all seven geometric pieces, but one design was more spread out than the other. Sheila asked the children to compare the area of the two designs. Even though there was a clear difference in the arrangement of the pieces, Sheila predicted that most of her children would conclude that both designs covered the same area (that is, that they would have a good concept of conservation of area). But the responses of her students varied:

"They are the same because they have used the same amount of space."
"They are the same, it's just that one is put together a different way." "One is
greater because it takes up more space." "One is greater because the shapes
are too bunched up—the more spread out the pieces are, the greater the
area." "I think it would be the same because they use all the pieces and they
equal together."

Sheila then asked the children to use some centimeter grid paper and find
the area of each individual tangram piece. After they had discussed their results together, she invited them to create their own tangram design and to
record it on centimeter paper, calculating both its perimeter and its area. As
the students were working on their designs, one child said to Sheila, "But Ms.
Hanley, won't the area be the same for everyone?" Sheila and her students discussed this question together. There were still a few students who insisted
that the designs would not all have the same area. At this point Sheila used
their desks as an analogy: "If we rearranged the desks in our classroom, would
we still be covering the same amount of carpet?" Most seemed to agree that
the covered area would be the same.

As the children completed their designs they shared their results with each
other. Many found their areas to be almost the same. Brad and Tiffany's designs appear in Figures 10–3 and 10–4. The children realized that the calculations for area would be slightly different because of the estimation required to
count partial squares. They did notice a significant variation in the perimeters
that each person obtained and related that finding to their previous comments

FIGURE 10–3

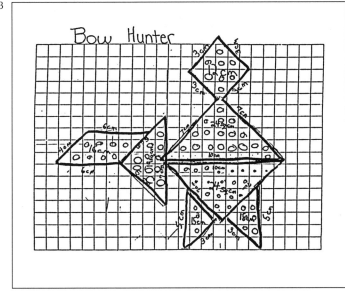

FIGURE 10-4

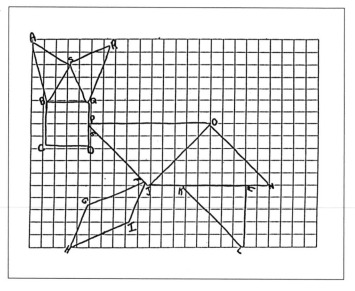

about designs being "spread onto" or "bunched up." Their investigations helped to highlight important distinctions between the concepts of area and perimeter.

Books in the classroom 5–6

Kathryn McColskey worked with David Whitin in exploring the concepts of area and perimeter with her fifth-grade students. Kathryn read aloud *The Village of Round and Square Houses* (Grifalconi, 1986), which tells a legendary story about why one African tribe's buildings are the shape they are. David then asked the children why they thought houses were built in different shapes. Their responses reflected a variety of cultural and practical justifications.

1. *The size of the family.* One child mentioned that he had a lot of brothers and sisters and needed more space for his family than if he were an only child.

2. *Environment.* The kind of houses people build depends on the kind of materials available; bamboo, thatch, wood, and brick all influence the shape of a culture's dwellings.

3. *Climate.* Humans try to build structures that will keep them cool in hot weather and warm in cold weather. One child mentioned the usefulness of porches, which catch cooling breezes by the ocean. She also mentioned that "if you're building a house along the shore, and you don't want the wind to blow it over, you might build round walls instead of flat ones." Her thoughts perhaps grew out of discussions that occurred in South Carolina

after Hurricane Hugo caused such devastating damage along the coast. The shape of beachfront homes was a major concern for people who were rebuilding.

4. *Terrain.* Another child mentioned that the type of land people live on may affect the kind of houses they build; a house in the jungle may differ in shape from houses on mountaintops or in the desert.

5. *Culture.* Another child mentioned that the beliefs of a people can influence how they build their houses. David mentioned Black Elk, a Native American leader, who once said, "We have made these little gray houses of logs that you see, and they are square. It is a bad way to live, for there can be no power in a square. You have noticed that everything an Indian does is in a circle, and that is because the Power of the World always works in circles and everything tries to be round" (cited in Zaslavsky, 1989, p. 18).

6. *Psychological factors.* "Sometimes you just don't want to be like everybody else," explained one student, "so you build a house that is different."

7. *Historical tradition.* "It might be the only way you know how to build a house; your father taught you, and his father taught him, and you've always done it that way," reasoned another child. His justification paralleled the historical tradition described in *The Village of Round and Square Houses.*

8. *Way of life.* "If you're a migrant worker and always moving around, you would build something different; they don't want to build a huge mansion, so they build different shapes that are easy to set up and take down," explained another child.

After the children shared these possible reasons for architectural shape and style, Kathryn and David gave each child a sheet of centimeter square paper and a piece of string 32 centimeters long and presented them with the following challenge: "Pretend that you live in a society in which people must produce almost everything they need by their own efforts. Your family is planning to build a house. You and your family must gather all the materials, perhaps with the help of your neighbors. Some of the materials may be hard to come by, and you want to use as little as possible. Pretend that you have collected a certain amount of material for the walls (the piece of string). Figure out what shape will give you the largest floor space with this quantity of material." (This idea comes from Zaslavsky, 1989.)

As the children set to work, they posed some interesting questions to help them clarify and extend the investigation. Sheri asked, "Can we leave a gap for the doorway?" John's question was, "Can we pretend we have other houses already built, and use some of their walls as sides for this house we're building now?" His question highlighted the notion that buildings may be either free-standing or connected. Rebecca asked, "Can I unravel the string and use the little strands for building?" trying to increase the amount of building material available.

One of the children's major findings was that the area of their shapes increased as they began to approximate a circle. Rebecca created two shapes
and noted the difference, as seen in Figure 10–5. She nicely captured the
unique attribute of a circle, which "stays the same all the way around."
Megan created a triangle, a square, and a circle and recorded the area for
each (Figure 10–6). As the children recorded what they had learned from this
experience, Ben noted the relationship between shape and area when he
wrote, "I learned triangles have a smaller area than a circle. A square has more
than a triangle but less than a circle. A circle has the greatest amount of the
three."

Katie learned about a different kind of relationship when she wrote, "Circles have more space than squares do. I thought it would be the other way
around because circles can fit into squares," (she drew a circle inside a square
to explain her reasoning, not realizing that squares can also be inscribed inside circles).

After the students discussed their findings about area, David asked the class,
"Why do you suppose that we build mostly square and rectangular houses in
the United States, when we know that circular houses would give us a greater

FIGURE 10-5

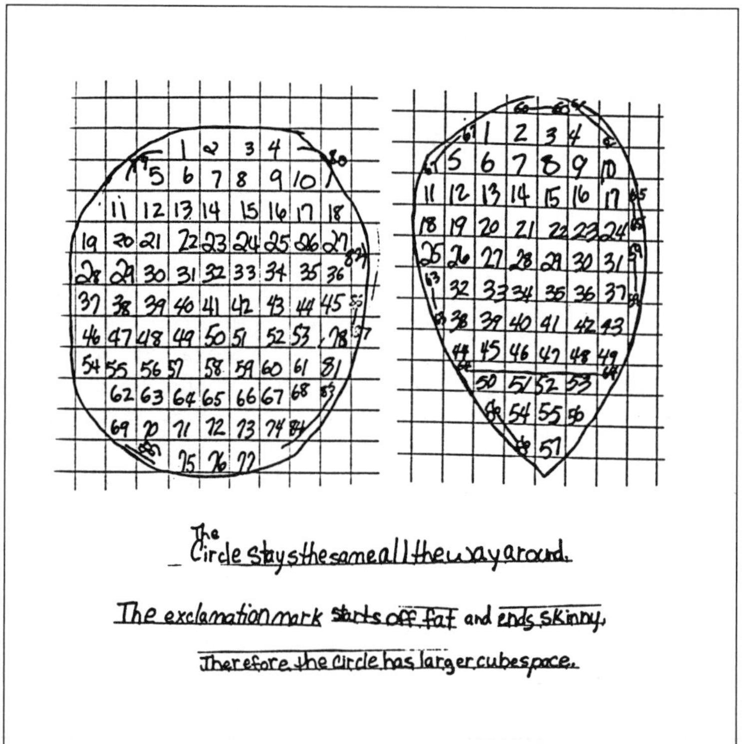

The Circle stays the same all the way around.

The exclamation mark starts off fat and ends skinny.

Therefore the circle has larger cube space.

FIGURE 10–6

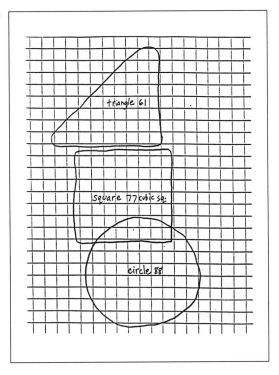

area for a given perimeter?" (The round houses of other cultures, such as the igloo, tipi, Central Asian yurt, and African cylindrical house, were cited as examples.) The class again offered reasons that reflected varying cultural values:

1. *Aesthetics.* "Maybe they want to make it pretty for other people."

2. *Nature of materials.* "It's harder to build a circle with wooden planks."

3. *Efficiency.* "It's faster to build straight houses."

4. *Economy.* "A circle gives the biggest area but some people don't care about saving material." Aslinn went on to explain this idea further: "I learned that we can be more resourceful of our natural resources. We don't always need everything to be big. We need to save our earth." Her comment underscored the role of values in architectural design.

This fifth-grade class used mathematics as a lens to look at culture and gained an increased awareness of the values that underlie the shape and structure of the dwellings favored by different societies.

Further explorations

1. When beginning exploration of geometry with young children, you can provide many opportunities to observe and discuss shapes in the world

around them. You might invite them to go on a shape walk, send them on a shape detective hunt at home, and so on. You can mesh these activities with Tana Hoban's shape books and invite children to bring in photographs or drawings of the different shapes they see.

2. Older children might be interested in using some of the geometry picture books discussed in this chapter to make their own books for sharing with younger children. They could take photographs like Hoban and McMillan do, make mirror puzzles like Walter's, create rotating pictures like Gardner's, or, if they are really ambitious, design reversible books like Jonas's.

3. Students working with David Macaulay's architectural books might want to research the construction of a building in their own community and write a book about it following Macaulay's style. If they are lucky enough to have a new building going up near the school, they may be able to document the construction as it happens.

4. You might want to look in the adult section of the library for books on architecture, both to stimulate your own thinking about the structural use of shape and to find books that children might enjoy looking at, even if they're too hard to read. Books on two architects as different as Frank Lloyd Wright and Antonin Gaudi, for example, would help children see that there are many possible choices about how to use shapes in building.

5. Why are objects shaped the way they are? You can invite children to bring interesting shapes to school for discussion. The emphasis should not be on naming the shape but on analyzing why the object has this particular shape. What function does the shape serve? Such a question can provide a framework for discussing the shape of any object, from coat hangers to dinosaur teeth. Some of the books involving shape and architectural design could be helpful resources, as sources of more shapes to examine and as explorations of architectural principles.

Children's books

SHAPES

Anno, Mitsumasa. 1970. *Topsy-turvies: Pictures to stretch the imagination*. New York: Walker.

———— . 1988. *In shadowland*. New York: Orchard.

———— . 1991. *Anno's math games III*. New York: Philomel.

Brown, Marcia. 1979. *Listen to a shape*. New York: Franklin Watts.

Carle, Eric. 1972. *The secret birthday message*. New York: Crowell.

———— . 1974. *My very first book of shapes*. New York: Harper Collins.

————. 1986. *Papa, please get the moon for me*. Natick, MA: Picture Book Studio.

Charlip, Remy, and Jerry Joyner. 1975. *Thirteen*. New York: Parents' Magazine Press.

Charosh, Mannis. 1971. *The ellipse*. New York: Crowell.

Dunbar, Fiona. 1991. *You'll never guess!*. New York: Dial.

Ehlert, Lois. 1989. *Color zoo*. New York: Lippincott.

————. 1990. *Color farm*. New York: Lippincott.

Emberley, Edward. 1961. *The wing on a flea: A book about shapes*. Boston: Little, Brown.

————. 1979. *Ed Emberley's big green drawing book*. Boston: Little, Brown.

————. 1980. *Ed Emberley's big orange drawing book*. Boston: Little, Brown.

————. 1984. *Ed Emberley's picture pie: A circle drawing book*. Boston: Little, Brown.

Fisher, Leonard. 1984. *Boxes! Boxes!* New York: Viking.

————. 1987. *Look around!* New York: Viking Kestrel.

Freeman, Mae, and Ira Freeman. 1946. *Fun with figures*. New York: Random House.

Goor, Ron, and Nancy Goor. 1981. *Shadows, here, there and everywhere*. New York: Crowell.

Hoban, Tana. 1970. *Shapes and things*. New York: Macmillan.

————. 1971. *Look again!* New York: Macmillan.

————. 1974. *Circles, triangles, and squares*. New York: Macmillan.

————. 1981. *Take another look*. New York: Greenwillow.

————. 1982. *A, B, see!* New York: Greenwillow.

————. 1983a. *Round and round and round*. New York: Greenwillow.

————. 1983b. *I read symbols*. New York: Greenwillow.

————. 1986. *Shapes, shapes, shapes*. New York: Greenwillow.

————. 1987. *Dots, spots, speckles, and stripes*. New York: Greenwillow.

————. 1988. *Look! look! look!* New York: Greenwillow.

————. 1990. *Shadows and reflections*. New York: Greenwillow.

Jonas, Ann. 1984. *Holes and peeks*. New York: Greenwillow.

Kline, Suzy. 1989. *The hole book*. New York: Putnam.

McMillan, Bruce. 1988. *Fire engine shapes*. New York: Lothrop, Lee and Shepard.

Oakley, Graham. 1979. *Magical changes*. New York: Macmillan.

Phillips, Louis. 1982. *The upside down riddle book*. New York: Lothrop, Lee and Shepard.

Rahn, Joan. 1984. *Holes*. Boston: Houghton Mifflin.

Read, Ronald C. 1965. *Tangrams, 330 puzzles*. New York: Dover.

Reiss, John J. 1974. *Shapes*. Scarsdale, NY: Bradbury.

Rogers, Paul. 1989. *The shapes game*. New York: Holt.

Seuss, Dr. 1973. *The shape of me and other stuff*. New York: Random House.

Shaw, Charles. 1947. *It looked like spilt milk*. New York: Harper and Row.

Silverstein, Shel. 1976. *The missing piece*. New York: Harper and Row.

———. 1981. *The missing piece meets the Big O*. New York: Harper and Row.

———. 1981. Shapes. In *A light in the attic*. New York: Harper and Row.

Sitomer, Mindel, and Harry Sitomer. 1971. *Circles*. New York: Crowell.

Snape, Juliet, and Charles Snape. 1987. *The boy with square eyes*. New York: Simon and Schuster.

Sullivan, Joan. 1963. *Round is a pancake*. New York: Holt, Rinehart and Winston.

Testa, Fulvio. 1983. *If you look around you*. New York: Dial.

Tombert, Ann. 1990. *Grandfather Tang's story*. New York: Crown.

Van Note, Peter, 1968. *Sam Loyd's book of tangram puzzles*. New York: Dover.

Vreuls, Diane. 1977. *Sums: A looking game*. New York: Macmillan.

Webster, David. 1968. *Snow stumpers*. Garden City, NY: Natural History Press.

Wildsmith, Brian. 1980. *Animal shapes*. New York: Oxford.

Yenawine, Philip. 1991. *Shapes*. New York: Delacorte Press.

Ziebel, Peter. 1989. *Look closer!* New York: Clarion.

LINES AND ANGLES

Charosh, Mannis. 1970. *Straight lines, parallel lines, perpendicular lines*. New York: Crowell.

Froman, Robert. 1975. *Angles are easy as pie*. New York: Harper and Row.

Juster, Norton. 1963. *The dot and the line*. New York: Random House.

Prelutsky, Jack. 1990. My snake. In *Something big has been here*. New York: Greenwillow.

Sitomer, Mindel, and Harry Sitomer. 1972. *Lines, segments, polygons*. New York: Crowell.

———. 1974. *Spirals*. New York: Crowell.

Yenawine, Philip. 1991. *Lines*. New York: Delacorte Press.

SPATIAL CONCEPTS

Anno, Mitsumasa. 1971. *Upside-downers: More pictures to stretch the imagination*. New York: Walker/Weatherhill.

———. 1991. *Anno's math games III*. New York: Philomel.

Froman, Robert. 1972. *Rubber bands, baseballs and doughnuts: A book about topology*. New York: Crowell.

Hill, Eric. 1980. *Where's Spot?* New York: Putnam.

Hoban, Tana. 1972. *Push-pull, empty-full*. New York: Macmillan.

———— . 1973. *Over, under and through, and other spatial concepts.* New York: Macmillan.

———— . 1979. *One little kitten.* New York: Greenwillow.

———— . 1983. *Here a chick, there a chick.* New York: Lothrop, Lee and Shepard.

———— . 1990. *Exactly the opposite.* New York: Greenwillow.

———— . 1991. *All about where.* New York: Greenwillow.

Holt, Michael. 1975. *Maps, tracks and the bridges of Königsberg: A book about networks.* New York: Crowell.

MacDonald, Suse. 1989. *Puzzlers.* New York: Dial.

McMillan, Bruce. 1986 *Becca backward, Becca frontward: A book of concept pairs.* New York: Lothrop, Lee and Shepard.

Srivastava, Jane. 1974. *Area.* New York: Crowell.

———— . 1980. *Spaces, shapes and sizes.* New York: Crowell.

SYMMETRY

Birmingham, Duncan. 1988. *'M' is for mirror.* Norfolk, England: Tarquin Publications.

Gardner, Beau. 1980. *The turn about, think about, look about book.* New York: Lothrop, Lee and Shepard.

———— . 1984. *The look again . . . and again, and again, and again book.* New York: Lothrop, Lee and Shepard.

———— . 1989. *What is it? A spin-about book.* New York: Putnam.

Jonas, Ann. 1983. *Round trip.* New York: Greenwillow.

———— . 1987. *Reflections.* New York: Greenwillow.

Silverstein, Shel. 1981. Reflection. In *A light in the attic.* New York: Harper and Row.

Sitomer, Mindel, and Harry Sitomer. 1970. *What is symmetry?* New York: Crowell.

Walter, Marion. 1971a. *Look at Annette.* New York: M. Evans. Reissued as *Another magic mirror book.* New York: Scholastic.

———— . 1971b. *Make a bigger puddle, make a smaller worm.* New York: M. Evans. Reissued as *The magic mirror book.* New York: Scholastic.

———— . 1975. *Another, another, another and more.* London: Andre Deutsch.

———— . 1985. *The mirror puzzle book.* Norfolk, England: Tarquin Publications.

PAPER FOLDING

Coerr, Eleanor. 1977. *Sadako and the thousand paper cranes.* New York: Putnam.

Phillips, Jo. 1972. *Right angles: Paper-folding geometry.* New York: Crowell.

————. 1975. *Exploring triangles: Paper-folding geometry*. New York: Crowell.

Sarasas, Claude. 1964. *The abc's of origami: Paper-folding for children*. Rutland, VT: Charles E. Tuttle.

BUILDING AND ARCHITECTURE

Giblin, James. 1988. *Let there be light*. New York: Crowell.

Grifalconi, Ann. 1986. *The village of round and square houses*. Boston: Little, Brown.

Hutchins, Pat. 1971. *Changes, changes*. New York: Macmillan.

Isaacson, Philip M. 1988. *Round buildings, square buildings, and buildings that wiggle like a fish*. New York: Knopf.

Korab, Balthazar. 1985. *Archabet*. Washington, DC: National Trust for Historic Preservation.

Macaulay, David. 1973. *Cathedral*. Boston: Houghton Mifflin.

————. 1974. *City*. Boston: Houghton Mifflin.

————. 1975. *Pyramid*. Boston: Houghton Mifflin.

————. 1976. *Underground*. Boston: Houghton Mifflin.

————. 1977. *Castle*. Boston: Houghton Mifflin.

————. 1980. *Unbuilding*. Boston: Houghton Mifflin.

Maddex, Diane. 1986. *Architects make zigzags*. Washington, DC: National Trust for Historic Preservation.

Munro, Roxie. 1985. *The inside-outside book of New York City*. New York: Dodd, Mead.

Stevenson, Robert L. 1988. *Block city*. New York: Dutton.

Wilson, Forrest. 1968. *Architecture: A book of projects for young adults*. New York: Reinhold.

Teacher resource

Zaslavsky, Claudia. 1989. People who live in round houses. *Arithmetic Teacher, 37*: 18–21.

A third-grade teacher asked her class to write about why people measure. Although some of the students referred to making lemonade and figuring out what size clothes to buy, most of them responded by saying that people measure so they can find out how long something is. Children's literature can expand students' understanding of measurement by allowing them to explore different types of measurement and to recognize the many different contexts in which measurement operates in everyday life. We measure one or two dimensions (length and area) when we buy fabric or carpeting; we move into a third dimension when we measure volume, as we do in cooking. We measure weight when we buy vegetables or mail packages. In a sense, we also measure when we keep track of time and money. An excellent resource that demonstrates how much is encompassed by the idea of measurement is *Comparisons* (Diagram Group, 1980), a profusely illustrated source book with sections on distance, size, area and volume, weight, energy, temperature, time, speed, and number. The chapter on size has a two-page spread showing buildings and monuments drawn to scale, from Cleopatra's Needle in London (68 feet) to the Warsaw Radio Mast (2,120 feet), while the chapter on time includes a geological time chart representing hundreds of millions of years, with pictures of animals that lived during each period at appropriate points.

Big and small: comparisons

Young children might begin to examine measurement simply by considering what it means for something to be bigger or smaller than something else. Tana Hoban's *Is It Larger? Is It Smaller?* (1985) is a good place for children to start thinking about the importance of size in the world around us. Hoban's imaginative photographs are a thought-provoking meditation on all the ways and reasons that one thing is bigger or smaller than another. Baby pigs are smaller than their mother for a different reason than a toy car is smaller than a real one. A boy is bigger than a rabbit, but the rabbit's ears are bigger. This single book is so rich in detail it could be the centerpiece for an exploration of measurement that expanded into every possible concept: length, area, volume, weight, time, and even money (How do the prices of large and small suitcases or real and toy boats relate to their respective sizes?). *Super Super Superwords* (McMillan, 1989) would be a good

11

measurement

book to follow Hoban's. In photographs taken at a kindergarten, McMillan illustrates comparative and superlative words, many of them related to things we measure. Photos of stacks of books show us what we can't feel directly (heavy, heavier, heaviest), while a measuring cup that goes from full to fuller to fullest illustrates volume. The words *big* and *small* are used in two sets of pictures, and McMillan also illustrates the more precise terms *tall* (block castles), *long* (a set of pop-together cubes), and *short* (a pencil that keeps shrinking as it's sharpened).

Sometimes we measure changes that occur over time. *Changes* (Allen and Rotner, 1991) is a good way for beginners to see that size is one quality that may change over time. The book's vivid color photographs show plants and animals changing by growing bigger. Eric Carle's *The Tiny Seed* (1987b) follows the life cycle of a flower through an entire year, beginning and ending with a seed's being carried by the wind in autumn, and bringing out the contrast between a tiny seed and the "tallest flower that people have ever seen" that grows from it. The theme of growth from smaller to bigger as part of the life cycle also appears in *You'll Soon Grow into Them, Titch* (Hutchins, 1983), in which Titch, the youngest of three children, always has to wear hand-me-down clothes that are a little too big for him. Finally, when a new baby is born, Titch gets some brand-new clothes and has someone to hand *his* old ones down to. Children might enjoy writing about how they've grown over the years, and keep track of their height and other measurements throughout the school year in order to see that they're still growing. Titch is also the subject of an earlier book (Hutchins, 1971) in which his possessions are always smaller than those of his bigger siblings: their big bikes overshadow his little tricycle, and while they have a hammer and saw, he just has little nails. Finally, though, Titch ends up with something bigger: their spade and flowerpot help provide a home for his tiny seed, which "grew and grew and grew." Young children are acutely aware of their small size in relation to the adults and older children around them. These two Titch books can help them to think about both the mathematical and the psychological concepts of big and small.

Several picture books explore large and small in exaggerated ways. *Titch*, ending with the growth of a flower, might be followed by a reading of *The Carrot Seed* (Krauss, 1945), which echoes the experience of many gardeners in its story of a carrot seed that doesn't seem to grow at all and then becomes huge overnight. If students do any planting of seeds as part of their science curriculum, regular measuring and charting should certainly be part of it. (Can plants *really* grow huge in one night, or does it just seem that way?) *The King's Flower* (Anno, 1979) is a more normal-sized plant, but much of what surrounds it is big. The king of the title "had to have everything bigger and better than everyone else," such as a giant knife and fork that he needed pulleys and a team of helpers to use. When the king decided he should only be catching big fish in his pond, his servants secretly stocked it with a whale, but they were unable to influence the seed planted in the king's giant flowerpot, which grew up to be "small but beautiful" and completely acceptable to the king. In a charming afterword, Anno describes the pleasure he experienced in imagining huge human-made objects, but also his realization that "even the most powerful human beings cannot produce life. We must be content, and recognize that each flower, each worm, is something natural and indispensable." *The Biggest House in the World* (Lionni, 1968) also explores the concept of the appropriateness of size. A young snail who is dissatisfied with the small size of the home he carries on his back hears from his father the story of another snail who discovered that through willpower and wishing he could produce a gargantuan, bulging, multicolored shell that was admired far and wide but was unfortunately too heavy for him to move, so that he died when he couldn't move on to a new food source.

Moving further into the realm of animals and people, some books by Steven Kellogg deal with creatures that are, in reality or imagination, bigger than the norm. In *Can I Keep Him?* (1971), Arnold keeps bringing home potential pets that his mother always has some reason for rejecting. He starts with a cat and a dog, but the pets keep getting bigger and more improbable: a deer, a bear, a tiger, a python, and finally a defrosted dinosaur. Students might enjoy thinking and writing about what it would be like to have a really large pet. (Like many children's books, this one calls all animals "he"; the teacher reading it aloud might choose to alternate pronouns or to use "it.") Like Titch, the narrator of *Much Bigger than Martin* (1976) gets tired of always being smaller than his brother and deals with it by imagining what it would be like to grow bigger than he is. One delightful set of four pictures shows him at first just a little taller than Martin and eventually big enough to carry his flabbergasted brother around in his shirt pocket. Kellogg has also created a new version of *Paul Bunyan* (1984), in which much of the fun comes from the wealth of visual detail used to picture a life lived at much larger than normal size. The giant flapjack griddle is greased by kitchen helpers, organized into teams of "Mops" and "Brooms," playing hockey with slabs of bacon for skates. One final note on big things: Shel Silverstein's poem "Longmobile" (1981, p. 39) shows that, if a car is big enough, it may not need to move at all!

At the other end of the size scale, there are two books for somewhat older readers that use the common children's literature theme of very small people. The classic *Borrowers* (Norton, 1953; there are also several sequels), about a family of small people living in the walls of a house, is especially delightful for its portrayal of a household assembled from odds and ends "borrowed" from full-size humans; wallpaper made from old letters (the handwriting creating stripes) with postage stamps hung up as paintings, a cooking-pot made from a thimble, and a blotting-paper carpet that conveniently soaks up spills. (Shel Silverstein's poem about shortness, "One Inch Tall" [1974, p. 55], has similar images: "If you were only one inch tall, you'd ride a worm to school. / The teardrop of a crying ant would be your swimming pool.") Some students might even want to create their own Borrowers house out of found objects from their classroom and homes, perhaps using measurement to ensure that the scale is consistent. *The Shrinking of Treehorn* (Heide, 1971) is a satire about a young boy who gradually starts growing smaller. When he tries to tell the adults around him about it, they all respond inappropriately. His parents at first don't believe him ("Nobody shrinks"), then worry about what people will say, and ask him if he's doing it on purpose. Finally, Treehorn solves the problem himself by getting out his "game for kids to grow on." After playing for a while, he grows back to normal size (after remembering he'd moved back seven spaces in the board game the day before!).

When children are ready to explore concepts of size more precisely, *Bigger and Smaller* (Froman, 1971) provides a good summary of what we mean when we use these terms. As Froman points out, they are comparative words, and we may want to measure size along more than one dimension, such as height and weight. He then explores some examples of big and small, gradually going both bigger and smaller. Big animals (in comparison to other animals) are outclassed by bigger trees and bigger buildings, while small dogs (compared to other dogs) look big next to smaller rodents and even smaller insects.

Linear measurement: length, area, and volume

Children who have a good general sense of what big and small mean can be encouraged to think about particular kinds of big and small and to learn about ways to measure them. The most obvious starting point is length and its extensions into area and volume. *3D, 2D, 1D* (Adler, 1975) is an excellent introduction. This book examines the three dimensions of height, width, and thickness as the three components of linear measurement, and conceptualizes volume, area, and length in concrete terms. Volume can be seen as the number of blocks that can fit into a box, area as the number of tiles that cover a surface, and length as the number of units that can fit along a line. As the beginning of an exploration of linear measurement, you might want to brainstorm with students the variety of everyday situations where we want to know length, area, or volume, and the reasons why each type of measure is appropriate for its own situation.

Inch by Inch (Lionni, 1960), the story of an inchworm who measures other animals, can help young children see that measuring involves laying out units of a uniform size end to end over and over again. Children can explore measuring with units of their own invention and gradually discover for themselves the need for more standard units of length. *How Big Is a Foot?* (Myller, 1962) is a good introduction to this topic that makes an implicit connection to the original derivation of "foot" as a measure based on the size of a king's foot. This brief story shows the disastrous result when a bed is built by an apprentice based on the length of his own foot, when the dimensions had originally been determined using the king's foot. Another excellent book that introduces readers to the use of nonstandard units of measure is *The Line Up Book* (Russo, 1986), in which a young boy named Sam stretches a continuous line of objects from his bedroom to the kitchen. He uses boots, blocks, bath toys, and finally his own body length to reach the kitchen (just in time for lunch!). Children enjoy the predictable structure of this story and often suggest other possible objects to use as measuring units as they hear it read aloud.

The theme of standard measurements is developed at length in *Long, Short, High, Low, Thin, Wide* (Fey, 1971), which explores some of the history of how our current measuring units for length were developed. Fey begins with thoughts about what kinds of measuring units might be appropriate (toothpicks are too short; shoes are too variable), then shows how units of length have become more and more standard over time, and discusses the origins of the inch, foot, yard, and mile.

Area (Srivastava, 1974) is a good introduction to measurement in two dimensions. Since instruction about area often moves far too quickly into using abstract formulas like "length times width" without building sufficient understanding of how and when those formulas work, a book like this one can be very useful. It operates entirely on the concept level with no formulas at all. Srivastava begins by defining area as a space with edges, then poses the problem of how we might measure such a space. The discussion reviews a variety of topics: the general principle of covering a space with a number of smaller shapes; the benefits of shapes like triangles and squares that can cover a surface completely (unlike circles, which leave bare spots) and of standard-sized units; and an awareness that different shapes can have the same area. This book would be a good basis for an extensive set of area measurement activities, which might include having students discover and develop their own formulas for various regular shapes, like rectangles, triangles, circles, and so on.

A book that can get students to start thinking about volume is *The Mysterious Tadpole* (Kellogg, 1977), in which the title character outgrows a jar, the sink, the bathtub, and an apartment, and ends up going to live in a swimming pool. How does one measure whether a container is big enough to hold something? Extending the ideas in *Area* (Srivastava, 1974) can help students answer this question through exploration and discovery. Cooking is one of the most important purposes for which we measure volume in daily life. A book that imbeds cooking in a story context is de Paola's virtually wordless *Pancakes for Breakfast* (1978a), in which the cook gathers some of her ingredients by going out to the henhouse, getting milk from the cow, and skimming off the cream to churn into butter. The book includes a recipe with several volume measurements.

Weight

Sometimes what something weighs is the measurement we are most interested in knowing. In *The Three Billy Goats Gruff* (Asbjornsen and Moe, 1957; other versions also exist), the bigger and heavier a goat is, the more noise it makes crossing the bridge and the more appetizing it seems to the troll. In *The Story of Ferdinand* (Leaf, 1936), the bull captured for a bullfight because he's the "largest and fiercest" confounds expectations when he turns out to be too gentle to fight. *8,000 Stones* (Wolkstein, 1972) leads the reader through a discovery process about how to weigh something very large; it is also one of the few books that introduces students to the use of nonstandard yet regular units of measure. This folktale tells the story of how the Supreme Governor of China received a huge elephant as a gift but had no way of knowing how much it weighed since there were no scales big enough for it. Finally the emperor's son solves the problem by discovering that a small ivory elephant placed on a toy sailboat consistently sinks in water to the same level, thus demonstrating the principle of water displacement. He explains to the king's advisors: "No matter how many times I sailed [the] elephant on my boat, it always weighed the boat down to that line . . . . If you want to weigh the big elephant, you can do the same thing. And if you need to know the exact weight of the elephant, then pile stones on the boat until the boat sinks to [the right level]" (p. 20). The answer is the book's title. This book is an obvious lead-in for children's own experiments with water displacement. Choosing some small, consistent-weight units of measure to compare the weights of objects, whether used with water displacement or on a balance scale, is a valuable method of developing concepts about weight, particularly when learners are just beginning, since it is far more concrete than the abstract numbers on a bathroom scale. As *Weighing and Balancing* (Srivastava, 1970) explains, people used to compare the weights of objects by simply holding them in their hands, but now we have balances and scales. Much of the book is devoted to hands-on ideas for making and using balances, primarily to compare objects with each other rather than to standard units of weight. For instance, the author suggests trying to find a variety of objects that will balance a small apple. The book also suggests that readers look for weighing machines in the world around them—at the supermarket, the drugstore, and the doctor's office. If teachers want to help students explore relationships between weight and volume, this book is helpful in its discussion of how objects may be large yet light, or small but heavy.

Time

Time is the dimension of measurement we use most often in our daily lives. We are always aware of its passage, and it marks the events of each day and year as well as special occasions. The young child walking with a grandparent in *A Little at a Time* (D. Adler, 1976) learns that much of what we see in the world around us became that way over a long time, changing almost imperceptibly from day to day:

How did that tree get to be so tall, Grandpa?
How did it get so tall?
When it started
  it was just a seed.
Then it grew
  and grew and grew and grew,
  but it only grew
  a little at a time.

Everett Anderson's Nine Month Long (Clifton, 1978) explores a period of some-what more rapid change in the life of a young boy whose mother is expecting a new baby. Nine sensitive poems explore Everett's emotions as they change over the nine months. This would be a nice accompaniment to a class's study of the physical changes that occur in the nine months before birth.

Time is commemorated in special ways on birthdays and holidays. *I'm in Charge of Celebrations* (Baylor, 1986) creates some new holidays in response to the narrator's experience of the natural beauty of the desert: Dust Devil Day, Green Cloud Day, The Time of Falling Stars, and others. Her descriptions have a special resonance because they comprise specific memories rather than generic scenes, and they occurred on particular days she intends to com-memorate for the rest of her life.

Several books are useful for children who are becoming aware of clocks and learning to tell time. *The Scarecrow Clock* (Mendoza, 1971) is a predictable book (see Rhodes, 1981, for a definition and discussion of predictable books) in which one creature after another asks a scarecrow where the previous char-acter has gone. The scarecrow becomes a clock by virtue of its pointing hands. On each page the hour is indicated in five ways: in the text ("He pointed one hand toward eight, and the other hand at twelve"), a drawing of a clock, a numeral (8:00), words (eight o'clock), and a picture of the scarecrow. Chil-dren who have begun to notice all the clocks in the world around them might enjoy *The Clock Shop* (Henwood, 1989), in which a clockmaker looks after all the clocks in town, including the milkman's waterproof one (it falls into the milk a lot), and especially his own, which gets a little bit of extra care be-cause all the others are set by it. A clockmaker also appears in *Clocks and More Clocks* (Hutchins, 1970), coming to the home of Mr. Higgins, who thinks his many clocks are out of synchrony because when he checks the time on one, by the time he gets to a clock in another room it's a few minutes later. The clock-maker solves the problem by using a watch to check the clocks as he goes from one to another. Young children might want to see if they can figure out what Mr. Higgins's problem is before the book provides the answer. In *The Ten-Alarm Camp-Out* (Warren, 1983), clocks are a constantly ticking presence in the plot. A large family of armadillos have camped out overnight, each one curled up around its own alarm clock. They roll into town overnight, are discovered in different spots by people who, seeing a ticking scaly ball, are sure they've found a bomb, and eventually get deposited back on their hill just before the alarms go off. (There's an unintentional mistake in the plot; the armadillos fall asleep at eight o'clock with their clocks set for nine o'clock, but the alarms ring not one but thirteen hours later. See if your students catch this!)

Learning about clocks might include an exploration of sundials, the historical precursor of clocks. *Anno's Sundial* (Anno, 1987) is informative enough for adults to learn from but, particularly in its pictures, can also be used very effectively with children. This is one of the few pop-up books in which the paper engineering actually supports concept development rather than being merely decorative. The book provides various working models of sundials, including a set calibrated for use at latitudes ranging from 30° to 60° north or south.

One of the concepts discussed and explained in *Anno's Sundial,* time zones, is the subject of *All in a Day* (Anno, 1986). Double-page spreads illustrate the lives of children in nine locations throughout the world: a child in Chicago rides a sled at 9:00 A.M., a Brazilian child is playing on the beach at 6:00 P.M., and a child in Tokyo is asleep at midnight, all on the same January day. An excellent afterword explains how time zones work and a time-zone map of the world shows each location in the book. Students might enjoy working with maps and globes to create their own stories involving people living in different time zones.

A number of books can help to build students' knowledge base about the role of time in our lives and how we measure it. *How Long? To Go, to Grow, to Know* (Olney and Olney, 1984) is a good introduction to time in the natural world. Plants and animals vary widely in how quickly they grow and how long they live. Animals (including humans) travel at different rates, rocks last longer than snowflakes, and light travels much, much faster than sound. All of these are illustrated here. Two older books, *Time in Your Life* (I. Adler, 1955) and *The Calendar* (Adler and Adler, 1967), are excellent comprehensive explorations of how humans measure time. *Time in Your Life* deals with the earth as the original clock (one we "never wind"), telling time by the stars, a brief history of clocks, and the rhythms of time found in living creatures, geology, and the atom. *The Calendar* talks about the day, month, and year as units of time grounded in the natural world and how calendars developed to integrate these three time spans, including the problems inherent in bringing them into synchrony with each other, since they don't mesh exactly. (A lunar month is about $29\frac{1}{3}$ days long, and a solar year $365\frac{1}{4}$ days, about $12\frac{1}{2}$ lunar months.) Students might enjoy trying to figure out alternatives to our present conceptions of day, month, and year before reading about those embodied in the calendars that preceded our own. Both books also contain a cut-out perpetual calendar. Because of the publication dates of the books, these calendars cover the time period from 1951 to 1999. It would be a simple project for students to design an updated one, perhaps beginning with 1980 so that the years in which they were born would be included. (In doing so, they should be sure to research what happens to leap year in years ending with

"00," since the calendar will include the year 2000.) *This Book Is About Time* (Burns, 1978) incorporates many topics relating to time in a mixture of information and activities. Students are encouraged to think about their own awareness of time. They also learn about time zones, clocks and watches, calendars, and time in nature, investigate how long various events take, and determine how old they are in days, or how old they would be on other planets. This is probably the most comprehensive single book on time available.

Finally, four remarkable books deal with the human and social dimensions of time in socially and culturally conscious ways. *Annie and the Old One* (Miles, 1971) is the story of a young Navajo girl who is unwilling to accept the impending death of her grandmother, who helps her understand that death is part of the cycle of life and time: Annie "understood many things. The sun rose but it also set. The cactus did not bloom forever. Petals dried and fell to earth. She knew that she was a part of the earth and the things on it. She would always be a part of the earth, just as her grandmother had always been, just as her grandmother would always be, always and forever. And Annie was breathless with the wonder of it" (p. 41).

Window (Baker, 1991), by an Australian illustrator, focuses on environmental change in wordless pictures. It uses collage to show the view from the same window every two years, beginning with the year a baby is born into a lush rural landscape. By the time the child is twenty-two, that landscape has become urbanized into a city complete with litter, graffiti, and pollution. The boy's family is not a wealthy one, as the outhouse in the earlier pictures and the peeling paint and mixed-use neighborhood of the later ones reveal. The artist thus makes a subtle statement that environmental issues may have the most impact on the poor. (*The Little House*, Burton, 1942, would be a good companion piece, showing as it does the same rural to urban transformation from another perspective.)

New Providence (von Tscharner, Fleming, and the Townscape Institute, 1987) illustrates and describes an imaginary American downtown at six points from 1910 to 1987. This fascinating portrait of the passage of time is also a mini-history of urban development and change as buildings fall into temporary disrepair, neon and electric signs appear, streets are turned into pedestrian malls, and storefronts are boarded up. The book ends on a hopeful note, with old buildings restored, closed streets reopened, and the downtown area revitalized. An afterword lists the real buildings and other structures that were used to design the imaginary New Providence. (One of us lives in a city whose pedestrian mall has some of the same problems as that of New Providence. Its centerpiece is the "harsh concrete fountain" that first appears in the 1970 scene in the book but is gone by 1987.) This would be an excellent inspiration for students to create a timeline of their own town or city.

Finally, in *My Place* (Wheatley and Rawlins, 1987), created for Australia's bicentennial, time is an organizing device in portraying the history of a whole country over two hundred years. The book begins with a double-page spread set in 1988 in which an Aboriginal child describes her urban neighborhood, illustrated by a map. Going back ten years at a time, we meet a whole series of children, reflecting Australia's multiple cultures, who describe "my place" in the same, usually working-class, neighborhood. The maps become simpler and simpler as we move from a city to a town to a village to a rural area. The book ends, as it began, with an Aboriginal child, but this one living in 1788, before any Europeans had arrived. Seeing time in reverse order gives *My Place* a tremendous emotional impact. We are made aware of all that lies behind modern "civilization" and has been lost because of it.

Money

Two useful books for children who are beginning to understand the relative values of different coins and bills are *26 Letters and 99 Cents* (Hoban, 1987), which uses simple, appealing photographs to represent different amounts of money, and *Dollars and Cents for Harriet* (Maestro and Maestro, 1988), whose full-size illustrations show one hundred pennies, twenty nickels, ten dimes, four quarters, and two fifty-cent pieces, each one making up one of the five dollars Harriet needs to buy a kite. Young children can use these books as adjuncts to their own counting of real or play money. Money (spending it, earning it, and being gypped out of it) is an element in the plot of several fictional books of various lengths. The title character in *Alexander, Who Used to Be Rich Last Sunday* (Viorst, 1978) is no longer rich because the dollar his grandparents gave him went a little at a time to buy bubble gum, to pay off a bet, to rent a snake for an hour, (literally) down the toilet, and so on, with nothing left to show for it except a few pitiful purchases from a garage sale. Students might find it interesting to track their own income and spending for a week or so. *A Bargain for Frances* (Hoban, 1970) is a cautionary tale about how Frances gets tricked by her friend Thelma into buying an inferior plastic tea set; a similar theme appears in Shel Silverstein's poem "Smart" (1974, p. 34), whose narrator started out with a dollar bill and made successive trades, thinking he was smart because he ended up with five pennies, and "five is more than four" (than three, than two, than one)! *The Toothpaste Millionaire* (Merrill, 1972) is a charming short novel about a child inventor who becomes a millionaire selling toothpaste at fifteen cents a tube. Money mathematics, such as a statement of expenses per tube of toothpaste, is sprinkled throughout the book, especially once Rufus's teacher starts intercepting the notes he passes and turning them into math problems for the class:

The message from Rufus that Mr. Conti got to read that day said:
  If there are 2½ billion tubes of toothpaste sold in the U.S. in one year, and 1 out of 10 people switched to a new brand, how many tubes of the new brand would they be buying?

The right answer is 250 million. It took the class a while to figure that out. Some peo-
ple have trouble remembering how many zeros there are in a billion. Then there
was a second part to the note:

   If the inventor of the new toothpaste made a profit of 1¢ a tube on his toothpaste,
   what would his profit be at the end of a year?

And it turns out that the inventor of this new toothpaste would make a two-and-a-
half million dollar profit! (p. 26)

Informational books about money help children understand it and use it better. *Money* (Cribb, 1990), in the Eyewitness series published by Knopf, explores
money primarily as a visual object and includes photographs of coins and bills
from all over the world (as well as checks and credit cards) laid out attractively
on the page. The text focuses on history, but it also discusses making, storing,
and counterfeiting money. *If You Made a Million* (Schwartz, 1989) develops the
concept of large amounts ranging from one to a million dollars. What is each
one equal to? The number of pennies in $1 can be arranged in a life-size pho-
tograph that takes up less than a page, while the pennies in $100 would
make a fifty-foot stack. How much interest will this money earn? At 5 percent,
$1 will earn $6.40 in ten years, and $128.04 in fifty years. The book also ex-
plores how checking accounts and mortgages work, and an afterword provides
more detail about these topics and several others, such as income tax.

   The increasing disposable income of many of today's children has, sadly, led
corporations, occasionally unscrupulous ones, to see them as a promising market. Therefore, once children have a sense of money itself, a book like *Smart*
Spending (Schmitt, 1989) can help them use it better. Chapters on topics like
money management, consumer fraud, and warranties help children protect
themselves from some of the abuses of the marketplace. The book's multiple
case studies of children being cheated because they didn't understand their
rights or how to read advertising read like minidramas. *Zillions* (P.O. Box
51777, Boulder, CO 80323-1777), the children's magazine of the Consumer's
Union, would be worth a classroom subscription. Regular features like ''The
Sneaky Sell'' and ''Bug Squad'' (readers' pet consumer peeves), as well as reviews of products, help children become more sophisticated in their use of
money. Students might want to produce an in-house consumer newsletter for
kids as an ongoing project.

   Finally, two fiction books include money in serious narrative contexts.
Money and time are linked in *The Hundred Penny Box* (Mathis, 1975), in
which an elderly African-American woman uses a box of pennies to tell and re-
tell the stories of the hundred years of her life. In *A Chair for My Mother*
(Williams, 1982), a poor urban family saves coins in a jar to buy a new arm-
chair after most of their possessions burn in a house fire. In a life with little cash
to spare, the child narrator's earnings from odd jobs, the waitress mother's
tips, and the grandmother's savings from bargains at the supermarket all go
into the jar. The book also presents a good model of community sharing. After

the fire, "The first day we moved in, the neighbors brought pizza and cake and ice cream. And they brought a lot of other things too. The family across the street brought a table and three kitchen chairs. The very old man next door gave us a bed from when his children were little." In a consumerist society where people are often measured by their possessions, a book like this one is an excellent opportunity to help children think about values and about how little money many people have.

Multiple dimensions of measurement

Some books are not limited to a single type of measurement but instead explore a topic in ways that bring in different concepts such as length, weight, and time. We have already mentioned *Comparisons* (Diagram Group, 1980). Another is *Animal Superstars* (Freedman, 1981), which has chapters on the many ways that animals can be superlative: biggest eaters, smartest, strongest, and so on. Almost every chapter has one or more numerical tables, and the index is excellent. One can, for instance, look up "elephant" and find that its brain weight compared to its body weight is only one twentieth of ours; that its top running speed is 24 miles per hour (close to that of humans), that it can live up to about seventy-seven years (second only to humans among mammals), that it eats about 350 pounds of food a day, and that its maximum recorded weight is about 26,000 pounds. (A related book with a smaller scope is *The Racers: Speed in the Animal World* [Simon, 1980], which has short sections on each of several animals describing how and how fast they move.)

How Much and How Many (Bendick, 1989) is a sourcebook on weights and measures. It includes chapters on the metric, avoirdupois, and other systems, and on the use of weights and measures in the contexts of building, clothes, cooking, science, maps, weather, time, speed, and communication. Each chapter has information on the units of measure used in each field; thus the chapter on building explains that different materials are measured by weight (tons of steel and ninety-four-pound bags of cement), number (thousands of bricks), volume (board feet of wood), or thickness (thousandths of an inch of wire).

Another adult book, *Reading the Numbers* (Blocksma, 1989) is a fascinating "survival guide to the measurements, numbers, and signs encountered in everyday life." In more than a hundred brief sections ranging from age to earthquakes to pencils to zip codes, Blocksma explains how and why various elements of daily life are numbered and measured. It might be fun to pick one of these to explore for each week of the school year; one week have students bring in items with bar codes to decipher, another week explore how vitamins and minerals are listed on food package labels.

Books in the classroom K-2

The students in Carla Morgan's first-grade class had already been discussing time and using clocks when Carla decided to introduce *All in a Day* (Anno, 1986) to broaden their understanding of the concept of time. Before reading the book aloud, Carla used a globe and a flashlight to demonstrate that at any given moment the earth is partially in sunlight and partially in darkness. The class also discussed how the earth's rotation would affect the time on a clock throughout the world. Then as Carla read the story, the children were quick to notice that not only the time on the clock but also the weather was quite different in different countries. Paige remarked, "It looks like winter in Russia but the children in Australia are wearing shorts and playing in the water." Her observation caused other children to think that the pictures on each page represented different times of the year, since various seasons were depicted simultaneously. However, Carla pointed out the date, January 1, at the top of each page. The children were intrigued by this idea, and were surprised to find that the weather in other parts of the world was not necessarily the same as the weather in Sumter, South Carolina, on any given day.

After Carla had finished the story, the children continued their discussion about how time differs throughout the world. Some students were still not quite sure how daylight and darkness occurred. Shawn thought the sun literally rose and set, and his comment highlighted for his classmates the problem with using the commonplace terms of "sunrise" and "sunset" to describe the movements of the sun and earth. Jason was so disturbed by the fact that time differed drastically throughout the world that he devised a plan to make time more uniform. He said he would construct huge mirrors in outer space to reflect the sun's rays everywhere on earth at the same time. (He was not certain, however, how to achieve darkness in all places at the same time.) The children also wondered about the location of the shipwrecked boy on a remote island in the book. They shined the flashlight on the globe and predicted how the light might be projected on their town at 3:00 P.M. From the way the light hit the globe, they could approximate the location of the island at 9:00 A.M.

Books in the classroom 3-4

One of the best predictable stories about measurement and the use of non-standard units is *The Line Up Book* (Russo, 1986), in which Sam uses a variety of household objects to create a line from his bedroom to the kitchen. As JoAnn Reynolds shared this story with some of her third-grade students, she noticed that they became quite interested in predicting events. When Sam finished measuring with one kind of object, he looked around the house for something else. As Sam reached the bathroom, for example, several of the children suggested "bath toys" as the next object to use; as Sam reached the front door, some of the children noticed a large container of umbrellas in the illustration and recommended these as an appropriate measuring tool; when Sam finally entered the living room one child suggested using pillows (there were no pictures of pillows in the story but this child remembered them in his own living room). As Sam looked around the living room for a suitable unit of measure, the children were already anticipating trouble, and when he spied some fragile objects on the mantel, they moaned in unison, "Oh no, not that!"

JoAnn built on the children's predictions by asking them to suggest classroom objects Sam might have used. They listed such items as pencils, erasers, stuffed animals, feet, and hands. To demonstrate one kind of measuring unit, JoAnn began to measure the width of a student's desk with her stapler. When she finished, several of the children protested, "Hey, that's not the way Sam did it!" "What do you mean?" asked JoAnn. "Well, he used all different sizes of things [not just a single stapler that is repeated], and he didn't put it end-to-end like you did," they responded. The differences the children noted inspired further discussion on the importance of a single unit of measure and the need for continuous measurement.

JoAnn invited the children to find their own measuring tool and to do some measuring around the room. Katisha used a stuffed "Snoopy" to measure various objects, including a small Christmas tree, her desk top, and a large paper model of Snoopy (Figure 11–1). When she compared the cardboard Snoopy with her stuffed Snoopy and discovered a two-to-one ratio, she shared this

FIGURE 11-1

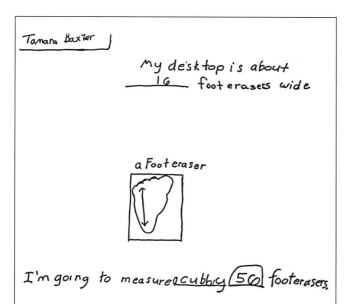

FIGURE 11-2

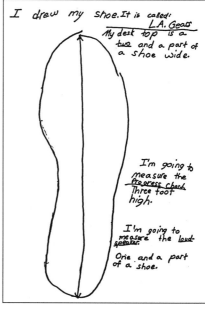

FIGURE 11-3

equivalence by writing "2 little snoopie equals 1 big snoopie." In this way Katisha was beginning to establish equivalent relationships between nonstandard units of measure.

Tamara and Lucretia both measured their desk tops but obtained very different answers (Figures 11–2 and 11–3). When JoAnn asked them if they could explain this discrepancy, they realized that the length of the measuring device was the determining factor. Thus their own explorations with nonstandard units helped them discover an important underlying principle: there is an inverse relationship between the size of the measuring unit and the number of units.

In the present example the children saw that a small pencil eraser (in the shape of a foot, and therefore called a "foot eraser") needed to be repeated more frequently than the length of a large shoe. Lucretia also began to investigate the need for partitioning a whole into smaller units of a measure, describing her findings as "two and a part of a shoe wide."

Books in the classroom 5–6

Teacher Leah Roof read *8,000 Stones* (Wolkstein, 1972) to Mandy, a fifth-grade student, and then invited her to use the emperor's strategy to weigh an unknown object. They gathered together a pan of water, a plastic boat, a toy figurine, some equal-sized rocks, and a marker. To begin her experiment, Mandy floated the plastic boat in the water, placed the figurine inside the boat, and marked the water line on the side of the hull. She then removed the figurine and began filling the boat with rocks until the water line matched the same mark. She determined that the figurine must weigh approximately two stones.

"Is there a way we could determine the actual weight of the figurine in pounds and ounces by using only the stones?" Leah asked.

"Let's weigh the stones on a scale," said Mandy, "and that should be the same as the figurine." She used a scale to weigh the two stones and found that they weighed slightly over two ounces. "The figurine must weigh the same," she replied.

As Mandy logically reasoned:

    If $a = b$ (the figurine weighs the same as two stones)
    and $b = c$ (two stones weigh two ounces)
    then $a = c$ (the figurine weighs two ounces).

To check her prediction she placed the figurine on the scale and found that its weight was almost exactly two ounces.

"If the stones that the Chinese used in the book were this size, could we figure the weight of the elephant?" asked Leah.

"Sure we could," said Mandy. "It would weigh about 8,000 ounces because each stone would weigh about one ounce. But how many pounds is that?" Together they converted ounces to pounds, arriving at a weight of 500 pounds. Mandy knew that elephants weighed much more than that, and so she reasoned that the stones in the story probably weighed more than the ones she had used. Her conclusion demonstrated good number sense; she recognized that the total weight was dependent on both the number of stones and the weight of each stone.

Another fifth-grade teacher, Rick DuVall, used the fairy tale *Melisande* (Nesbit, 1989), discussed in Chapter 6, to explore concepts of length and progression with his students. Princess Melisande, cursed by an evil fairy at her christening, grows up beautiful but bald. When she is finally granted one wish, she asks for golden hair a yard long that grows an inch every day and twice as fast when it is cut. After Rick had read this story to his children he showed them a foot of yarn and asked, "If we doubled the length of this piece of yarn from one foot to two feet, then to four feet and so on, how many times would we have to double it so we would have a piece long enough to circle the earth?" After some initial estimates of from 1,000 to 300,000 doublings, Rick revealed that it would take only 27! The children were a bit skeptical and decided to test it out with some measuring of their own. They decided to see how many doublings it would take to reach from their classroom to the cafeteria. Some predicted at least 100 doublings, but they were amazed to discover that in just five doublings they had exceeded the length of the classroom and in just two more they had reached the cafeteria, with plenty of feet to spare.

The children then organized themselves into groups of four and used the progression of doubling to measure the distance from their classroom to other points on campus, such as the library, playground, office, music room, and kindergarten building.

Further explorations

1. If you read folktales and fairy tales with your students, you might want to seek out those in which size or measurement is an element of the plot; tales of giants and little people, stories featuring magical coins, the suspended time of "Sleeping Beauty," and the importance of midnight in "Cinderella."

2. When using children's books that have food as part of the story, consider doing some cooking as one of the activities connected with the book, as a way of exploring volume measurement. Children's cookbooks can be a useful addition to a classroom library because they are not only fun to read but can lead to many measurement-related activities. (Several representative cookbooks are among the children's books listed at the end of this chapter.)

3. Invite children to create timelines of their own days, both weekdays and weekends, and to think, and perhaps write, about how fictional characters spend their time each day. The section in *Charlotte's Web* (White, 1952), describing a typical day in the life of Wilbur the pig is a good model.

4. The newspaper is another source of measurement activities. Features like sports scores, stock market reports, the prices of houses and cars in the classified ads, and scale maps in news stories can provide students with opportunities to measure and to work with numbers derived from measurement.

5. A class interested in further investigating the role of weights and measures in everyday life might invite speakers to talk about how they use them in their work—perhaps a pediatrician who tracks children's growth, a building contractor, and a chef.

6. What kinds of watches do most of your students have? You might use what students know about their own watches, along with books about time, to begin a discussion of the different ways that cultures have tried to keep track of time. How would students figure out the time if they had no watches or clocks? (You might want to try a "day with no watches," and cover the classroom clock as well.) After reading about other timepieces, students might enjoy creating their own water, sand, or candle clocks, as well as sundials.

7. What things change in your classroom, schoolyard, and community? Children might use concepts of measurement to document such changes. Books that highlight changes in people, plants, and animals can be a beginning point for such discussions.

8. Do your students have any real-life math problems involving money that they'd like to ask the class for help with? How do they know how many things they can buy if they go to a store with a five-dollar bill, and how can they tell if they've gotten the the correct change? How many hours of lawn-mowing or baby-sitting will it take to earn enough for a new bicycle? What are the trade-offs in buying something new (a book, a toy, a cassette tape) versus buying it used?

Children's books

COMPARISONS

Allen, Marjorie N., and Shelley Rotner. 1991. *Changes*. New York: Macmillan.

Anno, Mitsumasa. 1979. *The king's flower*. New York: Collins.

——— . 1987. *Anno's math games*. New York: Philomel.

Barrett, Judy. 1981. *I'm too small. You're too big*. New York: Atheneum.

Carle, Eric. 1977. *The grouchy ladybug*. New York: Crowell.

——— . 1987a. *A house for hermit crab*. Natick, MA: Picture Book Studio.

——— . 1987b. *The tiny seed*. Natick, MA: Picture Book Studio.

Diagram Group. 1980. *Comparisons*. New York: St. Martin's Press.

Dodge, Bertha. 1972. *Big is so big*. New York: Coward, McCann, and Geoghegan.

Freedman, Russell. 1981. *Animal superstars: Biggest, strongest, fastest, smartest*. Englewood Cliffs, NJ: Prentice-Hall.

Froman, Robert. 1971. *Bigger and smaller*. New York: Crowell.

Ginsburg, Mirra. 1982. *Across the stream*. New York: Greenwillow.

Heide, Florence P. 1971. *The shrinking of Treehorn*. New York: Holiday House.

Heide, Florence and Sylvia Van Clief. 1968. *How big am I?* Chicago: Follett Publishing.

Hennessy, B. G. 1988. *The dinosaur who lived in my backyard*. New York: Viking Kestrel.

Hoban, Tana. 1976. *Big ones little ones*. New York: Greenwillow.

——— . 1985. *Is it larger? Is it smaller?* New York: Greenwillow.

Hutchins, Pat. 1971. *Titch*. New York: Macmillan.

——— . 1983. *You'll soon grow into them, Titch*. New York: Greenwillow.

Kalan, Robert. 1979. *Blue sea*. New York: Greenwillow.

Kellogg, Steven. 1971. *Can I keep him?* New York: Dial.

——— . 1976. *Much bigger than Martin*. New York: Dial.

———— . 1984. *Paul Bunyan: A tall tale*. New York: William Morrow.

Krauss Ruth. 1945. *The carrot seed*. New York: Harper and Row.

Lionni, Leo. 1968. *The biggest house in the world*. New York: Pantheon.

McMillan, Bruce. 1989. *Super super superwords*. New York: Lothrop, Lee and Shepard.

Norton, Mary. 1953. *The Borrowers*. New York: Harcourt Brace and World.

Silverstein, Shel. 1974. One inch tall. In *Where the sidewalk ends*. New York: Harper and Row.

———— . 1981. Longmobile. In *A light in the attic*. New York: Harper and Row.

Simon, Hilda. 1980. *The racers: Speed in the animal world*. New York: Lothrop, Lee and Shepard.

Simon, Seymour. 1984. *The dinosaur is the biggest animal that ever lived, and other wrong ideas you thought were true*. New York: Lippincott.

Spier, Peter. 1972. *Fast-slow, high-low*. Garden City, NY: Doubleday.

Ueno, Noriko. 1973. *Elephant buttons. New York: Harper and Row*.

Wing, Henry. 1972. What is big? In Bill Martin, Jr., ed., *Sounds of number*. New York: Holt, Rinehart and Winston.

Wolkstein, Diane. 1972. *8,000 stones*. Garden City, NY: Doubleday.

LINEAR MEASUREMENT

Adler, David. 1975. *3D, 2D, 1D*. New York: Crowell.

Aliki. 1990. *My feet*. New York: HarperCollins.

Allen, Pamela. 1980. *Mr. Archimedes' bath*. New York: Lothrop, Lee and Shepard.

Anno, Mitsumasa. 1989. *Anno's math games II*. New York: Philomel.

Carle, Eric. 1987. *The tiny seed*. Natick, MA: Picture Book Studio.

Caple, Kathy. 1985. *The biggest nose*. Boston: Houghton Mifflin.

de Paola, Tomie. 1978a. *Pancakes for breakfast*. New York: Harcourt Brace Jovanovich.

de Paola, Tomie. 1978b. *The popcorn book*. New York: Holiday House.

Fey, James T. 1971. *Long, short, high, low, thin, wide*. New York: Crowell.

Heide, Florence P. 1971. *The shrinking of Treehorn*. New York: Holiday House.

Hutchins, Pat. 1978. *Happy birthday, Sam*. New York: Greenwillow.

Johnston, Tony. 1986. *Farmer Mack measures his pig*. New York: Harper and Row.

Kellogg, Steven. 1976. *Much bigger than Martin*. New York: Dial.

———— . 1977. *The mysterious tadpole*. New York: Dial.

———— . 1984. *Paul Bunyan: A tall tale*. New York: Willliam Morrow.

Kajima, Naomi. 1986. *The chef's hat*. San Francisco: Chronicle Books.

Krauss, Ruth. 1945. *The carrot seed*. New York: Harper and Row.

Laithwaite, Eric. 1987. *Size: The measure of things*. New York: Franklin Watts.

Lionni, Leo. 1960. *Inch by inch*. New York: Astor-Honor.

Myller, Rolf. 1962. *How big is a foot?* Bloomfield, CT: Atheneum.

Nesbit, E. 1989. *Melisande*. San Diego: Harcourt Brace Jovanovich.

Norton, Mary. 1953. *The Borrowers*. New York: Harcourt Brace, and World.

Raffi. 1989. *Everything grows*. New York: Crown.

Russo, Marisabina. 1986. *The line up book*. New York: Greenwillow.

Seuss, Dr. 1958. *Yertle the turtle and other stories*. New York: Random House.

Silverstein, Shel. 1974. One inch tall. In *Where the sidewalk ends*. New York: Harper and Row.

———. 1981a. Longmobile. In *A light in the attic*. New York: Harper and Row.

———. 1981b. Snake problem. In *A light in the attic*. New York: Harper and Row.

Srivastava, Jane. 1974. *Area*. New York: Crowell.

Zolotow, Charlotte. 1981. *One step, two . . .* New York: Lothrop, Lee and Shepard.

WEIGHT

Allen, Pamela. 1983. *Who sank the boat?* New York: Coward, McCann, and Geoghegan.

Asbjornsen, Peter C., and J. E. Moe. 1957. *The three billy goats gruff*. New York: Harcourt Brace Jovanovich.

Bendick, Jeanne. 1989. *How much and how many*. Rev. ed. New York: Franklin Watts.

Dahl, Roald. 1990. *Esio trot*. New York: Viking.

Galdone, Paul. 1981. *The three billy goats gruff*. San Antonio, TX: Willow.

Leaf, Munro. 1936. *The story of Ferdinand*. New York: Viking.

Srivastava, Jane. 1970. *Weighing and balancing*. New York: Harper and Row.

Wolkstein, Diane. 1972. *8,000 stones*. Garden City, NY: Doubleday.

TIME

Adler, David A. 1976. *A little at a time*. New York: Random House.

Adler, Irving. 1955. *Time in your life*. New York: John Day.

Adler, Irving, and Ruth Adler. 1967. *The calendar*. New York: John Day.

Allison, Linda. 1975. *The reasons for seasons*. Boston: Little, Brown.

Anno, Mitsumasa. 1986. *All in a day*. New York: Philomel.

———. 1987. *Anno's sundial*. New York: Philomel.

Apfel, Necia. 1985. *Calendars*. New York: Franklin Watts.

Baker, Jeannie. 1991. *Window*. New York: Greenwillow.

Baylor, Byrd. 1986. *I'm in charge of celebrations*. New York: Scribner.

Blackburn, Carol. 1991. *Waiting for Sunday*. New York: Scholastic.

Burns, Marilyn. 1978. *This book is about time*. Boston: Little, Brown.

Burton, Virginia L. 1942. *The little house*. Boston: Houghton Mifflin.

Carle, Eric. 1969. *The very hungry caterpillar*. New York: Putnam.

——— . 1977. *The grouchy ladybug*. New York: Crowell.

Clifton, Lucille. 1970. *Some of the days of Everett Anderson*. New York: Holt, Rinehart and Winston.

——— . 1978. *Everett Anderson's nine month long*. New York: Holt, Rinehart and Winston.

Fisher, Leonard. 1987. *Calendar art: Thirteen days, weeks, months, and years from around the world*. New York: Four Winds.

Galdone, Paul. 1973. *The little red hen*. New York: Seabury.

Gerstein, Mordicai. 1989. *The sun's day*. New York: Harper and Row.

Gibbons, Gail. 1979. *Clocks and how they go*. New York: Crowell.

Goodall, John. 1979. *The story of an English village*. New York: Atheneum.

——— . 1987. *The story of a main street*. New York: Margaret McElderry.

Henwood, Simon. 1989. *The clock shop*. New York: Farrar, Straus and Giroux.

Hutchins, Pat. 1970. *Clocks and more clocks*. New York: Macmillan.

Johnson, Chester. 1969. *What makes a clock tick?* Boston: Little, Brown.

Knapp, Edward. 1987. *How speedy is a cheetah?* New York: Platt and Munk.

Krensky, Stephen. 1989. *Big time bears*. Boston: Little, Brown.

Lesser, Carolyn. 1984 *The goodnight circle*. San Diego: Harcourt Brace Jovanovich.

Lloyd, David. 1986. *The stopwatch*. New York: Lippincott.

Maestro, Betsy and Giulio. 1984. *Around the clock with Harriet: A book about telling time*. New York: Crown.

Martin, Bill. 1970a. *Monday, Monday, I like Monday*. New York: Holt, Rinehart and Winston.

——— . 1970b. *The turning of the year*. New York: Holt, Rinehart and Winston.

Mathis, Sharon Bell. 1975. *The hundred penny box*. New York: Viking.

McMillan, Bruce. 1989. *Time to . . .* New York: Lothrop, Lee and Shepard.

Mendoza, George. 1971. *The scarecrow clock*. New York: Holt, Rinehart and Winston.

Miles, Miska. 1971. *Annie and the old one*. Boston: Little, Brown.

Olney, Ross, and Patricia Olney. 1984. *How long? To go, to grow, to know*. New York: Morrow.

Paine, Penelope. 1990. *Time for Horatio*. Santa Barbara, CA: Advocacy.

Parish, Peggy. 1979. *Be ready at eight*. New York: Macmillan.

Perl, Lila. 1986. *Blue Monday and Friday the thirteenth*. New York: Clarion.

Quinn, John R. 1977. *Nature's world records*. New York: Walker.

Rockwell, Anne. 1987. *Bear child's book of hours*. New York: HarperCollins.

Russo, Marisabina. 1988. *Only six more days*. New York: Greenwillow.

Sendak, Maurice. 1962. *Chicken soup with rice: A book of months*. New York: Harper and Row.

Sherrow, Victoria. 1990. *Wilbur waits*. New York: Harper and Row.

Shulevitz, Uri. 1967. *One Monday morning*. New York: Scribner.

Silverstein, Shel. 1981. Shadow race. In *A light in the attic*. New York: Harper and Row.

von Tscharner, Renata, Ronald L. Fleming, and the Townscape Institute. 1987. *New Providence: A changing cityscape*. San Diego: Harcourt Brace Jovanovich.

Warren, Cathy. 1983. *The ten-alarm camp-out*. New York: Lothrop, Lee and Shepard.

Wheatley, Nadia, and Donna Rawlins. 1987. *My place*. Long Beach, CA: Australia in Print.

White, E. B. 1952. *Charlotte's web*. New York: Harper.

Williams, Vera. 1981. *Three days on a river in a red canoe*. New York: Greenwillow.

Ziner, Feenie, and Elizabeth Thompson. 1982. *Time*. Chicago: Children's Press.

Zubrowski, Bernie. 1988. *Clocks: Building and experimenting with model timepieces*. New York: Morrow Junior Books.

MONEY

Barkin, Carol, and Elizabeth James. 1990. *Jobs for kids*. New York: Lothrop, Lee and Shepard.

Belliston, Larry, and Kurt Hanks. 1989. *Extra cash for kids*. Brentwood, TN: Wolgemuth and Hyatt.

Brown, Marc. 1990. *Arthur's pet business*. Boston: Little, Brown.

Cribb, Joe. 1990. *Money* (Eyewitness Books). New York: Knopf.

Hoban, Lillian. 1981. *Arthur's funny money*. New York: Harper and Row.

Hoban, Russell. 1970. *A bargain for Frances*. New York: Harper and Row.

Hoban, Tana. 1987. *26 letters and 99 cents*. New York: Greenwillow.

Kimmel, Eric. 1989. *Four dollars and fifty cents*. New York: Holiday House.

Maestro, Betsy, and Giulio Maestro. 1988. *Dollars and cents for Harriet: A money concept book*. New York: Crown.

Martin, Bill. 1963. *Ten pennies for candy*. New York: Holt, Rinehart and Winston.

Mathis, Sharon Bell. 1975. *The hundred penny box*. New York: Viking.

Medearis, Angela. 1990. *Picking peas for a penny*. Austin, TX: State House.

Merrill, Jean. 1972. *The toothpaste millionaire*. Boston: Houghton Mifflin.

Pomerantz, Charlotte. 1977. *The mango tooth*. New York: Greenwillow.

Schmitt, Lois. 1989. *Smart spending: A young consumer's guide*. New York: Scribner.

Schwartz, David. 1989. *If you made a million*. New York: Lothrop, Lee and Shepard.

Sharmat, Marjorie. 1983. *Rich Mitch*. New York: Morrow.

Silverstein, Shel. 1974. Smart. In *Where the sidewalk ends*. New York: Harper and Row.

Viorst, Judith. 1978. *Alexander, who used to be rich last Sunday*. New York: Macmillan.

Wilkinson, Elizabeth. 1989. *Making cents. Every kid's guide to money, how to make it, what to do with it*. Boston: Little, Brown.

Williams, Vera. 1982. *A chair for my mother*. New York: Greenwillow.

————. 1983. *Something special for me*. New York: Greenwillow.

COOKBOOKS

Bjork, Christina, and Lena Anderson. 1990. *Elliot's extraordinary cookbook*. New York: Farrar, Straus and Giroux.

Cayle, Rena. 1985. *My first cookbook*. New York: Workman.

Darling, Abigail, and Alexandra Day. 1991. *Teddy bears' picnic cookbook*. New York: Viking.

Perl, Lila. 1975. *Slumps, grunts and snickerdoodles*. New York: Seabury.

Watson, N. 1987. *The little pigs' first cookbook*. Boston: Little, Brown.

Teacher resources

Blocksma, Mary. 1989. *Reading the numbers: A survival guide to the measurements, numbers, and sizes encountered in everyday life*. New York: Viking Penguin.

Rhodes, Lynn. 1981. I can read! Predictable books as resources for reading and writing instruction. *ReadingTeacher, 34:* 511–518.

Zillions (magazine). P.O. Box 51777, Boulder, CO 80323-1777.

How much is 1 x 2 x 3 x 4 x 5 x 6 x 7 x 8 x 9 x 0?
(Gardner, 1969, p. 38)
Using only 4's, write a number that equals 100.
(Fixx, 1978, p. 50)

Games and puzzles are an especially valuable part of a mathematics program. They are a way to implement many of the goals proposed by the National Council of Teachers of Mathematics in their *Curriculum and Evaluation Standards for School Mathematics* (1989). Games foster the flexible use of various problem-solving strategies—simplifying a problem, working backward, looking for a pattern, and guess and check—and they can provide historical perspectives on different cultures. Games also emphasize the importance of learning to reason mathematically and support learners in becoming more confident in their mathematical abilities. Many games and puzzles require a lot of time to figure out, and learners can develop a healthy patience and persistence as they work through them. Puzzles also encourage a tolerance for ambiguity ("I'm not sure that what I'm doing is getting me anywhere, but I'll keep going anyway"), an important part of a risk-taking attitude. In addition, the intriguing nature of games often helps learners to focus on the process and to pose such questions as: How was my opponent able to win? How could I have avoided that situation? Does it matter who goes first? How could I guarantee a win? Is this game fair? The issue of fairness can center attention on process in a very authentic way.

Students who are good at math may pick up a book of puzzles and spend days with it, working on every single one, looking at the answers only when absolutely necessary. Children who haven't had as much success with mathematics may be attracted by a book that provides a chance to play around with numbers, shapes, and logical thinking in activities that can't be solved by a formula but reward exploration, creativity, or a flash of insight. Three authors are especially well known for their mathematical puzzle books: Martin Gardner, Mitsumasa Anno, and Marilyn Burns.

12

games, puzzles, and other explorations

Martin Gardner

Martin Gardner, who has written an extensive series of mathematics game and puzzle books for adults drawn from the

191

"Mathematical Games" column he wrote for *Scientific American* for many years (see the teacher resources at the end of this chapter), has also produced puzzle books for children. *Perplexing Puzzles and Tantalizing Teasers* (Gardner, 1969a) is a good starting point for novices, particularly those who aren't sure how they feel about math. The book begins with some really silly riddles (What is yellow and always points north? A magnetic banana) and provides a mix of word puzzles, logic problems, and a few geometric puzzles. Many of the puzzles and teasers have sneaky twists to them, which makes them fun for students to try out on their friends. Gardner has also written two *Aha!* books (*Aha! Insight* [1978] and *Aha! Gotcha* [1982]) that focus on problem solving. Although many of the concepts are quite sophisticated and the books are most suitable for older students (upper elementary and above), many of the puzzles are quite accessible because they are presented in storyboard form with accompanying cartoons. (The cartoons are based on filmstrips produced in conjunction with each book but unnecessary for appreciating the books.)

Aha! Insight is a collection of puzzles that in most cases are solvable by a flash of intuition. They are grouped into chapters by topic: combinations, geometry, numbers, logic, procedures, and words. A teacher could keep the book on hand as a source of puzzles for students to work out together or play around with on their own. The answers and explanations are very detailed, and the puzzles range widely in difficulty, so that the book will be useful to all teachers, not just those who are good at puzzles themselves. *Aha! Gotcha* follows a similar format but deals with paradoxes of various kinds. Unlike the "insight" puzzles, which for the most part have simple, satisfying answers, these paradoxes are often enjoyably maddening, since they have no answer at all, which is of course their point. Consider the sentence: "This sentence contains seven words." It's obviously false, so presumably its opposite is true: "This sentence does not contain seven words." False again, so that two sentences with opposite meanings are both false! Many apparent paradoxes, however, are really cases of flawed reasoning and disappear when they are examined more logically. One of the real benefits of *Aha! Gotcha* is its ability to support critical thinking, which it does by discussing many common fallacies. For instance, it is not true that a couple who have had five daughters are almost certain to have a son next (since the odds against six daughters in a row are so high), or that there is bound to be a deeper meaning in apparent coincidences, like the common experience of meeting a stranger on an airplane who happens to know a friend of a friend. Even the odd fact that the initials of the nine planets contain the sequence SUN (**S**aturn, **U**ranus, **N**eptune) isn't really very surprising after Gardner's examination of it. (Similarly, by the way, the initials of the twelve months of the year contain a common boy's name.) In its exploration of logic, number, geometry, probability, statistics, and time, this book also considers fascinating topics like infinite numbers, antimatter, and time travel, which form the basis of a good deal of science fiction. (One last paradox: Who shaves the barber who shaves all the men who don't shave themselves?)

One further book by Gardner, *Puzzles from Other Worlds* (1984), is somewhat more difficult. Although most elementary school students wouldn't be able to understand it on their own, some of the puzzles are easy enough that a teacher (particularly one who enjoys puzzles) could present them as an activity for a group of students. Each puzzle is set in the context of a short science fiction story, and the answer is followed by a second, third, and sometimes a fourth puzzle. For instance, a puzzle about how a TV audience on earth knows if a spaceship's report of a temperature of −40° is Fahrenheit or Celsius (it is either, since the Fahrenheit and Celsius scales intersect at −40°) is followed by a question about why fever thermometers need to be shaken down after use and a rebus that represents a temperature:

$$\frac{BABS}{0}$$

(Two degrees [Bachelor of Arts and Bachelor of Science!] above zero.)

Mitsumasa Anno

Anno, a well-known Japanese author-illustrator, has produced a number of books involving mathematical games and puzzles. His three-book *Anno's math game* series (1982, 1989, 1991) draws on his unique visual talents: he is a master at illustrating complex information in a way that is both clear and striking. A typical chapter from the first book in the series explores the concept of putting together and taking apart from a variety of perspectives. Kriss and Kross, two characters who manipulate objects and ideas in all three books, have invented a magical glue that works on anything. Following pictures of mythical "stuck-together" creatures from the past, like a winged horse and a centaur, Anno explores familiar objects that can be seen as combinations of other items (for example, a clock and a bell equal an alarm clock), imagines what everyday items might look like with wheels or handles stuck on, and uses grids to stimulate thinking about various combinations of items and attributes. A picture of four children in brightly colored outfits is related to a grid with outlines of clothing down the side and colors across the top. This could also be related to the Cartesian product model of multiplication (mentioned by Anno in the afterword to the book), which represents the product of two numbers as the number of possible ways they can be combined. In this case, five items of clothing times five colors equals twenty-five different items. This could be extended to determining how many different outfits could be made from a hat, shirt, pants, socks, and shoes, each of which can be one of five colors. (The answer is 5^5 or 3,125.) The chapter concludes with a tangram-type puzzle in which a square is cut into five pieces that are then combined to make a variety of other shapes. Each chapter in these books thus takes a basic concept and suggests several directions to explore. There is also a somewhat more technical exploration of each topic at the back of the book.

The most open-ended chapter in *Anno's Math Games II* (1989) is called "Dots, Dots, and More Dots." Kriss and Kross first show us some long lines that are really made up of many small, discrete parts: a seam sewn in fabric, the perforations on a sheet of stamps, and a line of ants carrying cookie crumbs. They display a variety of pictures created from dots or other small shapes, including examples made from typewriter letters, sesame seeds, cross stitch, and beads. Anno also demonstrates how to break a picture into a grid layout so that it can be copied a square at a time. Students might enjoy using a magnifying glass to examine pictures in newspapers, books, and magazines to see if they are made up of dots, and creating their own pictures made up of smaller units, whether as small as dots or as large as mosaic tiles. (The paintings of the Impressionist artist Georges Seurat, which are made up of small dots, would also be of interest here.)

Anno has also written two books that examine a single exploratory problem at great length. *Anno's Hat Trick* (1985) presents a set of logical puzzles that involve trying to deduce the color of the hat one character is wearing based on both the color hat that other characters are wearing and whether those other characters can deduce what color their own hats are. The book begins with simple problems but soon becomes challenging even for adults. Children might enjoy acting out these puzzles as a way of solving them, as well as making up their own. *Socrates and the Three Little Pigs* (1986) uses diagrams of three pigs and five houses to explore permutations and combinations. Socrates the wolf, in trying to figure out where the three little pigs are sleeping in order to catch one for his supper, ends up staying up all night trying to figure out all the different possibilities. They range from 10 (if only one pig can be in each house and Socrates doesn't care which pig is which) to 210 (if there can be more than one pig per house and order matters both within and between houses). It would be interesting to present this book by reading just the first few pages and then ask students to work in groups to find their own answers, perhaps by using actual models of houses and pigs and figuring out a systematic way to make sure they have explored all possibilities. They can then return to the book to explore Anno's solutions.

Marilyn Burns

Marilyn Burns is well known for her three recreational mathematics books in the Brown Paper School series: *The I Hate Mathematics! Book* (1975), *The*

Book of Think (1976), and *Math for Smarty Pants* (1982). Laid out as a series of explorations of varying length and complexity and appealingly illustrated with cartoons, they are designed to be browsed through and skipped around in, rather than necessarily read in sequence. *The I Hate Mathematics! Book* (1975) begins with street math, so that kids who don't really feel like sitting inside can conduct statistical investigations of how tame their local pigeons are and whether it takes more paces to walk down a sidewalk stepping on *none* of the cracks or on *all* of them. Children who have spent much of their school lives feeling unsuccessful at mathematics might enjoy the chapters on "Maybe Grownups Aren't as Smart as You Think," "Mathe-Magic," and "How to Always Be a Winner," which present, respectively, riddles and trick questions, tricks to perform before an audience, and game-playing strategies, all with a mathematical theme. A clever coin trick with a psychological twist is to tell a friend you will guess which of her hands hides a nickel and which one a penny. You say, "Multiply what's in your right hand by 14. Now multiply what's in your left hand by 14. Add them together and tell me the total." You then tell her which hand holds the nickel, which you knew from watching her face to see when she is struggling to multiply 14×5 in her head! This book will also be of interest to students who are strong in mathematics, since it includes thought-provoking problems that are challenging for anyone (for instance, what is the relationship between the volume of two cylinders created by rolling up identical rectangles, one the short way and the other the long way), as well as brief digressions on topics such as primes and the numbers googol (one followed by one hundred zeroes) and pi. (Unfortunately, the explanation of pi, which is shown written to one hundred decimal places, is described as if its value had been determined by measuring circumferences and diameters and then dividing, which of course could never produce a precise enough answer.) *Math for Smarty Pants* (1982) is a longer, more complex collection of both classic and newer puzzles and explorations. Although this book will be especially interesting for students who enjoy mathematics, much of it is accessible to everyone, particularly if used as a springboard for class discussion and activities. For instance, one section helps students explore tests for determining if a number is divisible by each of the digits from 2 to 7. This could be figured out together by the class, with students encouraged to discover the easy ones, like 2 and 5, themselves, and the teacher giving more support on the harder ones, like 3 and 4. (The test for 7 is so complicated that it may not be worth pursuing except for fairly small numbers.) A classic puzzle included in the book is one in which an 8×8 checkerboard (64 squares) is cut into four pieces that are then rearranged to form a 5×13 rectangle (65 squares). Where did the extra square come from? This would be a good puzzle to explore with graph paper. For the teacher who is looking for a comprehensive resource for thought-provoking puzzles and activities to have on hand for the entire year, this may be the best choice available, particularly for intermediate grades. But the book has one somewhat annoying feature: the answers to the puzzles are scattered, unindexed, throughout the book, rather than being gathered in one easy-to-find location. They are also written upside down and in mirror writing to prevent inadvertent peeks. A teacher who plans to use this book frequently might ask for a few student volunteers to compile an index of puzzles and solutions.

Crowell young math books

Three titles from the young math book series published by Crowell deal with game and puzzle topics. The title of *Mathematical Games for One or Two* (Charosh, 1972) is self-explanatory. These simple games, which use common materials, emphasize logic, strategy, and looking for underlying patterns. One example is a magic trick. Cards are arranged in three rows, as seen below:

A	B	C
1	2	4
3	3	5
5	6	6
7	7	7

The magician turns his back, asks a friend to think of a number between one and seven and tell him which rows it's in, and then miraculously guesses the number! The trick is to add the numbers at the top of each column selected.

Yes-No; Stop-Go: Some Patterns in Mathematical Logic (Gersting and Kuczkowski, 1977) uses examples of drawbridges over a moat and switches on railroad tracks to explore "and" and "or" statements and how they combine in mathematical logic. The book concludes with truth tables showing that if two statements are combined with "or," only one statement has to be true for the combined statement to be true, while both must be true if combined with "and." (For instance, "Dogs bark or cats have wings" is true, but the same sentence with "and" is false.)

Maps, Tracks, and the Bridges of Königsberg: A Book About Networks (Holt, 1975) explores the mathematical theory describing how points in a network can be connected. It uses a series of puzzles, such as how many games there are in a checkers match in which each of five children plays every other child, and the classic example of the bridges in the city of Königsberg. The mathematician Leonhard Euler solved the problem of whether it's possible to cross its seven bridges exactly once each (because of their layout, it is impossible). Students who enjoy this book might try creating similar puzzles of their own, such as drawing geometric patterns that can or cannot be traced over with a single line. (For the first of the shapes below it is possible; for the second it is not.)

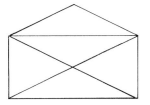 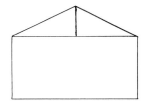

Other game and puzzle books

Irving Adler, who has written numerous books for children on scientific and mathematical topics, has produced a few game and puzzle books that, although older and lacking the kind of livelier illustrations that appear in more recent books, are still worthwhile. His *Magic House of Numbers* (1974) is really an exploration of the number system in the guise of recreational mathematics and includes many classic mathematical patterns and puzzles. For instance, the number 12,345,679, when multiplied by 9, 18, or any other multiple of 9, produces some surprising results. Students who still have trouble remembering the times tables between 6 and 9 might enjoy learning a quick method for multiplying on their fingers for those times when they just can't remember what 7 × 9 equals. The book also shows how to make some good math games out of simple materials, including Oware, an African counting game that can be made from an egg carton, and the Towers of Hanoi, made from dowels and cardboard discs. Adler explores bases other than 10 as well as the patterns that triangular, square, cubic, and perfect numbers form. This, like Burns's *Math for Smarty Pants,* is one of the best single game and puzzle books to have available in the classroom. It is a useful resource for the teacher and a good introduction to the quirks and pleasures of mathematics for children. Sandra Wilde recalls getting this book from the library as a child (in its 1957 edition) and developing a life-long interest in mathematics partly because of it. Irving and Peggy Adler also have a more recent book of short *Math Puzzles* (1978) that are fun to browse through. Two examples are a connect-the-dots puzzle with a twist (the solver has to find all the prime numbers and connect them) and a classic problem in which the reader is asked to imagine pouring some orange juice into a container of apple cider, then some of the resulting mixture back into the original container, and so on, and figuring out which liquid contains more of the other one.

Another Adler, David this time, has written a book called *Calculator Fun* (1981). Several of these kinds of books came out when calculators first became common; this book and others like it are likely to be available in many libraries. Adler includes some arithmetic problems that produce surprising results, such as $100 \div 81$ and $1,371,742 \times 9$. These would be tedious to do by hand but are pure pleasure on the calculator. He also has a selection of riddles whose answers are found by doing arithmetic problems on the calculator, then turning it upside down to read the resulting "words." For instance, add 357 and 636 to find out the answer to "the more you cook it, the harder it gets," and multiply 51×18 to find out what has only three letters but is not small. Students might enjoy making up their own riddles. A good starting point is the list of letters that an upside-down calculator can produce. Riddle writers are limited to answers spelled with B, E, G, H, I, L, O, and S (produced by the numbers 8, 3, 9, 4, 1, 7, 0, and 5 respectively).

One more recreational mathematics book is *Math Menagerie* (Kadesch, 1970), which includes explorations of various topics such as probability, binary and unusual numbers, interesting shapes, and mathematical machines. Several of the chapters include instructions for building models or conducting experiments. Students can use a small metal globe to make projection maps of various kinds or use BB's and straight pins to make a probability machine. There is also a whole section on soap-film mathematics with instructions for making various kinds of frames out of wire. This book is a rich source of ideas for several fairly ambitious projects. Intermediate-grade students might enjoy working in teams to construct various models, experiment with them, and present their findings.

Sideways Arithmetic from Wayside School (Sachar, 1989) is a good introduction to logical problems set in the context of a story; it also provides extensive puzzle-solving hints. The story line is minimal, about a class that does only "sideways" (puzzle-type) arithmetic, but the hints begin by taking the reader step-by-step through the first logic problem in the book, not only solving that problem but demonstrating a general model. The first puzzle is an addition problem in which every letter stands for a numeral:

$$
\begin{array}{r}
\mathrm{E\,L\,F} \\
+\ \mathrm{E\,L\,F} \\
\hline
\mathrm{F\,O\,O\,L}
\end{array}
$$

After showing that *F* has to represent 1, the author shows how the rest of the solution follows logically from that point. Progressively harder number arithmetic problems like these are followed by other kinds of logic problems. Although the book is very limited in scope, its funny tone may make it appealing to many students.

Finally, no discussion of games and puzzles can be complete without mentioning *Jumanji* (1981), Chris Van Allsburg's classic tale of the board game that came to life. Readers can imagine the horror of landing on spaces that speak of rhinoceroses stampeding and pythons sneaking into camp and having real animals appear in their living rooms! *Jumanji* might inspire students to create their own exotic board games.

Books in the classroom K–2

The game of Nim, discussed in *Mathematical Games for One or Two* (Charosh, 1972), is one of the oldest two-person games in the world. The simplest form of Nim is played with three rows of markers as illustrated:

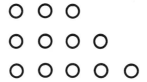

Each player in turn takes any number of markers from only one row. At least one marker must be removed each turn. The winner is the player who takes the last marker. (It is interesting to reverse the rules later and say that the player who removes the last marker is the *loser*. Students must rethink their game-playing strategies in order to accommodate this new set of rules.) David Whitin has often played this game with young children. He draws the set of 3-4-5 markers on the board and challenges students to try to beat him. As he and the children take turns erasing markers from the board, they test out different strategies. Sometimes children erase a whole row of markers, thinking that this move might get them closer to the final marker more quickly. When they see that this strategy does not always guarantee a win, they try erasing only a single marker. But after they play the game long enough, they begin to figure out some winning strategies. They notice that one winning strategy is a 1-2-3 arrangement (one marker in one row, two markers in another row, and three in the third); they realize that they can win if they create the 1-2-3 pattern at the end of their turn. No matter what their opponent does at this point, they can win if they use the correct strategy from then on. They also begin to notice another winning strategy: form two equal rows. Every time their opponent must respond to two equal rows, they can always make them equal again, and if their opponent takes all the markers of one row, they can win by taking all those remaining in the other row (thus creating two equal rows of zero). As children logically develop these winning strategies, their excitement for the game increases. They begin to analyze their moves more carefully and try to work backward even further to discover more winning situations. Sandra Wilde (1991) shows some older students' written responses to another variant of Nim known as "Poison."

Books in the classroom 3–4

Teacher Frank Jordan read *Anno's Hat Trick* (Anno, 1985) to his fourth-grade son Bryan. When Frank first read the story to himself he was intrigued by the

"Notes to Parents" at the back of the book. He found the chart showing all the different possibilities available when the hatter included a set of five-hat problems to be especially helpful. He and Bryan decided to make their own drawings to help them in solving some of the logic puzzles in the book. For instance, on page 35 of the text, both children in the drawing, Tom and Hannah, are wearing red hats but the color of the hat worn by Shadowchild (a stand-in for the reader) is unknown. Tom is asked, "What color is your hat?" and answers, "I don't know." (Tom does know that at least one hat is red.) Frank and Bryan realized that Tom could have seen either a white hat and a red hat or two red hats. (Tom would only have known the color of his own hat if the two he saw had been white; his would then have been the red one by default.) The only way to determine which of these alternatives was correct was to read Hannah's response (made after she heard Tom's) and to try to understand why she had also said, "I don't know." Frank described the deductive reasoning he and Bryan used to solve the problem: "From Tom's answer, Hannah knew that she and/or Shadowchild had a red hat. If Shadowchild's were white, then Hannah would know hers was red, but if Shadowchild's hat were red, then hers could be either color. Since Hannah's answer was 'I don't know,' then Shadowchild must have on a red hat." When Frank reflected on what his son had learned from the experience he wrote: "Bryan had to learn to put himself in the shoes of each person (Tom and Hannah) to see why they answered as they did and what they 'saw.' Then he realized that from their answers he could draw certain conclusions."

Books in the classroom 5–6

Rick DuVall used an activity with his fifth-grade students that Marilyn Burns describes in *Math for Smarty Pants* (1982). It is known as the "money alphabet" and involves assigning a monetary value to each letter of the alphabet (a = 1¢, b = 2¢, c = 3¢ . . . z = 26¢). Rick introduced the money alphabet to his class and told them how much his own name was "worth." That simple demonstration set the class going in many different directions. After tabulating the worth of their first names, students began to add up their last names. Still others wanted to include their middle names and began to figure that total as well. In the middle of these investigations, one child suddenly announced, "Hey, wait a minute! My last name has two A's in it that are worth only a penny each, and Jonathan's last name has two Z's in it. His two Z's are worth more than my whole last name!" Rick then suggested other challenges to pursue: Whose name was the least expensive? Whose name came closest to the value of one dollar? Could anyone find a word that was worth exactly one dollar? Who had similarly priced names? Whose name came closest to equaling the value of the teacher's name?

In addition to these challenges, the children began to explore the value of their parents' names, their brothers' and sisters' names, and any other names they could think of. They even began to look at other curricular areas through this quantitative lens. They calculated the names of several early explorers of North America, each of the fifty states and their capitals, the parts of an atom, and the titles of stories they were writing. They were even quick to advertise their services to other students in the school. Rick overheard one of his students say to a student from another class, as they were getting on the bus at the end of the day, "Hey, I can tell you how much your name costs!"

Further explorations

1. Invite children to join a "puzzler's club" that will research new puzzle books and share new mathematical puzzles regularly with the rest of the class.

2. Choose a time every week as math puzzle time, when students work in heterogeneous teams to solve one of the mathematical puzzles from the books discussed in this chapter.

3. You might want to develop your own logical abilities by exploring Martin Gardner's adult books of mathematical recreations. (See the reference list at the end of this chapter.) Each book varies enough in difficulty to provide something for everyone. You can browse among them, turning to topics that sound intriguing and peeking at the answers if they are too hard for you to solve on your own. Several of the books have trick puzzles created for the April (Fool's!) issue of *Scientific American* that are especially accessible to those with less background in mathematics.

4. You might also want to subscribe to *Games* magazine, which usually has some features that are adaptable for use with students. A recent issue had an interesting article on computer fraud, a punch-out tangramlike puzzle with a variety of shapes to make from it, and an order form for a variety of new puzzle books.

Children's books

Adler, David. 1981. *Calculator fun*. New York: Franklin Watts.

Adler, Irving. 1974. *Magic house of numbers*. Rev. ed. New York: John Day.

Adler, Irving, and Peggy Adler. 1978. *Math puzzles*. New York: Franklin Watts.

Anno, Mitsumasa. 1982. *Anno's math games*. New York: Philomel.

———. 1985. *Anno's hat trick*. New York: Philomel.

————— . 1986. *Socrates and the three little pigs*. New York: Philomel.

————— . 1989. *Anno's math games II*. New York: Philomel.

————— . 1991. *Anno's math games III*. New York: Philomel.

Bell, Robbie, and Michael Cornelius. 1988. *Board games round the world*. New York: Cambridge University Press.

Burns, Marilyn. 1975. *The I hate mathematics! book*. Boston: Little, Brown.

————— . 1976. *The book of think*. Boston: Little, Brown.

————— . 1982. *Math for smarty pants*. Boston: Little, Brown.

————— . 1990. *The $1.00 word riddle book*. New Rochelle, NY: Cuisenaire.

Charosh, Mannis. 1972. *Mathematical games for one or two*. New York: Crowell.

Fixx, James F. 1978. *Solve it! A perplexing profusion of puzzles*. Garden City, NY: Doubleday.

Gardner, Martin. 1969. *Perplexing puzzles and tantalizing teasers*. New York: Simon and Schuster.

————— . 1978. *Aha! Insight*. San Francisco: Freeman.

————— . 1982. *Aha! Gotcha*. San Francisco: Freeman.

————— . 1984. *Puzzles from other worlds*. New York: Vintage.

Gersting, Judith, and Joseph Kuczkowski. 1977. *Yes-no; stop-go: Some patterns in mathematical logic.*. New York: Crowell.

Holt, Michael. 1975. *Maps, tracks and the bridges of Königsberg: A book about networks*. New York: Crowell.

Kadesch, Robert R. 1970. *Math menagerie*. New York: Harper and Row.

Sachar, Louis. 1989. *Sideways arithmetic from Wayside School*. New York: Scholastic.

Sackson, Sid. 1991. *The book of classic board games*. Palo Alto, CA: Klutz Press.

Van Allsburg, Chris. 1981. *Jumanji*. Boston: Houghton Mifflin.

Teacher resources

Bell, R. C. 1979. *Board and table games from many civilizations*. New York: Dover.

Games (magazine). One Games Place, P.O. Box 55484, Boulder, CO 80323–5484.

Gardner, Martin. 1960. *The Scientific American book of mathematical puzzles and diversions*. New York: Simon and Schuster.

————— . 1964. *The second Scientific American book of mathematical puzzles and diversions*. New York: Simon and Schuster.

————— . 1966. *New mathematical diversions from Scientific American*. New York: Simon and Schuster.

————— . 1969a. *Perplexing puzzles and tantalizing teasers*. New York: Simon and Schuster.

———. 1969b. *The unexpected hanging and other mathematical diversions.* New York: Simon and Schuster.

———. 1971. *Martin Gardner's sixth book of mathematical games from Scientific American.* New York: Scribner.

———. 1975. *Mathematical carnival.* New York: Knopf.

———. 1979. *Mathematical circus.* New York: Knopf.

———. 1983. *Wheels, life, and other mathematical amusements.* New York: Freeman.

———. 1986. *Knotted doughnuts and other mathematical entertainments.* New York: Freeman.

———. 1988. *Time travel and other mathematical bewilderments.* New York: Freeman.

Wilde, Sandra. 1991. Learning to write about mathematics. *Arithmetic Teacher, 38:* 38–43.

afterword

This book is ending, but we hope your journey has just begun. Our intent has been to celebrate the many interesting and unusual possibilities children's literature offers for exploring mathematical concepts. The primary goal of a mathematical literacy program is to create a learning environment that encourages children to think like mathematicians. In order to be engaged in this kind of thinking, learners must grapple with the concepts that are basic to the mathematical system. Children's literature provides an exciting way to investigate these concepts and to understand the basic generalizations that underlie a mathematical view of the world.

Throughout these pages we have heard children telling mathematical stories that involve classifying sneakers, spending money, taking trips, sharing bananas, dividing candy bars, estimating jelly beans, noticing shapes, determining areas, measuring desktops, calculating grains of rice, and describing the infinite. As these children tell these stories they demonstrate in a dramatic way that mathematics is a system for making meaning that derives its very life from social situations. They are making sense of events in their lives. We hope that the classroom scenarios we have included make the true significance of story clear. A list of books alone does not demonstrate the central role stories play in the generation of mathematical understanding. If learners cannot tell stories to illustrate a mathematical concept, that concept has no meaning for them. Stories give us all a fresh perspective on our own thinking and that of our students. We urge you to continue this storytelling in your own classrooms.

This has been a noisy book. We have heard children sharing, debating, and extending their mathematical ideas. We have watched them representing their thinking through writing, drawing, drama, song, and classroom discourse. We have felt their excitement as they discovered a pattern, invented a new solution, or made an interesting connection. We hope this book will produce similar healthy and productive noise in your own classrooms.

No bibliography is ever complete. Although we have worked with teachers for over five years compiling this list of books, we know that there are good books we have omitted. If you are aware of any noteworthy omissions please write and tell us so we can include your entries in future editions. And as you share these books with children, send along the story of these experiences as well. We are fascinated by the potential that children's literature holds for fostering mathematical literacy, and your stories can help us all see that potential a little bit more clearly.

David J. Whitin
University of South Carolina
College of Education
Columbia, SC 29208

Sandra Wilde
University of Oregon
College of Education
Eugene, OR 97403